Revolution Stalled

OXFORD STUDIES IN DIGITAL POLITICS

Series Editor: Andrew Chadwick, Royal Holloway, University of London

Revolution Stalled

THE POLITICAL LIMITS OF THE INTERNET
IN THE POST-SOVIET SPHERE

SARAH OATES

OXFORD
UNIVERSITY PRESS

OXFORD
UNIVERSITY PRESS

Oxford University Press is a department of the University of Oxford.
It furthers the University's objective of excellence in research, scholarship,
and education by publishing worldwide.

Oxford New York
Auckland   Cape Town   Dar es Salaam   Hong Kong   Karachi
Kuala Lumpur   Madrid   Melbourne   Mexico City   Nairobi
New Delhi   Shanghai   Taipei   Toronto

With offices in
Argentina   Austria   Brazil   Chile   Czech Republic   France   Greece
Guatemala   Hungary   Italy   Japan   Poland   Portugal   Singapore
South Korea   Switzerland   Thailand   Turkey   Ukraine   Vietnam

Oxford is a registered trade mark of Oxford University Press in the UK
and certain other countries.

Published in the United States of America by
Oxford University Press
198 Madison Avenue, New York, NY 10016

Library of Congress Cataloging-in-Publication Data
Revolution stalled : the political limits of the internet in the post-Soviet
sphere / Sarah Oates.
p.   cm.
Includes bibliographical references and index.
ISBN 978–0–19–973595–2 (hardcover: alk paper)
1. Internet—Political aspects—Russia (Federation). 2. Internet—Access
control—Russia (Federation). 3. Internet in political campaigns—Russia
(Federation). I. Title.
HN530.2.Z9 I5665 2013
302.230947–dc23

                                            2012019437

9   8   7   6   5   4   3   2   1

Printed in the United States of America
on acid-free paper

Contents

Acknowledgments

This book was produced at a time of fundamental change in political communication. Not only was the internet transforming the information sphere, it was changing how people studied the information sphere as well. Thus, from a time when studying the Russian media meant huddling over VCRs in cold Moscow apartments and painstakingly gathering a handful of people for focus groups, the field has moved on to an embarrassment of research riches. Not only can one now watch (and record) Russian television online, the information sphere has widened out to the huge sprawl of the Russian internet. The lone scholar cannot hope to tame this information tide.

This book benefits from the work of a vast range of scholars and analysts, only some of whom I will be able to mention here. In-depth and interesting reports on the Russian internet from the Berkman Center for Internet & Society at Harvard, Internews, the *Digital Icons* online journal, the Reuters Institute for the Study of Journalism, and the Center for New Media and Society at the New Economic School in Moscow make a significant contribution to this book. In addition, I would like to thank individual scholars who have been helpful in collaboration, comments, answering endless questions, and helping me to keep up in the ever-changing sphere of internet studies (as well as Russian politics), including Luciano Floridi, Floriana Fossato, Sam Greene, Gillian McCormack, and Regina Smyth. Particular insight on contemporary Russian media was provided by faculty at the Higher School of Economics in Moscow, including Anna Kachkaeva (who kindly provided the photo for the book's cover) and Sergey Davydov. Insights from academics at the Higher School of Economics in St. Petersburg, including Olessia Koltseva, also were helpful in completing this book.

A special thanks to my current and former PhD students who struggled along with me in internet studies as their more nimble, less-tired brains so often provided great insights—Tetyana Lokot, Paul Reilly, and Filippo Trevisan. My colleagues in politics at the University of Glasgow have provided friendly support (as well as very valuable research leave while writing this book) and I am particularly grateful for the expertise and support of Ana Langer, Vikki Turbine, and Stephen White. A consultancy on the internet and public diplomacy exposed me to the insights and intelligence of the expert staff at InterMedia, a Washington, DC, research and consultancy firm with a specialty in post-Soviet media. I am grateful to Anna Kvit, who provided excellent research assistance in the field of Russian media law.

Over the course of writing this book, I attended many conferences and presented various aspects of this research (at varying stages of completion). I would like to thank panel organizers, copanelists, and panel attendees for the incredibly useful feedback received at conferences including the 2011 International Affairs Conference on Democratisation and New Media, The Royal Irish Academy, Dublin; the 2011 general conference of the European Consortium for Political Research, Reykjavik, Iceland; the Fourth Annual Research Forum for the Centre for Russian, Central and East European Studies, University of Glasgow (May 2011); The New Ethical Responsibilities of Internet Service Providers Conference, University of Hertfordshire, 2011; the Measuring Press Freedom workshop cosponsored by the American Political Science Association and the Annenberg Foundation, Annenberg School for Communication, University of Pennsylvania in 2010; the Political Communication section pre-conference for the American Political Science Association Annual Meeting (2010 and 2008); the New Media in New Europe–Asia Workshop at the University of Birmingham sponsored by the Centre for East European Language-Based Studies in 2010; Politics: Web 2.0 International Conference, Royal Holloway, University of London in 2008; and the Post-Soviet Media Research Methodology Workshop, Centre for Russian and East European Studies, University of Birmingham in 2008. Participants of the Google Forum UK meetings, which I chair, have been instrumental in fostering a more multidisciplinary approach to the study of the internet, including by highlighting the work of the "Reading the Riots" project at the London School of Economics and the University of Manchester.

The research for this project has been supported by a range of funding. Key to the work have been grants to study the Russian internet. These have included Grant RES-000-22-4159 from the U.K. Economic and Social Research Council to study the internet and everyday rights in Russia as well as a British Academy Research Grant to study the internet and attitudes to health care in Russia. The Carnegie Trust for the Universities of Scotland gave critical funds at the exploratory phase of the project.

This book would not have been possible without the inspiration and support of Andrew Chadwick, the Digital Politics series editor, and Angela Chnapko at Oxford University Press. I recently noted to them that they seem to commission a book and—the next thing you know—the region under study starts to have significant online protests. I do not think they can be held responsible for the Arab Spring or the Russian winter protests of 2011–12, but they are responsible for inspiring, coaxing, chivvying, encouraging, and generally bearing with the pangs of creating a book in a fast-moving, dynamic, and fascinating field.

Sarah Oates
Philip Merrill College of Journalism
University of Maryland, College Park

1

Introduction

In December 2011, the internet transformed a flawed Russian election into a massive protest movement, bringing huge street demonstrations, arrests, and clashes with police, and crystallizing online solidarity into a visible opposition to the Russian regime. In a matter of days, the expectations for routine, albeit rather unfair, elections were overturned and Russian leaders found themselves in uncharted political territory. Yet what seemed to be a wave of protest unleashed from the online sphere was, in fact, the result of several different factors within Russian politics and society that had been evolving over a number of years. The protests in the winter of 2011–12 were a manifestation of many forces, some of them grounded in the online sphere and some of them in traditional post-Soviet politics. This book seeks to define, explore, and analyze these factors. In doing this, not only can we understand the specific convergence of forces that created the Russian protests, but we also can apply comparative experience and theory to the Russian case. This can allow us to build a model for understanding how, why, and even when the online sphere becomes an overwhelming catalyst for protest and change in non-free states.

This "winter of discontent" in Russia took many by surprise, both inside and outside of the Russian Federation. Until December 2011, there was little compelling evidence that the internet had made a significant difference in Russian mainstream politics. The country remained a state in which there is relatively little opportunity for democratic movement and consolidation. While there are regular elections, a large media sphere, a parliament, and some debate in society, there is no consistent rule of law or widespread equality of political opportunity. Rather, Russia is an oligarchic regime with a market economy, relatively peaceful in the years of prosperity brought about by the booming world market for natural resources. The war in Chechnya continues—as do terrorist attacks on Russian soil—but there is little serious dissent or discussion about the war in Russian media or society. While Dmitri Medvedev was the first Russian president to launch a website and produce regular podcasts, they were top-down messages from a Kremlin elite that continues to manipulate the media, elections, parliament, and the regions for its own interests.

Medvedev's podcasts and the Kremlin website itself are emblematic of the challenge of analyzing the role of the internet in democracy, repression, and possible revolution. Cyber-optimists point to the democratizing elements of the internet that empower the common citizen. After all, Medvedev and the Kremlin website offered far more information and opportunity for engagement than any other national Russian leader had in the past, as do myriad websites from levels of Russian governance ranging from the national to the local. Yet what difference does this information make for the citizens of Russia? They are free to read about their president online, and millions more Russians have become active online since Medvedev gave his first podcast in 2008. Russians are even free to send him an e-mail and, unlike on the U.S. White House website, they are not even limited to a mere 2,500 characters.[1] However, in a society that lacks free elections, a robust party system, or rule of law, what real change can Russian citizens hope to bring about through e-mail? They are free to complain, but at best they must wait to see if the leadership chooses to act on their complaints. On a more worrying note, any interaction with the presidential website could bring them to the attention of the security services.

While there might be the temptation to assume that a lack of democratic institutions and a tradition of oligarchic rule would render the internet little more than political communication window dressing, there are two critical additions to the political sphere offered by information communication technologies that challenge this view. On the one hand, the online sphere offers a new way of creating and delivering information that is in many ways fundamentally different from the traditional relationship between news producer and media consumer. In addition, the series of political revolts against authoritarian regimes in the Middle East in 2011 suggest that online communication can provide unprecedented speed and dexterity in information management to those who oppose repressive regimes. In particular, the Egyptian and Tunisian governments were clearly caught off guard and out-maneuvered on both internal and external propaganda fronts by networked citizens. Thus, is online communication something that is particularly good at challenging—and even toppling—non-democratic regimes? This book will argue that online communication is not a "magic bullet" that can empower citizens and change regimes; rather, this study will present evidence at *how* and *when* the internet can influence political life in non-free states. Hence, the title of the book reflects the idea of a "stalled" revolution, recognizing both the potential and the barriers to the internet's ability to deliver democratization. Through this analysis, which includes a study of online content, networked communities, catalyzing events, state co-optation, and government control, there is the elucidation of factors that can allow social scientists, policy-makers, citizens, and political leaders to understand how, when, why, and where the internet can play a significant role in political change in non-free states.

While this book uses the Russian political communication experience to build useful tools for understanding the relative role of the internet in political change, this work also emphasizes the need to understand the role of information and communication technologies (ICTs) within national contexts. Throughout this book, it is argued that while there are universal characteristics of online communication, they must be analyzed within the context of national political and media systems. Thus, online content and even online platforms—ranging from micro-blogging tools such as Twitter to social-networking sites to forums—do not have the same resonance in different national settings. Their use and popularity shifts and adapts over time and space. In addition, studies also often make the assumption that the internet audience, defined through uptake of ICTs as well as by mea-suring trust and attitude toward online communication, are essentially the same from country to country. In fact, usage patterns and attitudes toward the internet differ widely from country to country, as well as within national populations themselves. Even a cursory examination of the online space in different countries will reveal profound differences in taste and culture in the virtual sphere.

The third key point about this study is that it has sought—and found—political engagement in what at first would seem unlikely places in the Russian online sphere long before people took to the streets in Moscow and other Rus-sian cities in 2011. The best evidence of political action on the part of Russian citizens is found not via political parties, candidates, or even in the lively world of political blogs on Russia's LiveJournal. You can find impassioned, angry Rus-sian citizens who use the internet to aggregate and fight for their rights, but these rights are not generally defined in broad philosophical terms or even in terms that many people would consider "political." Rather, there is striking evidence that Russians will use the internet to aggregate interests when faced with difficult personal issues, particularly relating to health. Thus, while Lonkila (2008) found Russians used the internet to search for ways to avoid the military draft, they generally did not use it to aggregate interests against the draft in principle. Rus-sian bloggers have enormous freedom of expression and will talk about a broad range of political ideals and principles (Etling et al., 2010; Fossato et al., 2009). However, there was little evidence that they were talking to anyone beyond a small circle of elites and virtually no evidence they were having a significant impact on the political agenda prior to the end of 2011.

While it would be hard to build a convincing argument that elite political forces—be they politicians, political parties, or even bloggers—were making a political impact via the internet prior to the end of 2011, there was promising evidence of online aggregation in Russia when one switched the focus from elite to grassroots online activity. The best way to find it was to look for social flashpoints such as the closure of a Russian dialysis center or the denial of medication to critically ill children and watch small, online communities of Russians start to use the internet to campaign for their rights. While these rights were defined in relatively narrow ways, i.e., the right to specific health-care treatments as opposed to the broader notion of the human right of care, evidence from content analysis of Russian web forums showed the distinctive way in which Russian citizens aggregated online and took action offline to secure what they perceived as their rights. This can help to explain why Russians, who were neither broadly dissatisfied with their society nor organized around a specific opposition, took to the streets in large numbers after reports of election falsification in December 2011.

This book cannot answer the question of whether enough Russians will use the online sphere to become engaged citizens and effectively demand a more democratic society. However, the analysis in this book does establish a visible pattern of how to detect and measure online protest in non-free states. This does not necessarily take place via standard political institutions, such as parties and the legislature, because these do not effectively interact with Russian citizens in a democratic way. It is not necessarily linked to the elite blogging world in Russia, although it is almost always connected to traditional media and society in some way. Prior to the December 2011 protests, it tended to center around relatively small but passionate issues. It often challenged the Russian state's complacency about poor services and response to citizen protests, including in the regions. And, just as the final, conclusive wave of online activism in the Arab Spring could be traced to the public suicide of a street peddler enraged at his treatment by a petty bureaucrat, these online campaigns were typically launched by catalyzing events that angered and energized a preexisting online community. Finally, there would appear to be a critical role for online social entrepreneurs, those who are willing to both spend much time moderating online interchanges as well as often lead in the confrontation that will take place in the offline world through protests, demonstrations, or even civic disobedience.

The Russian Case and Internet Studies: Cyber-optimism, pessimism, and skepticism

The way in which a Russian presidential website both challenges and consolidates information policy in the former Soviet sphere is emblematic of the core questions of this book. For many years, there has been a debate between cyber-optimists, who see the communication tools of the internet as a way to foster democracy, and cyber-pessimists, who fear that the internet works more for the consolidation of anti-state or dangerous forces (such as terrorism) within society. There are worries that unequal access to the internet (both between countries and within nations themselves) lead to what Norris dubbed the digital divide, a society of information haves and have-nots that further fosters worrying divisions in social capital (2001). Another grave concern is the often successful efforts of countries such as China to simultaneously censor web content as well as use the internet as a further means of identifying and punishing dissidents. As such, the internet becomes more a tool for repression than a beacon of democracy.

Much of the study of the internet as a political communication tool has examined the qualities of the medium that exist outside the normal ways in which we understand national media systems to function. The internet, by its ability to provide instant and simultaneous communication that blurs the line between news producers and consumers, fundamentally changes the way in which information is distributed. The extreme outcome of this conceptualization of the online sphere is the notion that this information can then rearrange power structures, taking control away from elites and spreading it amongst the masses in a more democratic manner. This is somewhat of an overstatement of cyber-optimism, in that those who study the internet seriously are cautious to test and measure the extent to which the internet has achieved these goals. However, many scholars do suggest that due to the particular features of the internet, the online sphere could deliver political change that has the potential—for better or worse—to transform or transcend national political institutions (Teubner, 2004). At the same time, there has been a relative neglect of trying to establish how existing media norms, particularly on the national level, have structured the use and influence of the internet within specific countries. Thus, assumptions about the availability of the internet are not enough to predict the role that the internet will play in the media sphere in a particular country. In addition to availability, key points to consider are the political environment and tolerance for free speech; the government's approach to internet regulation and surveillance; the type of content available online; and the perception of citizens about risks and rewards in engaging in the online world.

Christensen (2011) usefully identified a gap in the debate between what he termed "techno-utopians" and "techno-dystopians" (p. 239): "while techno-utopians overstate the affordances of new technologies (what these technologies can give us) and understate the material conditions of their use (e.g., how factors such as gender or economics can affect access), techno-dystopians do the reverse, misinterpreting a lack of results (such as the failure of the Iranian protesters to topple the Ahmadinejad regime) with the impotence of technology; and, also, forgetting how shifts within the realm of mediated political communication can be incremental rather than seismic in nature." This book attempts to fill that gap, weighing the global potential of the internet against factors at the national level in Russia that both shape and constrain that potential.

Both domestic and international factors are bringing the role of the internet in politics to the fore in Russia. Although extensive analysis of the events in the Middle East is still ongoing, it is clear that information communication technologies played a key part in both informing the public and organizing the protest on the ground. While Russia had taken a relatively relaxed approach toward overt policing of the internet (discussed in more depth in Chapter 4), the issue of internet surveillance and control moved up the agenda of all non-free states in 2011. In addition, there is compelling evidence (Deibert et al., 2010) that states such as Russia favor more effective, albeit less obvious, interventions in the online sphere in order to control its ability to inform the public and counter oppositional forces. This parallels the many ways in which the Russian state has constrained political and media openness in general in the past two decades.

At the same time, internet growth in Russia expanded with great rapidity from 2000 to 2010, as the country experienced the largest online growth of any major European country over the course of the decade. According to the measurement by the World Telecommunications/ICT Indicators Database, 43 percent of the Russian population was online by March 31, 2011, with an estimated 59.7 million users out of a population of 138.7 million.[2] The organization reported an increase in usage of 1,826 percent between 2000 and 2010. Russians made up the second-largest online population in Europe by mid-2011, trailing only Germany, and were on track to become the largest online population in the region. While various surveys reported slightly different penetration rates for Russian internet use, it is clear that the trend was toward very rapid growth, fueled by mobile internet access as well as by a Russian government policy to expand online access in general (discussed in more detail in Chapters 3 and 4). There is a parallel here to the policy of Soviet glasnost in the 1980s, in which Soviet leaders wanted to encourage more interesting debate and wound up with central media outlets that were highly critical of the serving leaders (Mickiewicz, 1988; 1997). The media played a key role in the collapse of the Soviet Union in 1991, a lesson that all of the Russian leadership must still remember, if even from their childhood. Thus, the internet offers the Russian government a tool that not only has proven itself effective in challenging apparently stable, non-free regimes, but it is presented to a country in which internet usage has exploded in the past few years. While Russian elites would appear to believe that they can harness these informational tools and have rejected widespread, overt control, the history of the Soviet media would suggest that elites can overestimate their ability to "spin" a population indefinitely, particularly when distribution of information is undergoing a rapid shift.

As of 2011, Russia remained a state in which some free circulation of information had not sparked the growth of robust, citizen-centered political institutions such as parties and social-action networks. Despite the presence of the internet, Russia has remained a relatively authoritarian state in which political parties and grassroots organizations have had little role to play. How well can the Russian experience help us to understand the way in which national political systems constrain and shape the democratizing features of the internet? Overall, there is little comparative work on how national political, media, and social structures may influence the role of the internet in a society, although some has begun to emerge (Giacomello, 2008; Goggin and McLelland, 2008). Rather, the study of the internet in society tends to focus on how the internet could transform society rather than how the society itself might shape and constrain the online world. While television, print media, and radio all are acknowledged to have particular national or cultural forms, the same often is not assumed about the internet. Yet even cursory evidence—such as the relevance of U.S. blogs versus the relative dearth of independent political blogging in the United Kingdom—would suggest that there is as much indication for the internet to be transformed by society as vice versa.

What is missing from much of the debate is the discussion of the role of state power and communication strategy in understanding the function of the internet in the political sphere. While there are studies of how states seek to control the internet, there is little discussion of how states actively use the internet to expand their communicative power, although Deibert et al. (2010) and the work of the OpenNet Initiative have contributed a great deal to this debate. It is recognized that there are certain universal properties of the internet as communication provider, a social networking tool, and even as a virtual sphere for democratic debate (for a good overview, see Polat, 2005). However, these features manifest themselves in different ways in various societies. By the same token, ways of monitoring or controlling the internet vary across country boundaries as well, with China recognized as a clear example of how to balance the rapid growth of the internet for consumers while limiting its use as a political tool for citizens. However, there has been little direct investigation of how state power manifests itself in the online sphere, although interest in this is rising quickly, in the United States in particular (Nye, 2004).

While this study is concerned with the general role of the internet in the political sphere, the book also needs to establish the specific political and media environment in which the internet functions. As such, the book will consider the state of freedom of speech and information distribution in Russia in comparison to both Western models as well as to the former Soviet sphere. While this book will highlight particular regulations and laws relating to the online sphere in Russia, it also contrasts how the Russian internet has developed in comparison with other countries. This study will make a direct analysis of how Russian state power is perpetuated online through a range of methodologies. This will include analysis of state policy, the content itself, the distribution of content, as well as audience consumption and engagement in the online sphere. This book approaches the examination of the online media and political sphere by emphasizing the study of political institutions and issues over the analysis of particular online sites. As such, while the project involves the study of web content, this is not limited to the scrutiny of a particular website or set of websites. Rather, the volume examines Russian political party websites as a way of comparing Russia with studies about parties online in the West. In addition, the book expands on web analysis techniques pioneered by Fossato et al. (2008) by tracing how issues critical to certain groups of citizens are discussed in the online sphere. This allows the project to examine how issues that are important to either particular segments of society (access to a particular hospital) or to all citizens (access to health care) are possibly affected by the online "virtual" sphere. It also allows the project to follow, as much as possible via word searches and web link analyses on the Russian internet, where there are issues of interest in the online sphere.

In order to carry out this analysis, the book provides an overview of the Russian online sphere, in the political, social, and media context of the country. It examines various levels of analysis and critical points of intersection of the online and offline world in a country defined both by its Soviet past and the failure of democratic institutions in the young Russian state. At the same time, the project is focused on exploring how state power and national politics shape and constrain the online sphere in a deliberate inversion of studies of how the internet affects national-level politics. Finally, this analysis is interested in advancing the field of internet studies by further developing and refining how to best isolate the role of the internet in the political sphere. In particular, this book will carry out this task by showing how citizens frame and talk about their rights in specific contexts in the online sphere. An additional chapter that analyzes the role of the internet in the 2011–12 protests will use both offline and online research to reflect on how the internet related to the protest. Overall, this book combines a range of methods, from the study of legal and media systems to internet content to the online audience and consumers themselves. Of particular interest is finding the critical synthesis between the online and offline worlds, so that it becomes possible to better model the democratizing potential of the internet within the constraints of national political systems.

On a final introductory note about methods, it must be said that technological advances in how to search, organize, and analyze online data have developed with great rapidity in recent years and even months. In fact, methods have changed so fast that a reviewer of an insightful book on American blogging (Davis, 2009) noted that while the book made an important intellectual contribution to the field, it seemed "almost quaint" to use only 2,951 posts for an analysis when computerized retrieval and software options for content analysis were available (Margolis, 2010, p. 220). The point is that Davis, along with others who use human coding, embedded the content analysis within broader discussion and research about blogging and its relationship to traditional U.S. journalism. Although the book by Davis effectively presents an elegant and compelling argument that blogs have been incorporated into the American political discourse rather than challenging that discourse, a few years on from this publication it is important to make use, where appropriate, of online analytics in support of research design. As such, this book uses online freeware for web link analysis called IssueCrawler[3] (where once web links would have been discussed, counted, or coded by hand) to provide the reader with an overview of how particular websites function within the broader information geography of the online world. In addition, this book has employed web analytics to triangulate websites and online platforms where political discourse and challenge to the Russian state is taking place. However, while this book reports on some useful and interesting computerized, semantic searches of the Russian online sphere, including work carried out by the Berkman Center for Internet & Society at Harvard University and the Center for New Media and Society at the New Economic School (Moscow), it relied on human coding of web content to measure the nature of online engagement in specific case studies. The trade-offs between automatic web tools and human content analysis will be discussed in more depth in Chapter 6.

International Internet Models vs. National Media Models

Although cyber-optimism and cyber-pessimism have pervaded much of the internet studies literature, it is now generally recognized that characterizing the internet as normatively good, bad, or perhaps indifferent is not that useful in terms of progressing social science inquiry. This is a bit of an unfair critique, as within these paradigms is some extremely useful research into the role of the internet in the political sphere. Notably, the discussion by Norris of the digital divide as well as her notion of the "virtuous circle" showing that media use enhances citizenship are both examples of useful ways to contribute to the understanding of the internet and the role of the media in the political sphere more generally (2001, 2000). In addition, the field has moved on to more specific hypothesis formation, including coding of how political parties use the web (such as Gibson and Ward, 2000; Gibson, Resnick, and Ward, 2003; Jankowski et al., 2005; Foot et al., 2010). Much of the study of the internet focuses on how it may enhance existing political institutions within a particular country (such as Linaa Jensen, 2006; Lusoli and Ward, 2006; Wright, 2006). There is some study of how the internet might bring democracy into a country that is undemocratic in nature. Unsurprisingly, there has been a focus on probing for signs that the internet is a democratizing force in China. Even in this rather compelling example (China has a combination of burgeoning internet use, a growing market economy, and repressive state laws to monitor the internet for spreading political dissent), there is no real agreement between cyber-optimists and cyber-pessimists. From the evidence gathered in China, it is not clear whether the internet can be a significant tool for delivering democratization to a country (Hartford, 2000; Polumbaum, 2001; Abbott, 2001; Harwit and Clark, 2001; Reporters Without Borders, 2005; Taubman, 1998). Arguably, most of these studies predate the advent of Web 2.0 and its greater potential to personalize, popularize, and spread political messages through social networks. However, it would be expected that the Chinese authorities could continue to monitor the internet with their multilevel filtering regime, from the production of internet content, to routine searches for words such as "democracy" in the content, to tracing of users themselves both online and via monitoring in cybercafes (Open Net Initiative, April 14, 2005; for an updated discussion see Deibert et al., 2009).

This leaves us with the issue of how one can structure a model of the democratizing potential of the internet. Existing cyber-paradigms are simply too broad, but other studies have generally dealt with only particular aspects of the online sphere. This is logical, in that trying to construct a sort of international meta-theory of the internet's democratizing ability would be a broad, difficult, and probably fruitless task. We are left with the basic qualities of the internet that we know offer the potential for democratization. Newhagen (1997) highlights the importance of going beyond current political communication studies of broadcasting, in that the internet functions as not only an information provider in the sense of "traditional" media but an advanced social communication tool as well. Polat expands this definition, pointing out that in addition to information and communication, the internet offers the opportunity to create a "virtual sphere." Davis makes the point that the introduction of a new media platform does not completely replace the audience for the previous media form—i.e., the introduction of television did not stop people from reading newspapers. He argues it is more useful to think of audiences as overlapping or augmented by a range of different media types (p. 190). In addition, aside from its interactive features, the internet has distinctive elements that make it different from traditional broadcast and print media. The internet also offers a low-cost (often virtually no-cost) ability to distribute information to a potentially limitless global audience. In addition, it allows for potential freedom from editorial filters and controls. Finally, the nature of the internet facilitates relative freedom from national media restraints as well as the ability to build an international audience.

How do these known elements of the internet map onto our understanding of the role of the media in the political sphere in terms of national media models? National media models are themselves rather contentious, in that some scholars feel that the relationship between the media and the state can be best understood via national models and culture (Siebert et al., 1994; Hallin and Mancini, 2004; Schudson, 1995) while others believe that it makes more sense to look at this as a power relationship that is not particularly tied to a specific national culture and structure (Herman and Chomsky, 2002; Sparks, 2000). It is clear that the elements of the internet listed above would intersect differently if one were conceptualizing of the media via a "national" system or a "power" system. However, in both cases it would appear that the particular features of the internet *should* allow citizens to circumvent barriers via news cycles, news norms, ownership controls, access, editorial issues, censorship, and other filters in order to communicate more freely with one another. Interestingly, there was a long gap in case studies in which there was some compelling evidence of the role of the internet in challenging regimes. The classic case study was the Chiapas people in Mexico, who used Web 1.0 and links to a U.S. university to attract international support to their cause in the mid-1990s. Surprisingly, there remained relatively few compelling case studies of broad challenge to non-free regimes via the internet from the Chiapas revolt until the Iranian elections in 2009 (and evidence remains mixed about the efficacy of the internet's role in the protest). However, by early 2011, there was significant evidence that the internet was being used as a key information conduit for anti-state protestors in the Middle East. What remains still in doubt is whether internet communication *followed* the protest or whether the internet *spurred* protest with rapid and critical information disbursal that was faster and more nimble than state propaganda efforts.

More ominously, Deibert et al. suggest that the internet can actually *impede* protest in non-free states, a conviction shared by Morozov (2011). They argue that the real asymmetry in power between repressive states and citizens lies in the ability of states to deploy the internet in a carefully choreographed manner that simultaneously promotes state interests through propaganda as well as discredits opponents via information campaigns or strategic takedowns of internet sites at critical political moments. At the same time, the state can use the internet to penetrate resistance organizations with ease, allowing them to selectively intimidate or arrest cyber-dissidents. The internet also allows repressive states to set up systems to coerce or encourage citizens to stay within national domains or particular types of websites in the online world, further promoting the distortion of information while they harvest online interactions to gain nuanced information on political actions and orientations of individual citizens. This raises the question about whether the potential of the internet to promote democratic protest is being subverted even before it can be effectively used by citizens (given the gap between the Chiapas uprising and the Arab Spring). All good social scientists must consider the null hypothesis: Will there be a time when we must ask ourselves if there are *fewer* democratic protests against authoritarian regimes because of the presence of the internet?

Even without the overt threat of what Deibert et al. call third-generation controls of the internet, in which "the focus is less on *denying* access than successfully *competing* with potential threats through effective counter-information campaigns that overwhelm, discredit, or demoralize opponents" (p. 27, emphasis in original), there needs to be careful attention paid to how national political institutions and culture shape—and apparently tame—the potential of the internet. The notion that a nation can subvert the democratizing potential of an international communications tool might at first seem unlikely in states without an overt, repressive control of the online sphere and beyond. However, using the Russian case to examine how communication tools can promote undemocratic notions provides compelling evidence for this idea. There are a range of different levels of analysis to consider, some of which are not an explicit part of the media models suggested by Hallin and Mancini (2004) or Siebert et al. (1963, reprinted in 1994). Those models tend to focus most closely on the relationship of the state to the media system. In fact, it is important to consider the different levels that define this relationship, from news production to the audience itself. In terms of research focus, it is key to consider the factors that shape the production of news within a country (such as political environment, media norms, media regulations, media ownership, and the journalistic profession), the media content itself, as well as the audience. These factors are not linear or static; rather, they shift and interact with one another constantly. Another factor is the way in which different national audiences embrace the internet. For example, researchers are aware that levels of trust in the internet vary both between countries and within countries themselves, particularly in terms of audience variables such as age, education, and length of time since entering the online sphere. However, there needs to be more analysis of trust and media generally. To explore the nature of the relationship between the user and the internet, this book includes a study of how those who are routinely online in Russia vary in key political attitudes (Chapter 3).

The Paradox of the Russian Media

From a distance, Russia provides a communications paradox in that there is so much information and so little democracy. The country has a wealth of media outlets and a range of opinions that are expressed in broadcast, print, and internet outlets. The economic stability of the Russian media, in particular television, increased steadily as the Russian economy improved under

Putin (Kachkaeva, Kiriya, and Libergal, 2006). Yet, in some ways, it would appear that the contemporary Russian media has more to do with the Soviet media than any Western model (Oates, 2007; Becker, 2004). In Soviet times, the media served the interests of the ruling elite in the Communist Party of the Soviet Union as described by the Soviet model of the press in Siebert et al. Even through the glasnost period of 1985 to 1991, the Soviet media failed to transform itself from a platform for political players to a voice of the citizens. Diversity of media did develop, yet the idea of the media as objective or balanced has never been widely adopted. As Becker notes, diversity is relatively well tolerated in some sectors (such as print), but not on key broadcast outlets. All segments of Russian society, from politicians to the public to the journalists themselves, perceive the mass media as a political player rather than as a watchdog that can provide a check on political power for the interest of citizens (Pasti, 2005; Voltmer, 2000; Oates, 2007).

Analysts long persisted in calling Russia a "developing" democracy, but there is significant evidence that the country has not developed meaningful democratic institutions such as effective political parties, a strong legislature, an independent judiciary, or a Fourth Estate in the media. There is the appearance of democratic institutions in form, including a range of media outlets with various types of ownership, elections, parliament, and a popularly elected president, but these institutions lack democratic content. The mass media generally echo a charade of democratic interaction, particularly on the influential state-run television channels. Attempts to challenge the government on key issues such as corruption at the top, the progress of war in Chechnya, bribery, or the unfairness of the leadership are not tolerated (Oates and McCormack, 2010). For example, the majority stockholder of the most prominent commercial television station was arrested in 2000 and majority ownership in the media group was transferred to forces friendly to the government (Oates, 2006). Russia has been labeled by international media freedom organizations as particularly bad in terms of treatment of journalists, for whom there is a real fear of menace, physical threat, and even death. It is not surprising that the media work virtually unanimously to support the policies of the central leaders in a disturbing echo of the Soviet model of the media.

If we are trying to see what part the internet can play in the Russian media sphere, what does the traditional media landscape in Russia look like? Russia has a mix of ownership across all levels of print and broadcasting. There is a wealth of media, including national newspapers, local newspapers, state radio, and commercial radio, as well as satellite and cable television that has become quite widely available in recent years. However, central television stations in Russia retain a particular political influence that they now lack in the United States and the United Kingdom. The dominant networks (broadcast on Channels 1 and 2 on the television dial) are the state-run First Channel and state-owned Rossiya-1. There has been steady growth in the television sphere, with the number of channels that half of the Russian nation could receive increasing from five in 2004 to nine in 2006 (Kachkaeva, Kiriya, and Libergal, 2006). Self-censorship is endemic in the journalism industry, with only a few examples of confrontation with the Kremlin line on sensitive subjects such as Chechnya.[4] Employees of all media outlets are well aware of the limits of what can be said on air or in print. This parallels the Soviet experience of journalists, in which the action of a censor was rarely needed as Soviet reporters understood the party line and the way all stories should be formulated from their first day on the job. Even if there are certain topics that get little meaningful coverage, there is a lot of news in general. There are more than 400 newspaper titles (more than during the Soviet era), but most of them are quite small and many struggle financially.[5] In addition, all prominent newspapers toe the Kremlin line. There is some radio news, including the relatively liberal Echo of Moscow radio station (for more on the traditional mass media audience, see Chapter 3).

So why can't the internet fill this gap? In order to address this query, it is important to consider the nature of the Russian internet. What is the character of internet content, control, and usage in Russia? Where does it fit in the media mix? Most importantly for this study, where does the Russian internet link into the political sphere? More than other types of media, the internet can be connected directly to political institutions (social action groups, NGOs, political parties, local governance, etc.) because of its low-cost ability to aggregate interests. Is there something distinctive about the Russian internet that is preventing it from becoming an effective tool for democratization and political mobilization? Is there something about the Russian media sphere in general? Or is the actual dearth of political outlets and opportunities for mobilization the relevant problem in blocking democratization? In other words, does the internet simply exist, like so many other political institutions in Russia, as an isolated element, unable to spark political change because aggregated interests have no ability to take action? On an even more worrying note, what happens in the (relatively rare) instance when interests are aggregated online? Does it result in effective political action or does it merely bring protestors unwelcome attention from security services? What has been the result of the protests in 2011–12?

The Russian Internet Audience

The general Russian media audience is particularly well-educated and attuned to political messages via the news (Oates, 2007). Connection to the internet, particularly the home-based broadband link that fosters in-depth online usage, was relatively low in Russia for many years. However, growth exploded in the past few years. In 2011, the Russian government produced an in-depth report on the country's online audience, persuasively predicting that the online penetration rate would grow to almost 100 percent for those under 40 in the next five years (Russian Federal Agency on the Press and Mass Communication, 2011). While it might appear illogical that Russian internet growth would not stall in the same way as the U.S. or British audiences before reaching full penetration, the growth in the Russian internet audience has been extraordinary. It does not follow the same pattern in parallel to economic development as suggested by Cooper (2008). It has defied expectations and met the optimistic prediction of Medvedev to bring the internet penetration rate in Russia to 40 percent in a few short years (Cooper). Indeed, Russia has moved from relatively low internet usage for the former Soviet region to the second-largest group of Europeans online. As noted above, however, quantitative measures such as rates of penetration are not enough. This book is also concerned with whether participation in the online sphere is a transformative political experience. As Chapter 3 notes, there are distinctive political characteristics of those who go online regularly in Russia, suggesting that this group is more liberal and challenging to the state in general. Will this connection between online use and democratic values continue to grow along with the explosion in internet use in Russia?

Russian Internet Content

While there are well-known, professional websites that address Russian news and politics on the Russian internet (nicknamed Runet), many of them reflect the limited spread of news found in the mainstream media. This is not surprising, in that the web also is dominated by mainstream media sites in countries such as the United States and the United Kingdom. A project by the Reuters Institute for the Study of Journalism at Oxford (Fossato et al., 2008) examined three Russian social movements and blogs in an attempt to understand the nature of Web 2.0 in Russia. What they found was a disturbing echo of the dynamics of the Russian traditional media and political elites. In the Reuters Institute project, researchers examined both the general state of the internet in Russia as well as the Russian blogosphere. They found that 75 percent of Russian language blogs were hosted on five platforms, with LiveJournal as the most popular blogging and social networking site. While there was evidence that the Russian blogosphere was growing at a modest pace (with an estimated 7,000 blogs created daily), the Reuters Institute report did not find evidence that Web 2.0 could launch any social change. The researchers noted that Western expectations about the internet's ability to deploy democratization mechanisms were not shared by many Russian analysts of the Russian online sphere. Notably, Russian analysts felt that Russian political norms would be more likely to be replicated rather than challenged online, such as by being used by elites to discuss politics within relatively closed circles (Fossato et al., 2008).

The report by Fossato et al. provides evidence that Russia is shaping the internet, rather than Russian society being shaped by the internet (Rohozinski, 2000). This is a particularly clear and convincing image of how the internet is constrained by domestic, rather than international, political communication norms, or as Rohozinski phrases it, how "the 'new dog' of the Internet was adapted and used to perform the 'old tricks' inherent to the Soviet system" (p. 334). Although Rohozinski wrote this more than a decade ago, the idea still has resonance. The Reuters Institute report found that new communications technology did not appear to break down "well-established patterns of power" (p. 53). Rather, the state (rather than "netizens" or even citizens) remained the "main mobilising agent" (p. 53). Although the Russian internet is a powerful disseminator of information, the Reuters Institute did not find evidence that this information mobilized the masses by any stretch of the imagination. Rather, the case studies analyzed by the researchers found that "this information mobilizes mainly closed clusters of like-minded users who only on rare occasions are able and willing to cooperate with other groups" (p. 53). While this lack of mobilization was one part of the story—and there is arguably widespread lack of evidence of internet mobilization in Western Europe as well—the Reuters Institute report made an important insight into the nature of the internet, governance, and power by pointing out that the Russian internet was developing as another platform that the state used increasingly successfully "to consolidate its power, manipulate, and spread messages of stability and unity among the growing number of Russians regularly accessing websites and blogs" (p. 53). Thus, Russians would appear to have been experiencing further political repression from the growth of online communication. At the same time, the Russian masses seemed to reap little to no benefit from the democratizing potential of the internet, while the state was successfully using the online world to further its non-democratic agenda of citizen compliance and control.

To any serious observers of the Russian political and media sphere, this would not seem to be surprising. In particular, studies of Russian television and the journalism profession more broadly in Russia show that the mass media have been political players allied with political factions in Russia as opposed to media in service to the greater political good or even in the interest of relatively disinterested dissemination of information (Oates, 2006; European Institute for the Media, March 2000, August 2000; Voltmer, 2000; Pasti, 2005). The same relationship that existed among the media, the political elites, and the public in the traditional print and broadcast media would appear to have manifested itself in the online world in Russia prior to the end of 2011. This raised the question of whether this was the case in other countries as well. Was Russia simply an extreme example of the ability of the government to conquer the "high ground" of the internet communication heights—or was there something about the Russian media sphere itself that seemed to make this inevitable? Was it the traditional relationship of a relatively passive Russian public that preferred "strong hands" over "more say" in governance (White, Miller, and Oates, 2003) that dictated this role of the internet in the contemporary Russian infosphere? Or does the internet tend to be shaped by national political forces in any country? The Russian case is particularly intriguing in that there is no widespread evidence of heavy-handed censorship through the Russian media sphere, both online and offline, prior to the protests in the end of 2011. Rather, the Russian elites effectively controlled the media messages through a strategy of inculcated self-censorship on the part of journalists, selective application of financial laws to shut down alternative voices, and the knowledge on the part of journalists that they could be killed in a relatively lawless state by those they might have angered with their coverage.

It must be acknowledged, however, that theories about top-down control of the media only go so far in explaining the state of a national civic sphere. Part of the puzzle of post–Soviet Russia has been the widespread lack of civic organization and protest in general. In a way that has surprised many Western analysts, robust civic organizations have failed to materialize in Russia since the collapse of the Soviet Union. In particular, political parties have not become a legitimate democratizing force. There are a number of reasons for this, which have been explored in depth in the political science literature (e.g., see Smyth, 2006; Hutcheson, 2003; White, 2011). To summarize the arguments, there was significant political maneuvering on the part of elites to avoid the creation of civic institutions that would encourage the transfer of real political power outside of a narrow oligarchy. A wide range of public opinion surveys suggest that the Russian public were relatively comfortable with this type of rule—and very supportive in particular of the way in which president and prime minister Vladimir Putin ruled the country and muzzled the powers of the parliament (for an overview, see White 2011). More worrying is the lack of an independent judiciary in Russia, which has left a disproportionately large amount of power in the hands of the Kremlin. The point is, however, that the failure to aggregate interests online is not isolated. Rather, it reflects a widespread attitude that permeates much of Russian political culture. In addition, however, it also echoes a particular pragmatism in that generating political capital with no practical purpose is not worthwhile. If there are no effective political parties, social groups, or a meaningful national parliament, for what purpose does one generate social capital online? It is like amassing a currency that cannot be spent anywhere. Unsurprisingly, Russians do not appear to value this particular social asset.

These ideas about Russian political culture were challenged by the protests at the end of 2011 and the beginning of 2012. To observers and analysts of Russian elections, it would appear that the widespread public protests to the reports of election falsification were quite surprising. There has been quite obvious electoral manipulation, notably biased television coverage as well as anomalous precinct results, in virtually all Russian elections. However, as discussed in more detail in Chapter 7, the internet was able to spur protest in several ways. One key way was the collection of video evidence of voter irregularity and fraud to post online, making it more difficult for the officials to refute or manipulate the information. The online sphere made the falsification visible to others, rendering it very hard to dismiss it as isolated. People could download and analyze the election results for themselves, as they were all posted online by the Central Election Commission of the Russian Federation. In addition, social-networking/blogging sites such as VKontakte and LiveJournal encouraged discussion of the issue and aggregation of interests, motivated and led by popular bloggers. Finally, the internet provided an excellent venue to subvert state media framing of the elections as orderly, as well as afforded a way in which to organize the protests themselves. Yet, were the winter of 2011–12 protests isolated events, specifically spurred by compelling evidence of electoral fraud? Or were they just the first manifestation of a rising political consciousness on the part of the Russian citizens who will no longer tolerate the gap between what their leaders say and what they do? This calls for an examination of the evidence at a range of levels of analysis, from patterns of internet use, to content analysis, to network analysis.

Internet Research Methodologies and the Russian Case

The case of the Russian internet illuminates some of the key challenges in the study of the online sphere. Some of the central work in the field has focused on the content analysis of web pages. This methodology provided a structured way to categorize, summarize, and analyze significant web content. The methodology has been applied to Russia, in particular by March (2006) to examine political party websites. While the Gibson and Ward (2000) web content analysis scheme offers some key basics in the field—i.e., one has to know what information is available online and how it is presented—there are two challenges to using this methodology to study the contemporary Russian political internet. The first one is a practical one, in that web content has now expanded so enormously that it is difficult to capture the relevant information. When Gibson and

Ward started their studies of parties online, their key findings were both how little information was available as well as the relatively static, non-dynamic nature of that data. Today, even minor political parties in most democracies have a huge amount of information online in formats ranging from video blogs to forums, making it significantly more difficult to perform a relevant content analysis. While some scholars approach this by filtering or word searches (such as the computerized filtering tools found in the Dark Web project that tracks potential terrorist groups, see Qin et al., 2007), the sheer volume is still overwhelming. A far greater challenge than quantity, however, is the changing qualitative nature of what takes place online. In particular, the challenges of Web 2.0—in which the internet has grown into a virtual information sphere with real and potential communities forming online—have not yet been met by internet scholars. There is a great deal of interest in the area, with vigorous debate and ideas launched at conferences and in journals, but a robust, valid, and reliable method of testing online social science phenomenon is still in its early stages. Interestingly, tools developed for marketing intelligence have developed far more rapidly, with companies and researchers offering a range of ways to "scrape" data from blog postings, Twitter, Facebook comments, and so on, and present summaries of data findings and trends. As discussed later in this book, however, the analysis of political content is more complex.

This book argues that online research tools must be integrated into a broader understanding of political institutions and communication within a particular society. This project builds on a body of work that has emerged to analyze the Russian web with a particular grounding in post-Soviet political communication (including Fossato et al., 2008; Rohozhinski, 2000; Semetko and Krasnoboka, 2003; Krasnoboka and Semetko, 2006; March, 2006; Schmidt, 2006; Lonkila, 2008). All of these works place the post-Soviet internet within its political context and the work seeks to find evidence that the internet has, in some way, enhanced civic life in countries such as Russia. All of these studies fail to find that the internet has enhanced civic life in Russia, although Krasnoboka and Semetko did find evidence that the internet has contributed in a significant way to freedom of speech in Ukraine. The methodology in the studies is similar, in that the researchers examine web content in order to find evidence of social network construction, alternative political viewpoints, or growth of social capital.

Work in *The Web That Failed* (Fossato et al., 2008) carried out innovative research in an attempt to understand the possible impact of the internet on Russian politics. The researchers limited their analysis to three social movements with blogs, each of which challenged the Kremlin elite on some level (as a nationalist movement, a liberal movement, and citizen group campaigning for fair treatment of motorists). What is elegant about the methodology in this relatively modest project is that the researchers developed two important research innovations. First, they focused on the quality of web content in discussions linked to particular blogs rather than a larger, more unmanageable quantity of web content. While they found many postings quite routine, there were identifiable "firestorms" in the blogosphere in which relatively passive networks of individuals were galvanized into particular action in the offline world (such as after the unfair arrest of a civilian motorist to cover up the fact that a car driven at an unsafe speed by a state official had caused a fatal accident). The nature and spread of the online firestorms—and how they could be "extinguished" by authorities in the offline or online world—provide promise as a way to analyze the effect of Web 2.0 on the Russian political sphere. The researchers also used knowledge of Russian conversation and interchange to categorize the typologies of online exchange in general. They examined the blogs to characterize whether the nature of these conversations could be described as dialogues, monologues, or discussions. They further refined this by coding exchanges as emotional, appeals for calm, or calls to protest. In their research, they did not mention just the appearance of news (as the Gibson and Ward scheme does), but noted whether the news was in the form of an eyewitness report. In addition, did the website offer audio or video reports, either from the central blogger or the participants on the blog? Were people more likely to provide information or to offer opinion? All of these types of questions are important for understanding the nature of online interchange in Russia and beyond.

The work by Fossato et al. highlights the importance of understanding how politics and media work in Russia in studying the online sphere. In addition to web content analysis, the researchers interviewed the central bloggers themselves, which turned out to be critical in explaining why the motorists' rights blog became far less political in the end of 2007. According to the blogger, he was asked by government officials to tone down the criticism on this blog—and he complied. This parallels the offline world, in which Russian journalists are particularly vulnerable to elite pressures. The report concluded that none of the blogs, despite being some of the more relevant and popular political blogs in Russia, had any real effect on the country's December 2007 Duma elections or March 2008 presidential elections. While some of the lack of influence could be ascribed to relatively low internet penetration in the country at the time, it was clear that there was a different dynamic relating to the online political world in Russia than in developed democracies. Although political web content is a relatively small part of the online sphere even in the United States, it is still possible to identify important online components of political phenomenon in most Western countries, particularly during elections.

Building on analytical tools, reports, and previous studies of the Russian internet, this book will examine how online communication could foster political change in the country. Throughout the analysis, the attempt is made to balance domestic factors with the global properties and potential of online communication. This book simultaneously considers the internet landscape in Russia, in particular by examining internet use, changes in this use, and attitudes of the online audience, as well as how government policy and laws may encourage or constrain online engagement. How does it fit within the Russian system of news production, news content, and audience? Russian online audience, attitudes, and policies are placed within the context of the post-Soviet sphere to examine how and why Russia's online audience and policy may have developed differently from other former Communist states. While making an overview of Runet content and activity, the project focuses on specific areas of the online sphere in an attempt to measure the intersection between political interest and online activity. One chapter is devoted to considering how political parties, including the Communist Party of the Russian Federation as the only viable opposition party, attempt to use the online sphere to garner support. Another chapter considers case studies of advocacy groups for children with disabilities as well as action by dialysis patients in Rostov-on-Don that successfully fought to keep a life-saving service open. These cases are examined within the broader context of how citizens may find online spaces in which to express and campaign for their rights, even in a system that offers little in terms of traditional political institutions and aggregation. A final chapter looking at Russian web activity uses studies of people both offline and online to reflect on the role of the internet in the winter 2011–12 protests.

Chapter Summaries

Chapter 2 provides an overview of the political communication literature on how national political and media norms define and constrain global information flow. The objective of this chapter is to map the international, democratizing potential of the internet onto the national constraints of media systems. While this is quite relevant to the specific case study of Russia, it also addresses a key gap in the internet studies literature. Although media models are recognized as central to understanding information provision on a national level, there has been little study of the effect of the state on a national online sphere. This chapter seeks to build a model of how to understand and analyze the relative significance of the internet in the political sphere within a nation. In contrast to the mobilizing potential of the online sphere, the chapter considers how national media management and systems challenge this potential. In addition, the chapter considers ways in which the state can mobilize the internet for its own interests (rather than assuming the internet is naturally a tool for citizen interest and activism). While this phenomenon may be more directly observed in states such as

Russia, it is important to reflect that states in a range of regimes deploy the internet as a tool of the state rather than as a beacon of democracy for the masses.

Chapter 3 provides an overview of Runet content and community, with a discussion of popular websites and trends in the Russian online sphere. Of particular note is the way in which Russia has evolved one of the world's most active blogging platforms through LiveJournal, as well as the way in which Russia has developed strong national brands in the search engine Yandex and social-networking site VKontakte (In Contact) that dominate over foreign platforms such as Google and Facebook. In addition to information from several studies of the Russian online audience, this chapter includes an analysis of a 2010 survey of 2,017 Russians that explored attitudes about social issues, political issues, and media use. Audience analysis is often neglected in cross-national studies, but research has shown that audience usage, engagement, and trust of media outlets are particularly important ways of understanding the nature of national media systems (Oates, 2006; Oates, 2007). The survey provides a comparison of critical attitudes between the online and offline audience just as the online audience in Russia reached a significant percentage of the population. Of particular note is the way in which regular internet users in Russia appear to hold attitudes that are more challenging to an authoritarian regime. As the internet population grows, will these more liberal values spread as well? Or are these liberal values merely a correlation with preexisting beliefs, i.e., those who were more questioning were more likely to go online in the first place?

Chapter 4 focuses on the controls that shape what Russians see and do in the online sphere. While a fundamental element of the online sphere is understanding the audience and content as discussed in Chapter 3, government policy and investment also shape the access and functionality of the online sphere. In addition, once internet access and functionality have been created within a particular country, how does the government attempt to monitor and control the activity in the online sphere? This chapter analyzes the evolving controls of the online sphere in Russia. The picture that emerges is at first confusing—in that Russia has invested heavily in increasing online connectivity while simultaneously limiting free speech online—unless it is viewed within the broader approach of the Russian state to citizen information control. As with the traditional mass media, the Russian state is confident that it can use the means of mass communication to create more supportive citizens in a non-democratic environment. As a result, Russia serves as a model for what Deibert et al. have defined as third-generation internet control, in which the use of the internet is encouraged as a way to spread government propaganda and disinformation. This chapter analyzes the way in which laws and policies have been created that undermines the value of the internet as a democratizing tool for citizens. Of particular interest is an analysis of how Russian authorities have chosen to implement laws. While there is not a persistent pattern of harassment and containment, which technically could be possible under Russian law, there is enough detection and pursuit of those labeled cyber-dissidents to create an atmosphere of repression for citizens wishing to mount a serious challenge to the Russian state. A lack of censorship does not indicate a dearth of control. Rather, Russia's online media management parallels its offline media controls, notably through norms of self-censorship and a fear of severe consequences (including assassination) for challenging elites on key issues such as the war in Chechnya. This chapter discusses the trajectory of internet freedom in Russia, with references to reports on internet freedom in neighboring post-Soviet countries.

With the key factors of internet content and control discussed in Chapters 3 and 4, Chapter 5 uses comparative studies and methods to examine how the internet may support political parties in Russia. This chapter draws on the extensive literature on the role of political parties in democratic development, and specifically in the Russian context (for example, White, Rose, and McAllister, 1996; Colton, 2000; Hutcheson, 2003; White, Wyman, and Oates, 1997; Rose and Munro, 2002; Smyth, 2006). Two decades after the end of Soviet rule, political parties appear to have done little to foster democracy in Russia. Indeed, successive Russian presidential administrations have used prime television networks to create and manipulate political images to the point that traditional political parties have essentially been replaced by shallow "broadcast parties" (Oates, 2006), parties that are promoted as champions of the people at elections but rarely work in the service of citizens. Rather, after extensive, positive campaign coverage and consistent positive framing on the influential television news, Russian parties serve as vehicles to carry out the will of a narrow, ruling elite. At the same time, gradually more restrictive laws on the formation and activity of opposition parties have limited the ability of grassroots political movements.

Chapter 5 considers to what degree the internet can serve as a way to redress this balance and to help political parties become vehicles for the aggregation of mass interest in Russia. The study focuses on the four political parties that held blocs of seats in the Duma (the lower house of the Russian parliament) from 2007 to 2011: United Russia, the Communist Party of the Russian Federation, the Liberal-Democratic Party of Russia, and A Just Russia. As Chapter 5 discusses, these were four distinctive parties that run the gamut from a Kremlin-backed powerhouse to a small center-left opposition party. The chapter analyzes how effective these Russian political parties were at providing information to citizens and potential voters. In addition, the chapter uses web analytics to consider how visible and connected the political party websites were within the political geography of Runet. Overall, it would appear that the internet tended to reflect, rather than challenge, offline political power and political communication. However, there were features of various political party web-sites, notably news and citizen observations on smaller party websites, that provided unique viewpoints and information to citizens in Russia.

If there is significant evidence that central party websites are "preaching to the converted," where should one look for relevant online engagement? The re-mainder of the book attempts to find this engagement in a different way from measurements related to information provision and engagement via particular web content linked to offline political actions. Chapter 6 examines the ability of the internet to spark action on specific issues across a range of different locations of the web in online "firestorms" (Fossato et al.). This chapter uses catalyzing events in the Russian online sphere, including a crisis in Rostov-on-Don over the closure of a dialysis center and anger over a newspaper columnist who suggested that disabled children could be killed at birth. What sorts of online exchanges do these events spark? More broadly, what types of government policies, incidents, reports, or experiences will motivate Russians to go online—to complain, to post information, to engage in dialogue, to disagree? In particular, this chapter considers how the online engagement through Russian organizations and forums relating to health issues reflect on political engagement. Although there would seem to be relatively little interest and engagement with formal political institutions, there is passion, persuasion, and evidence of political action through these causes. According to work by Turbine (2007a, 2007b), Russians often have a more practical approach to the nature of rights in their society, using rights-based approaches to resolve concrete problems. By searching for clues of internet activism in a more specific way that reflects the nature of engagement in Russia, this project will be able to provide a better analysis of the role of the online sphere in political engagement in the post-Soviet context.

The work in Chapter 6 includes a range of data collection in five distinct ques-tions about the relationship between the issues and the online sphere: where is the information and discussion on the issue located online; who is talking about it via user-generated content; what is being said; why do the users feel moved to engage in online discussion; and how does the internet seem to have affected attitudes or even action? Chapter 6 also employs link analysis to examine where much of the discussion or information of these issues is disseminated on Runet. Both content analysis and user analysis will be employed to analyze who partici-pates in discussions about particular debates on these issues. Overall, the study of Russian web content and user-generated comments provides a backdrop to discuss broader issues of the relative merits of quantitative and qualitative analy-sis of the online sphere.

Chapter 7 examines what the winter protests in 2011–12 in Russia demon-strate about the role of the internet in Russian society and beyond. What were the protests about and how were they linked to the online sphere, both in terms of information provision and mobilization? How did the Russian government's reaction to the rising power of the internet alleviate or exacerbate political tensions? Do these protests provide compelling evidence that the internet has become embedded in the political life of Russian citizens, signaling a new era in political communication for the Russian state? What does this suggest for the future of Russian citizens, Russian leaders, and Russian democracy? The analysis in this chapter unpacks a combination of factors that all contributed to the Russian "winter of discontent." Some of these factors had been evolving in Russian society for some time, including the failure of state "soft" controls that relied on traditions of self-censorship to contain the online sphere; an online sphere that is freer than traditional mass media; as well as an explosion in internet use. At the same time, other factors were pivotal to the way in which the internet contributed to the protest, including a lack of understanding about citizen attitudes and the online sphere on the part of the Kremlin; the rise of crowd-sourcing; the strength of online political networks; and the role of online social entrepreneurs. In conjunction with these factors, studies of Russian attitudes and elections suggest that reports of widespread electoral falsification would serve as a particularly emotive and powerful trigger for Russian citizens. In the identification and analysis of these factors, we can recognize a pattern of online political evolution in general.

Summary: A Theoretical Framework for the Study of the Online Sphere in Non-Free States

The details of the study of the Russian internet in the context of post-Soviet politics can be summarized into five levels of analysis for greater clarity: content, community, catalyst, control, and co-optation. In this five-step analytical framework, content is just one factor in a range of elements that could possibly better illuminate the political power of the internet. At each level, there are specific methods although some of them overlap. As difficult as it can be to systematically analyze the huge amount of content on the blogosphere or on forums, this content holds vital evidence as to the function of the internet as a political tool. Fortunately, methodologies for taming the information overload of the blogosphere, and internet content in general, are emerging (Kelly et al., 2012; Greene, 2012, Suvorov, 2012; Etling et al., 2010; Qin et al., 2007; Li and Walejko, 2008; Hargittai and Walejko, 2008; Turnšek and Jankowski, 2008). Yet, it is not only the content itself but a broader notion of community that is important. Why do some people find internet content or interaction particularly meaningful? How are these users finding and expanding a sense of community online? How are online and offline communities connected? Community is a concept that has been linked to websites, but often not in any systematic way. It is important to consider both factors in the offline world that lead people to seek out online communities—and look more closely at the interaction among people via one-to-one, one-to-many, or even many-to-many online communication.

Much of what is understood about online/offline synergy comes about when there is a particular event that is a catalyst for an online community. In the report on the Russian blogosphere, anger over blatant attempts by the government to blame innocent drivers when government cars caused accidents was an important part of the dialogue on the motoring rights Free Choice website. Examples of the "power" of the internet are often cited through events or protests (such as Chiapas) that essentially only received significant attention due to online communication. However, firm examples of this interaction are relatively rare and almost always retrospective. By the same token, there is a need to "bring the state back in" to internet studies, in that there is significant variation in the use of the internet across country boundaries. While some of this is related to wealth and opportunity, the potential of the internet as a communication medium is significantly constrained in many countries by censorship and control. If we do not take this into account, we risk missing a significant element in understanding how the offline environment shapes online issues. In a world in which many people are jailed for what they post on the web in places such as China, we cannot pretend there is equal access and opportunity for social engagement online. Finally, a growing area of interest in comparative internet studies lies in conceptualizing how the internet can effectively be deployed by the powerful and/or the nefarious to consolidate information control. This can include the process of co-opting existing bloggers, websites, forums, and so on, and changing a democratic experience into propaganda.

The internet in the post-Soviet sphere shows us that while the online world offers essentially the same opportunities to different countries, national media and political systems themselves are key factors in shaping and constraining the internet within country borders. In particular, the Russian case proves that much of the democratizing potential of the internet may have been limited by the government's almost complete control of the national information sphere, an ingrained sense of self-censorship on the part of Russian "netizens," as well as a general lack of interest in the internet as an authoritative voice for citizens. Yet, this was not enough to stymie the ability of the internet to inculcate widespread protests in 2011–12. By reflecting on the developmental path of the internet across a range of post-Soviet countries, it is clear that it is not inevitable that the democratizing potential of the internet is tamed. In addition, examples from the Middle East suggest that the balance of power relating to the internet can shift very rapidly in certain situations, even when there has been scant hope for political change. Understanding how particular nations harness the power of the internet illuminates how national power can limit the international potential of a communications technology. At the same time, it should be clear that the development of new online tools and—even perhaps more importantly—new attitudes about the online sphere can truly challenge this relationship. Even a muted and controlled internet can harbor the potential for political events to be transformed online into political flashpoints. Is it possible for authoritarian states such as Russia to constrain and control that potential indefinitely? Evidence collected and analyzed in this book—with a parallel contribution to a further development of methodology—will allow us to address this key question in a more informed way.

2

The National Borders of the Internet

How the Russian State Shapes the Global Potential of ICTs

This chapter bridges the gap between comparative media and internet studies by analyzing the symbiotic relationship linking the domestic media sphere to contemporary online communication in Russia. The online sphere has many distinctive media features, including its low cost, ability to transcend borders, relative freedom from national media control, and interactivity. All of these features have the potential to map onto a wide range of media systems to create more informed—and potentially more empowered—citizens. There has been compelling evidence, particularly from the events of the Arab Spring, that the internet's flexibility as an information and mobilization tool can significantly increase the range and speed of protest against repressive leaders. Yet, there are a far greater number of cases in which the internet has clearly failed to spark democratic movements or has even worked against attempts by people to aggregate interests and claim their rights as citizens in a range of regimes.

This chapter, while presenting theories and cases behind both cyber-optimistic and cyber-pessimistic ideas, places the discussion about the political potential of the internet within the nature of an existing media system in a particular country. This chapter argues that the potential of the internet to foster more informed and engaged citizens can only be understood against the background of a specific country's media system. It is only then that one can show how the communicative potential of the internet has been shaped by national media systems and national audiences. The fact that the need to understand the internet against the background of national media and political environments has been relatively overlooked is not surprising, in that scholars and analysts have long struggled to judge the democratic potential of mass media against the opportunities and constraints of political communication in a range of states. In addition to discussing ideas of how the internet can augment or challenge democracy, this chapter will consider the utility of broad theories that address the role of media in democracy;

traditional models of the state-media relationship; and the role of the internet vis-à-vis the existing factors of political environment and media norms in Russia.

Information, Media, and Democracy

How much can the dissemination of information contribute to a civil society? How can it compete against state propaganda of the traditional mass media? Freedom of information is seen as a fundamental tenet of a free society, from the Constitution of the United States to the Universal Declaration of Human Rights by the United Nations.[1] Democratic theorists argue that the dissemination of information allows citizens to remain engaged and informed, guarding against excessive power and control by political leaders (i.e., Dahl, 2000; Habermas, 1989; Street, 2001). While it is clear that the view on what constitutes democracy is in many ways culturally specific, most critics agree that media play a crucial role in fostering civil society. Scholars vary somewhat on the exact nature of this role. While Dahl perceives democracy as an ideal rather than actual type of governance, he sees freedom of expression, media freedom, and the right to expression all as key components of civil society. Habermas argues that the media provide a critical "sphere" in which the public can debate and discuss policy as they continually forge a better society. Street provides a particularly useful overview of the arguments in support of how public information via the mass media is critical to democracy (2001, pp. 250–72), although his discussion is centered on the structure of public-service broadcasting as opposed to media in general. Street highlights two particularly useful arguments that relate to the discussion in this book. He points out that while there is bias and self-censorship in media in democratic states, states can actively take measures through media policy to create more democratic media systems. He emphasizes the ideas of Hirst (1994) that democracy needs to be defined in terms of communication and that "the state's responsibility is primarily to enable this communication to occur" (Street, p. 267). Street argues that a free media is a necessary, yet not sufficient, condition for a free society: "Democratic media do not, in and of themselves, create democracy. Democratic media need a democratic polity, and vice versa" (p. 271).

Unfortunately, states often struggle with both the concept and the reality of crafting media laws and policies that will foster an open communications sphere. On the one hand, many scholars believe that the media themselves often work against this idea. The concept of the media's role in enlightening citizens is countered by concerns that the media either seek power in their own right or are co-opted by powerful elites. Thus, rather than being informed and empowered by the media, citizens can be confused or even duped by the media in democracies. For example, Herman and Chomsky (2002) argue that the media "manufacture" consent for the elites due to pressures from owners, advertisers, public relations efforts, the drive for profit, and reliance on a closed circle of sources. Herman and Chomsky also have concerns about the pervasive way in which news framing is used to distort information, from the Cold War frame to the more recent War on Terror frame (Chomsky, 2006). Framing forms a key component of political communication theory, in that it is widely acknowledged that journalists must condense and present the information as they report the news. Many scholars have written about frames, noting that the way in which journalists develop a series of shortcuts to repetitively present selected facts in stories can lead to distorted or inadequate coverage of important issues (Altheide, 1997; Altheide and Michalowski, 1999; Glassner, 2000 on exaggerating or creating fear). In particular, scholars have extensively studied the use of framing to limit meaningful discussion about key issues (for example, see Entman, 2003, about the War on Terror or Iyengar, 1991, on U.S. political issues). When issues are reduced to convenient sound bites—such as crime is the fault of flawed individuals rather than flawed societies—it simplifies or distorts issues in ways that make engaged and meaningful political debate across a broad range of stakeholders in society very difficult.

In addition to the shortcomings on the level of the media, leaders themselves are prone to viewing the media as instruments of state power as opposed to watchdogs in service to the citizens. Indeed, the debates about media in democratic societies stand in stark contrast to the understood role of information in non-free states. In authoritarian states, information is understood as a key element in acquiring and maintaining power. Vladimir Lenin perceived the mass media itself as a central resource of the state, and the USSR deployed the Soviet media in a sophisticated propaganda campaign that glorified the Communist Party while spreading disinformation about the West and those who challenged the Soviet regime. Indeed, throughout the first half of the twentieth century, propaganda was seen as particularly powerful because audiences were generally deemed to be passive. This view started to change with post–World War II studies of the U.S. audience (Berelson et al., 1954) that found media use and its authority were tempered significantly by personal beliefs, experience, and the influence of family and friends. However, propaganda wars—between states and citizens as well as between states themselves with international broadcasters funded by governments—continue into the twenty-first century.

Theorizing the Internet's Democratic Role

Much of the initial writing about the role of the internet in society perceived ICTs as nothing short of revolutionary. There was initial enthusiasm for the idea that the communicative features of the internet could bring about significant and positive changes for society, in particular by shifting power from elites to citizens. Writings in cyber-optimism include Rheingold (1995), Toffler and Toffler (1995), Negroponte (1995), Rash (1997), and Dyson (1998). They argued that new digital technologies were central to the renewal of direct democracy and citizen empowerment. The inherent structural logic of new media, it was thought, would inexorably lead to the opening up of a decentralized interactive public space in which people, or even "netizens," would form new social bonds and create new fora for political decision making. The writings of political theorists such as Habermas were used to promote the idea that the internet would foster greater communication among citizens, perhaps even creating an enhanced "public sphere" (Brandenburg, 2006). Others adopted a less utopian perspective, seeing the potential of the new ICTs to lie in their ability to improve and streamline current governance apparatus rather than replace it entirely (Mulgan and Adonis, 1994; Heilemann, 1996; Poster, 1997; Shenk, 1997; Morris, 2000). There were still others, however, who saw the internet and its associated applications as inherently dangerous to democracy, reducing the possibility for collective action (Wu and Weaver, 1996; Lipow and Seyd, 1996) and eroding social capital and community ties (Etzioni and Etzioni, 1999; Galston, 2003). Others also perceived its problematic potential to reduce both the quality of political debate and discourse (Streck, 1999; Sunstein, 2009) as well as the accountability of government (Wilhelm, 2000; Lessig, 1999; Adkeniz, 2000; Elmer, 1997). Sunstein wrote about how the internet could draw people into informational echo chambers or "information cocoons" that would leave them with little energy or interest for broader social interaction and concerns (2009). Putnam (2001) was convinced that online activities could further distract and discourage people from taking part in traditional civic activities in the offline world.

From the more broadly philosophical work about the effect of normative implications of the communicative potential of the internet, the study of the online sphere has progressed very quickly as a field to focus on more defined research questions within the broader conceptualization of the internet as "good" or "bad" (Chadwick, 2006). In particular, there has been a growing depth to the study of the internet vis-à-vis "political institutions in their communications aspects," to borrow a term from Blumler and Gurevitch (1977: 273–74).[2] In other words, rather than thinking about the internet in broadly normative terms, it is more useful to fit the online sphere into a long tradition of study about political institutions. For example, how do political institutions such as parliaments, parties, presidents, prime ministers, candidates, and other political figures use the internet as part of their communication strategies? While this contributes to the larger question of how the internet may contribute to democracy, it also allows for a more focused approach with the possibility of falsifiable hypotheses. We can ask the big question—does the internet contribute to democracy or does it undermine it—but without evidence from a range of studies in the relationship between political institutions and the internet, we do not have a lot of data with which to answer this significant query.

Some of the most useful studies of the role of the internet in political institutions focus on how political parties and candidates (in a range of states) have incorporated ICTs into their operations (Anstead and Chadwick, 2009). Many of these studies have quantified and compared different factors on party websites into a cross-national comparison, finding that parties often fail to take advantage of the information provision opportunities offered by online spaces (Carlson and Djupsund, 2001; Strandberg, 2009). While some studies are finding evidence of change in political party campaigning, including greater opportunities for communication from smaller parties as well as more chance for dialogue between politicians and citizens, there is little evidence that the internet has fundamentally transformed party politics in democracies (De Zuniga and Rojas, 2009; Gibson and McAllister, 2008; Gibson et al., 2003). Political parties, members of legislatures, and the electorate have been relatively slow to take up the opportunity of interactivity offered by the online sphere (Lusoli and Ward, 2005), although there is evidence of cross-national conventions for web use by different political actors such as parties and candidates (Foot et al., 2010). Arguably, the advent of Web 2.0 and easy interactivity via social-networking and micro-blogging sites could spur more horizontal involvement and greater citizen engagement in political life. However, as noted by Gibson's research in particular (2010), it would appear that political parties have domesticated the web to their use, reproducing hierarchies and boundaries in the online world that exist between party insiders and outsiders in the non-wired environment. Although opinions differ on whether this is related to the wishes of parties to remain relatively aloof from the demands of citizens or whether it is down to a lack of interest on the part of most citizens, the internet had appeared to offer relatively little in the way of a significant broadening of traditional political involvement in western democracies until 2008.

As is often the case in internet studies, it would appear that actual evidence of change with a highly engaged online group of supporters for Barack Obama in the U.S. presidential race of 2008 outpaced scholarly understanding of politicized internet engagement. Here, the focus has shifted from how political institutions might use the internet to apparently seeing citizens create political capital through horizontal communication and interaction in the online sphere. In particular, the Obama campaign was noted for the large-scale creation of independent support groups for the presidential campaign via social-networking sites (Anstead and Chadwick). However, at the same time, reports suggested that the Obama campaign was able to harness the web, in particular for campaign management and fund-raising, more effectively than rivals in both the primary and general election (Steger et al., 2010). Thus, the internet became an asset for both the campaign manager and the supporters, with some difficulty in drawing a line between how much the internet supported organized *campaign* efforts and how much it enabled *individuals* to create a mass movement from the grass roots. While it would be enormously difficult to isolate the relative effect of the campaign efforts from individual interests, it is clear that ICTs enabled and intensified the efforts of both.

A fundamental question is whether Obama would have won the election without support of the internet campaign. Political communication scholars would be quick to point to traditional factors that favored Obama, including the economic crisis laid at the door of the incumbent Republican president and a traditional mass media that showed a bias against Democratic primary contender Hillary Clinton (Lawrence and Rose, 2010). One of the most compelling arguments that the internet made a fundamental change is the surge in the youth vote, which was linked by many to the way in which younger U.S. citizens are more likely to be engaged in web content production and interaction. However, it is likely that Obama's relative youth, image, and ideology would have energized the newest generation of voters at any rate. The scholarly analysis of the Obama victory attempts to gauge what factors may have significantly changed before or through the campaign—and what the legacy may be for online campaigning in general (Anstead and Chadwick, 2009; Anstead and Straw, 2009; Greengard, 2009; Harfoush, 2009; Haynes, 2009). It is not so much about winners and losers in elections, but whether the experience of a mass online political experience in the United States has permanently enhanced trust, value, and respect for the internet as a political player or catalyst.

How much does traditional social science help in the case of analyzing the effect of the online activity on U.S. politics (or politics in general) after the 2008 U.S. presidential elections? A central question in social science terms about the internet is whether one should build theory by considering the internet as a dependent variable (the phenomenon that is affected by other factors) or an independent variable (a factor that can affect the dependent variable). If Obama's victory were the dependent variable in a study, we would consider what measurable role the internet played in his victory vis-à-vis factors such as party identification, race, gender, wealth, education, other media use, and so on. If the internet itself is the dependent variable, we would consider the effect of a young, tech-savvy candidate and campaign team on how Americans engaged with politics in the online sphere. As a dependent variable, the internet itself is a political institution influenced by a range of national factors, including online access, censorship, democratic norms, online competency of citizens, trust in the medium, laws, and policing of the online sphere. At the same time, the internet is an independent variable, playing a role in deciding the outcome of elections, the delivery of government services, the spread of information, and even the mobilization of protest. Scholars in political communication have long struggled with the cause and effect of media. Are people mobilized by the media or do they choose media that best resonate with their preexisting beliefs? While it is impossible to tell the direction of the effect, it is still possible to measure the relationship. As Norris has demonstrated in *A Virtuous Circle* (2000), a greater range of choice and engagement with the media is correlated to more informed, engaged citizens in democracies. With the internet, all of this study is far more complicated due to the interactivity and speed of the medium—as well as by the fact that the online sphere has both domestic and transnational media features.

National Media Systems, Information, and Democracy in Russia

Russia is one of the most intriguing places to study the relationship between information and democracy because it subverts expectations: Although there is media diversity, the media do little to foster democracy. This is a particularly relevant question for this study, as Russia had achieved the rank of the seventh-largest online nation by March 31, 2011.[3] Russia has failed to develop a free media system since the collapse of the Soviet Union in 1991. Rather, state-controlled television, in particular, works at undermining democracy, particularly through biased and unfair coverage of Kremlin contenders during elections (Oates, 2006; European Institute for the Media, March 2000, August 2000; Organization for Security and Co-operation in Europe/Office for Democratic Institutions and Human Rights, January 27, 2004, June 2, 2004). In both Soviet and Western thought, the way in which the state communicates with citizens has been seen as crucial. In the Soviet system, Leninist philosophy called for the mass media to be a central tool in educating the public about the benefits and key role of communism for Russian society. This is codified in the "Soviet Communist" model of the press written about by Siebert et al. in 1963. In the Soviet media model, the media's central function is as an educational tool of the Communist Party. The media are there to continually provide propaganda about the party. There is no discussion of alternate views or debates as this is not necessary: The media exist to inform the public of the correct view and the audience is there to accept it. Siebert et al. contrasted this to other models, in particular drawing a distinction between Soviet and authoritarian models, noting that the Soviet model was coupled with state ideology while the authoritarian model relied more on repression and censorship linked to a ruling oligarchy. In reality, the systems both worked in the service of a ruling oligarchy, although the Soviet system was theoretically connected to the tenets of communism as opposed to the interests of a personal leader.

One of the greatest problems in understanding political communication within other countries is a failure to grasp the range of media norms in comparative perspective. It should be noted that the United States is unusual in having only a small public media sphere and no state-owned media for general consumption (leaving aside media produced by the military for its troops, etc.). Siebert et al. labeled the United States as having a Libertarian model, in which media freedom is created by a vibrant marketplace of media competition for audience. As the market provides a rich diversity of outlets, consumers are free to choose from a competitive range of sources. While the United States tends to score quite well in international media freedom measurements, there are strong critics of the commercial media system (notably Herman and Chomsky, discussed above, who argue that the nature of the U.S. media system reinforces the power of elites). In addition, international observers are concerned about the dearth of public media in the United States. Siebert et al. identified a fourth and final model as one of "social responsibility," in which the media work in the service of the public, filtering disturbing or distressing news in order to avoid public disorder, panic, or confusion. The United Kingdom, with the British Broadcasting Corporation's vast funding from a public tax on television ownership, is the most prominent example of socially responsible journalism, although all broadcasters in Britain must follow relatively close government supervision on public responsibility. This has spawned arguments (Miller, 1991; Philo, 1995) that the BBC is too close to the interests of the state at the expense of embracing political opposition or even a significant range of more radical ideas in Britain. It is fair to say that Siebert et al.'s 1963 *Four Theories of the Press* are outdated and have been challenged on key points (in particular by Hallin and Mancini, 2004) but they usefully highlight that democratic states have quite distinctive media systems—both different from authoritarian systems as well as distinct from each other.

If there is a significant difference in the traditional media between two democracies such as the United States and the United Kingdom, what can we expect of the online sphere? Will it parallel the differences, in that the U.S. audience is presumed to be more consumer-driven and the British audience more citizen-oriented? Putting the discussion of the internet aside for a moment, it must be said that traditional media are quite different in the two countries. Some key differences are in election news, which focuses more on personality than issues in the United States (Oates, Kaid and Berry, 2009). In addition, paid political advertising on television plays a high-profile role in U.S. elections, but is banned in British campaigns. The United States has significantly more local news, particularly on television. A recent study into whether the possible "Americanization" of British television news has led to less time for politicians to speak, more time for journalists to pontificate in front of the camera, and to turning elections from a discussion of issues into a "horse race" have not been proven (Ramsay, 2011). An analysis of both campaign systems in 2004 and 2005 found that British election coverage is much more focused on issues than was the U.S.

election news (Oates, Kaid, and Berry, 2009). This is also unsurprising in that political parties, not the public, select the final candidates for the race in the United Kingdom. Hence, there is far less need for public appeal of individual candidates, although the personalization of politics has increased somewhat in the United Kingdom (albeit not at the expense of political discussion, according to Langer, 2012). Although British television may be more measured, British newspapers are not. For most British newspapers—and particularly the tabloids—overt political bias pervades the entire issue in a way that American readers would find shocking when compared with the less overt framing that reflects political viewpoints in U.S. newspapers. The announcement in July 2011 of the breadth of phone-tapping scandal at a News Corporation newspaper in the United Kingdom only serves to underline the very different norms embraced by some at British tabloid newspapers.[4]

Given that the traditional media are so distinctive in the United States and the United Kingdom, how do the internet spheres compare? The countries have very similar levels of internet use and penetration, although penetration in the United Kingdom is now somewhat higher than in the United States, according to the International Telecommunications Union. The United States had an internet penetration rate of 74 percent in 2010, compared with 84 percent in the United Kingdom in the same year.[5] This subverts the theory that internet penetration tracks gross domestic product per person, as this is higher in the United States. It does show that there are factors in the United Kingdom that have fostered greater internet penetration, possibly a more active government policy on universal internet access or the fact that mobile internet has been much more affordable in the United Kingdom than the United States for some time. Yet, online differences go far beyond the small variation in online penetration. In particular, the political web is far more developed in the United States. The United States lacks highly structured political parties and public media to inform citizens in elections in the same way as the British voters. As a result, U.S. candidates would be far more likely to use the internet to organize campaigns as well as inform voters of their policies and positions. Given that U.S. newspapers do not provide a forum for overtly political news, it is unsurprising that several U.S. political bloggers have achieved significant followings in the United States (Davis, 2009). There is more news broken in the online sphere, with a more robust interaction between offline and online news media in the United States than in the United Kingdom. It is clear that the internet functions here as a dependent variable, shaped and constrained by national media and political factors.

The broader question is how the internet might fit into the existing understanding, expressed through various models, of the relationship between the media and politics within particular countries. While acknowledging the role of the state, my earlier work (Oates 2008, 2011) attempts to create a template through which news production can be understood in a range of regimes through a News Production Model. The News Production Model presents a series of five filters through which news is shaped within a particular country: (1) political environment; (2) media norms; (3) media regulation/law; (4) media ownership; and (5) the profession of journalism and public relations. The filters start at the widest point of political environment and narrow down to focus on journalism and public relations. The model, based particularly on a comparison of Russian news production with that in the United States and the United Kingdom, is an attempt to show how the constraints of a political environment operate on the production of news. It follows the same logic as the "funnel of causality" that models how U.S. voters make individual vote choices as shaped by a range of preexisting factors including socioeconomic status and party identification (Campbell et al., 1960). In particular, the News Production Model suggests that journalists are influenced by a range of factors "above" them in the model and that media freedom is not just about giving them the ability to report via social networking, blogging, and so on. Journalists are shaped by—and must survive in—specific political and media environments. This does not change with the advent of new media technologies; rather, the faster pace and wider spread of ICTs make the need for a clear model of the forces that shape news production that much more pressing. This is exacerbated by the way in which the internet further blurs the lines between producer, audience/journalist, and citizen, drawing a far wider range of content-producers into the public sphere.

The interesting question is where we may be able to fit online informational and organizational tools into the News Production Model to analyze how the internet reinforces or challenges the historic relationship among states, media outlets, journalists, and citizens. The online sphere cannot really affect the first four filters of the political environment, norms, laws, and ownership, although the internet can provide quite low-cost ways to produce and distribute news (hence influencing the layer of media ownership to a degree). However, most influential news production relies on quite expensive content production by professionals. As such, it would appear that the greatest influence of the online sphere on the model would be in the final category of journalism and public relations. The existence of the internet both challenges and supports traditional journalism and PR. It means a far greater range of information, sources, and distribution networks. However, just as information sources and networks explode, journalists face plummeting budgets and shrinking newsrooms. In the United States alone, newsrooms shed 10 percent of their staff in 2009 (after a similar percentage cut in 2008), bringing the number of jobs in U.S. newspapers down to about 41,000.[6] The internet can be seen as a challenge to commercial journalism in all countries, democratic or not, because it undermines the economic model for media outlet survival. In addition, a particular danger lies in perceiving online crowd-sourcing as a replacement for journalism. As Graber (2009) argues, society needs journalists to filter and sort through information to present it in a useful way to the audience.

Ironically, however, the very things that might threaten journalism in democratic states could actually contribute to more media freedom in non-democratic states by breaking dependence on the need for economic and political sponsors in order to distribute the news. At the same time that journalists are under personal and targeted threat, the expansion of information provision to crowd-sourcing can provide an important alternative challenge to state hegemony on information. However, as discussed below through the case of Russian blogger Alexey Navalny and via the studies in Fossato et al. (as well as in greater detail in Chapter 4), once citizens cross the line from commentator to journalist, they become vulnerable to the same threats and even violence that is the fate of many journalists in countries such as Russia.

Putting Runet in Post-Soviet Context

If there is compelling evidence that the internet is more shaped by national factors than a broader ideal of its universal communicative potential in the United States and the United Kingdom, how do we measure the effect of the Russian political environment, the media system, and its norms on the Russian internet? Following on from the information on the Russian political and media environment presented in Chapter 1, the discussion below focuses on theories and analyses of the Russian media and internet. In particular, this discussion explores whether the Russian media is so rooted in the Soviet past that the Russian internet is destined to follow the same course. Is there a useful parallel between the understanding of the late Soviet media period—in which a government policy of transparency has often been mistaken by analysts as a type of media freedom—and the conceptualization of the internet in contemporary Russian society?

The Soviet policy of glasnost is a useful model for understanding how different interpretations of political communication can blur important distinctions between the West and Russia. Much like the internet, the exact nature and role of Soviet glasnost was widely misunderstood in the West, often interpreted and represented as freedom of speech. The Russian word *glasnost* is often translated as "freedom" or "openness," but these are somewhat misleading translations. While a reasonable translation is "transparency," the word can best be understood as "giving voice" to something (or even by a translation of "publicity"). Glasnost was introduced by Soviet leader Mikhail Gorbachev in the 1980s in order to allow a broader debate about the function of the Communist Party of the Soviet Union. Given that the CPSU ran the country as a dictatorship and tolerated no political opposition, the move was profoundly significant at the time. Gorbachev expected to foster the constructive potential within the Party. However, the greater openness and discussion instead unleashed a torrent of revelations about the corrupt nature of the Party, which ultimately served to destroy the leadership rather than support it. In a matter of a few years, glasnost transformed the Soviet media sphere from a rigidly controlled, relatively monolithic institution in which little deviation was tolerated to an arena for intense debate, anti-state rhetoric, nationalism, and virtually no limits on what could be said or shown (Mickiewicz, 1988, 1997; McNair, 1991). When the CPSU attempted to retake control of the country and the media in August 1991, state television was able to defy the CPSU armed guards in their control rooms and broadcast public resistance to the Party.

Yet the profound richness of content and debate in the Russian media did not breed a democratic state. A closer examination of the glasnost era shows that, as in Soviet times, different media outlets were allied with various political factions (Oates, 2006). While these differences were much more overt in the glasnost period, an analysis of the Soviet media reveals differences in information provision by various media outlets over distinct epochs in the Soviet period. The orthodoxy and obsessive control of the Stalinist period aside, Soviet citizens could glean a large amount of useful information about political maneuvering within the Party, local affairs, international events, and other news through a wide range of television offerings, newspapers, periodicals, and local publications. It could be argued that in many ways the glasnost era merely amplified these variations. Glasnost vastly broadened the range and nature of the political debate, but still tied particular media outlets to power struggles within the state. This is unsurprising, as media tend to be either explicitly or implicitly allied with political causes, outlooks, or even political parties in a range of states. From a distance, it would appear that the late Soviet era had produced a pluralistic media. However, the eventual analysis should be that the post-Soviet media never moved from a focus on serving the state to an interest in serving the citizens (Lipman, 2005; Lipman and McFaul, 2010; Oates and McCormack, 2010).

What many analysts have since argued is that glasnost and the collapse of the Soviet state did not bring about a fundamental change in the character of Russian journalism either (Becker, 2004; Pasti, 2005; Voltmer, 2000). Journalists still view themselves as working for the interests of political or economic sponsors. Even if one puts aside an alleged "neo-Soviet news model" (Oates, 2007), the landscape of Russian news production still remains a battleground between various agenda of power (Koltsova, 2006). At the same time, many Russians view the role of the media as a tool for the state rather than a voice for the people (Oates, 2006). The question is whether the Soviet and post-Soviet experience of the media, especially the way in which an abundance of information gave a false impression of democratic media development during the glasnost era, is now paralleled by the development of the internet. As is clear from the rich content of the Russian internet, and particularly the Russian blogosphere discussed below, Runet offers broad, diverse information to post-Soviet citizens. However, a large amount of information did not lead to a fundamental change in either the control of critical news outlets or—according to earlier research—a shift in the conviction that the media should work in service of the citizens in the glasnost and early Russian period. Rather, media have remained political players, albeit reflecting a broader range of political views than during Soviet times. Will the development of the Russian internet follow the experience of the Soviet media in glasnost, in which the appearance of a large volume of information will have little effect on political life in Russia? One could argue that the much more chaotic and uncontrolled nature of the internet makes it far more difficult to predict. By the same token, this very chaos can serve the purpose of non-democratic leaders and institutions, as they are able more easily to "colonize" a burgeoning online public sphere through both soft and hard controls (discussed in Chapter 4).

The Internet and Democracy in National Context

If these democratizing elements of the internet were indeed deployed more or less equally across national boundaries, one would perhaps expect national challenge to political elites and the status quo to develop more rapidly than has actually occurred. Yet, examples of the power of the internet to play a high-profile part in regime change in non-democratic states had been relatively rare up until the Arab Spring of 2011. There have been numerous examples of online protests within authoritarian states. The list of these includes the way in which the Chiapas revolt in Mexico used relatively early internet technology (particularly Listservs and e-mail) to attract international support to their cause in the 1990s to the role of the online sphere in dissemination of alternative news in the Orange Revolution in Ukraine (2004–05) to networking of opposition opinion via Twitter (and the tragic video of the murder of a young woman on the street) in Iran in 2009–10. These events were paralleled by the rapid development and refinement of internet communication tools into the formidable networks of information and communication fostered by internet providers such as Google, Facebook, and Twitter.

Thus, attempts to understand the role of the internet in the Chiapas revolt—in which the internet was used to keep the Mexican government in check by focusing media attention on the injustices in the region—are quite different from attempting to analyze how the networking of individuals and information functioned during the Arab Spring in 2011. While authoritarian leaders were coming to terms with dealing with the internet as an external threat, the notion that a technology viewed internally as primarily an economic and social tool could be controlled by the government (by censorship, manipulation, or cutting off access) was a lesson learned in the Arab Spring in Egypt. Both analysts and policy-makers alike were astounded by the speed and flexibility of the resistance movement. The Arab Spring has been the attention of numerous studies attempting to weigh the relative value of the internet against a range of other factors in democratization including cultural shifts, elite behavior, interaction with the Arab traditional mass media, transnational forces for change in the region, rising levels of education, generational change, and other issues (studies include Howard and Parks, 2012; Heydemann and Leenders, 2011; Trombetta, 2012; Hamdy and Gomaa, 2012; Khamis and Vaughn, 2012, Lewiński and Mohammed, 2012).[7] The main finding that emerges from this research is that the internet mattered, but that its effects are difficult to predict (and hence replicate) because of the way in which the internet is embedded within political culture. In addition, this strand of research into the Arab Spring has highlighted the difficulty of online 'democracy by design,' in that commercial tools such as Facebook took on a transformative political role that dwarfed any attempts by political opponents or social action groups to deploy specific online tools to advance their causes. The experience of citizens and states alike in the Arab Spring underlines the challenge of calculating the opportunity offered by communication technology against the demands of citizens and the capacity of states. As Howard and Parks write, this complex puzzle demands a new approach to scholarship, with more collaborative, multidisciplinary approaches to both build theory and deploy research methods in the multilevel communication environment engendered by the online sphere, looking at the "linkages between tools, content, producers, consumers, and consequences" (p. 362).

Russian officials no doubt never imagined they would be facing a "Moscow Spring" less than a year after the fall of the Mubarak regime in Egypt. All of the indicators, as discussed in this book, were there for the internet to play a role in challenge to a non-democratic regime. In particular, Russia shared with Egypt a relatively relaxed approach to policing the internet (discussed in Chapter 4) coupled with a sharp spike in internet usage. Russian leadership also shared a relative complacency—albeit with a much higher approval rating and less overt violations of human rights—about its ability to win elections and manipulate the key sectors of the traditional mass media. Until the Arab Spring, there were no compelling examples of major regime transition fostered in the online sphere. Indeed, there were pervasive examples of the ability of states to use the online sphere to maintain power, in part through allowing dissident voices to both employ the internet as a "safety value" as well as reveal the most pervasive critics (and their networks) to state security forces (Morozov, 2011). Yet, the communicative potential of the internet had been changing swiftly and radically since the 1990s, when only a fraction of domestic populations in places such as Mexico and Egypt had internet access. In particular with the advent of the mobile internet and Web 2.0, the communication environment and the size of its audience have undergone fundamental changes. It is enormously difficult to gauge the power of information to transform citizen support for their regime as well as the ability of state media systems to tame the communicative potential of information challenges in general, and ICTs in particular (discussed further in Chapter 4, but challenged in Chapters 6 and 7). All of this is currently at stake in Russia, which is why a discussion of internet content for Russian citizens is the next important area to consider.

Online Content in Russia: Why Is LiveJournal So Popular?

On the one hand, the internet is a place in which information is vertically integrated. The websites of those who have offline power and organization project that presence to the online world. Thus, there are discrete locations, from the website of *The New York Times* to the website of the U.S. Internal Revenue Service, that are the online aspects of powerful organizations. On the other hand, the internet is extremely horizontal because of the way in which web pages are connected, both overtly through links that are clicked by users and rather less obviously via the way in which search engines use web links to rank web pages in their results. Thus, the web offers both the opportunity for enhanced information provision from a single source, as well as the relatively easy aggregation of information from a vast range of sources: One can delve deeply into one website or sample freely from a large number. It is difficult to know how to assess the relative value of vertical and horizontal web content in a national media system, particularly absent a study of how users interact with the web in a particular country. This section will consider both the development of web information provision for Russian entities as well as the way in which the Russian internet is linked together for the user.

The list of the ten most popular websites in Russia as of July 2011 differed relatively little from the list of the ten most popular websites worldwide, according to the web ranking company Alexa (see Table 2.1: Top Websites in Russia and Worldwide as of July 2011). While online preferences can shift relatively quickly (particularly when compared with traditional mass media preferences), this provides a reasonable comparison of the Russian online preferences with global preferences. The two most popular websites in Russia as of July 2011

Table 2.1 **Top Websites in Russia and Worldwide as of July 2011**

Russia		Worldwide	
Name	Primary function	Name	Description
1. Yandex yandex.ru	Search	1. Google Google.com	Search
2. Google (Russia) google.ru	Search	2. Facebook Facebook.com	Social networking
3. Pochta@Mail.ru Mail.ru	E-mail/internet service portal	3. YouTube YouTube.com	Video
4. Google (US) Google.com	Search	4. Yahoo! Yahoo.com	Search
5. V Kontakte [In Touch] VKontakte.ru	Social networking	5. Blogger.com Blogspot.com	Blogging
6. YouTube YouTube.com	Video	6. Baidu.com baidu.com	Search (China)
7. Facebook Facebook.com	Social networking	7. Wikipedia Wikipedia.org	Encyclopedia
8. Wikipedia Wikipedia.org	Encyclopedia	8. Windows Live Live.com	Search
9. LiveJournal Livejournal.ru	Blogging	9. Twitter Twitter.com	Micro-blogging/ social networking
10. Odnoklassniki (Classmates) Odnoklassniki.ru	Social networking	10. QQ QQ.com	E-mail/internet service portal

Source: Alexa
For Russia: http://www.alexa.com/topsites/countries/RU
Worldwide: http://www.alexa.com/topsites/global
(Accessed July 15, 2011)

were both Russian-language search engines, one a Russian company (Yandex) and the other the Russian branch of Google (Google.ru). While Yandex was the most popular search engine in Russia in July 2011, both Google.ru and Google.com were among the top ten websites. In addition, a Russian social-networking site (VKontakte, or "In Contact" in English) beats Facebook in popularity in Russia, while another Russian social-networking site (Odnoklassniki, or "Classmates") made the top ten. Russian online interests would appear to parallel internet interests globally, with sites founded and developed in Russia dominating the market in many cases. Domestic interests will shape online global trends to a degree. For example, Alexa statistics show that the online retailing giant

Amazon, as well as the classified listings Craigslist and eBay, all made the top ten in the United States during the same period. In Britain, BBC Online was a top ten site.[8]

The problem with assessing the role of web content in democratization in a particular country is that it is not just about finding and using sites with overtly political content. While a 2011 Russian telecommunications report did find that reading the news was one of the most popular online activities in Russia, there was no mention of political interest in the report. Finding out about politics online certainly did not figure in the top ten interests for the online sphere, which included interest in cars, holidays, real estate, beauty, health, medicine, and financial affairs (Russian Federal Agency on the Press and Mass Communication, 2011, p. 57). Again, this parallels global norms, in which politics has relatively little visibility in the online sphere (Hindman, 2009). Yet, despite people not being primarily drawn to the internet to learn about politics, their exposure to political information is likely, due to the structure of information in the online sphere. The design of the internet both pulls and pushes people toward various interests. The online sphere pulls people toward particular websites by providing suggested sites during searches, as well as via links listed on particular pages. Thus, people can drill down quite narrowly into specific topics, although web usage statistics such as these suggest that people are more interested in commerce or entertainment. On the other hand, people are "pushed" toward information if they become curious about a topic on one website and seek more information. They can then launch new searches with other terms or use their knowledge of the world to look for web information linked to offline organizations such as government agencies, political parties, leaders, campaigns, social-action groups, and so on. Thus, content cannot be considered in isolation. The amount and type of information offered in the online sphere is one way of understanding the transformative information potential of the online sphere (Brandenburg, 2006). But as the type of information available is so broad, it is really impossible to separate the existence of particular content from the behavior of the audience.

That being said, internet audiences can be surprisingly domesticated. Part of this is for linguistic reasons, in that people generally prefer to search and read information in their native languages. Another element of this is the attraction of relevant news—either local or national—or news that is filtered and viewed through a nationalistic viewpoint. With some curious exceptions,[9] people continue to turn to online domestic news outlets despite the availability of news from sources around the globe. Indeed, countries such as Russia that have biased news systems but few barriers to internet access (Deibert et al., 2009) are particularly intriguing. In early 2011, there did not seem to be a larger number of Russians—who are generally aware that their news is biased and incomplete (Oates, 2006)—turning to the internet to seek a broader range of political information. Despite the wealth of options that would provide far more balanced and extensive material, Russian internet users were more interested in domestic sites. This will be discussed in more depth by examining the Russian media audience both offline and online (Chapter 3) as well as analyzing how catalyzing events such as protest affect user behavior on Runet (Chapters 6 and 7). It should be noted, however, that Russian online behavior is more limited to native-language sources in a distinctive way from the use of the internet in countries with a higher proficiency in English (such as in northern Europe). A lower proficiency in English will limit the influence of non-Russian online content, further reinforcing the national-linguistic borders of the Russian online audience.

Where can we turn for a more in-depth analysis of Russians online than is offered by the identification of popular websites? The activities of Russians online have been the subject of the useful and timely Digital Icons project, which has published several studies of the Russian internet.[10] Saunders (2009) makes the point that the content and role of the internet varies a great deal across post-Soviet countries, underlining the idea that it is important to understand the political role of the online sphere in national perspective. He highlights the theory of digital divide as codified by Norris (2001) with three critical dimensions: "This divide is not simply one of information 'haves' and 'have-nots,' but a multidimensional phenomenon that encompasses three distinct aspects: a *global divide*, a *social divide* and a *democratic divide*" (Saunders, p. 12, emphasis in original). Goroshko and Zhigalina (2009) were more optimistic that Runet can provide a place for political aggregation that is relatively free from government oversight. Certainly, they found evidence of its great popularity, which is particularly interesting given the relative lack of online commerce that has blanketed the Western internet.

Figures from Goroshko and Zhigalina suggested that 11 percent of the world's blogs could be found on LiveJournal by 2009 and quoted Natalya Kurchakova (2006, p. 134) about the flexible nature of LiveJournal: "LiveJournal is used not only as private or public diary, but also as a means of socialization, a way of obtaining information and news, a way to acquire new friends, a place for discussion and the creation of joint projects."[11] Goroshko and Zhigalina concluded that Russian blogs were growing very fast; that more parties and politicians were involved in blogging; and that Russian blogs were closing the boundary between the personal and the public. Indeed, they speculated that engagement online had become critical for politicians and that blogs could provide effective political debate and alternative views for Russians, aggregate interests for the Russian audience, and provide for the "education of a virtual political society and social networks" (p. 97). This is quite a promising framework and Goroshko and

Zhigalina present some quantitative and qualitative analysis of blogs in their article. However, their theories bear more empirical investigation, particularly in terms of understanding who is consolidating and maintaining political influence online. Golynko-Volfson (2009) was far less convinced that the discourse on the Russian blogosphere was leading to any sort of enhanced public sphere crucial to a modern democracy: "The liberal myth about the Internet as a conduit for grassroots, spontaneous democracy and environment of formation of autonomous communities in Russia does not work, and sometimes turns out to be the complete opposite" (Golynko-Volfson, p. 103).

In fact, the people dubbed the "bloggentsiya" by Golynko-Volfson (p. 103) could be dangerous for democracy, as they might develop as yet another group of elites that further block the ability to hear the wishes of the masses. As does Saunders, Golynko-Volfson emphasized the need to understand the Russian internet within its cultural context. For example, he noted that VKontakte was originally associated with the St. Petersburg "artistic and bohemian lifestyle," while Odnoklassniki was linked to the Moscow "managerial and office type" (pp. 104–5). Golynko-Volfson identified a different dominant ideology amongst the two web platforms, perceiving VKontakte as having values that were more "pro-Western" and linked to "civilization and educational values of social intercourse." He described Odnoklassniki, however, as a "mouthpiece of Asian, despotic and obscurantist side of social relations." He also noted that cyber crime was linked more to Odnoklassniki (pp. 104–5). While this was an interesting perspective from a knowledgeable observer of the Russian internet, a further step of systematic study of linkages and content analysis would be needed to test the differences between the two sites. Overall, Golynko-Volfson perceived social-networking sites as another way to "brainwash" society into particular values (p. 109), paralleling the concept of "third-generation" controls described by Deibert et al. as proactive propaganda efforts online by repressive states (2010).

Fossato (2009) noted that on the Russian internet the "debates and disputes are indeed intense and at times fierce, but they are far from mobilizing long-lasting forms of activism, particularly activism with tangible social and political repercussions offline" (p. 4). Calvert (2010) also struck a note of caution about the ability of internet discourse to support democratization in Russia. While he found evidence that LiveJournal blogs can provide supportive online spaces for alternative viewpoints for anti-capitalists, anarchists, and environmental protesters, their online activity also attracted unwanted attention from political opponents. Calvert found that there remained a significant disconnect between the supportive, online environment and the persecution faced by political outsiders in Russia. Overall, the general lack of experience or confidence in grassroots civic culture limited the ability of the online sphere to inculcate change in the offline world in Russia. Fossato argued it would be far more useful to study how the Russian internet empowers Russian citizens in their ability to petition the state for privileges and power rather than look for ways that Runet fosters alternative political power. In analyzing how Russians used the web to cope with compulsory military duty, Lonkila (2008) echoed this argument by finding that people were using it more for information on how to gain individual exemptions than to challenge the brutal conditions or unfairness of compulsory military service on human rights grounds. These predictions seem particularly apt given that it was well-founded suspicion of electoral falsification—coupled with evidence presented via online sources—that spurred massive street demonstrations in Russia in late 2011 and early 2012.

There was also evidence of the political potential of the online sphere found in a two-year study of the Russian internet conducted by the Berkman Center for Internet & Society at Harvard University. Etling et al. (2010) reported on the findings in the first part of the study, which looked specifically at the Russian blogosphere. The Berkman report highlighted political content in the Russian blogosphere, notably campaigns against corruption and abuse of power by elites, the government, and the police. The report found extensive, politicized use of YouTube videos. The researchers also found evidence of political and social mobilization, particularly in blogging clusters affiliated with offline political and social movements. However, the report did not specifically study direct linkages between web content and offline protests at the time (a current project to do this is under way between Berkman and the Center for the Study of New Media at the New Economic School in Russia). The Berkman researchers found that online news consumption of Russian bloggers was "more independent, international, and oppositional than that of Russian Internet users overall, and far more so than that of non-Internet users, who are more reliant upon state-controlled federal TV channels" (p. 3). Unlike the report by Fossato et al., there were some findings in the Berkman report to support the idea that the Russian internet challenged the government via its utilization as a tool by offline social movements; the creation of online news consumers who are more independent-minded than those who rely on traditional media; and a burgeoning use of You-Tube for political purposes.

Unlike their counterparts in the United States and elsewhere, the Berkman report found that Russian bloggers prefer platforms that combine features typical of blogs with features of social-networking services. In this way, bloggers tended to remain within a known circle rather than push their blogs into the general news arena. The Berkman Center used automated web link analysis to establish the topography of the Russian blogosphere, in addition to using human coders to establish the content of some of the blogs. The researchers found that blogs on the Russian internet (with a core located on the LiveJournal platform) fell into four major groups: (1) politics and public affairs; (2) culture; (3) Russian-language bloggers in others states such as Belarus, Ukraine, Armenia, and Israel; and (4) "instrumental" bloggers who were paid to blog for other external incentives. Given the interest in the ability of the Russian internet to foster democracy, the report was particularly focused on the nature of blogging on politics and public affairs. Through the automated link analysis as well as human content analysis, the report found bloggers who supported particular political views, notably the democratic opposition and the nationalist cluster. However, the web link analysis suggested that there was not a particularly well-defined or prominent group of bloggers who consistently linked to each other and promoted a political ideology. Although the report authors note that this suggests an agreeable lack of political polarization and the closed "echo chambers" as discussed by Sunstein, it could equally suggest that political discussion online in Russia lacks political focus and strength. Or, it might imply that the Russian blogosphere needed to find a common cause, which arguably it did in the election falsification and discontent with the United Russia party in late 2011 and early 2012.

The Berkman report into the content of the Russian blogosphere was countered by Zygar's argument that the large volume of discussion on the Russian internet was unlikely to lead to political action (2009). Pointing to examples of Russian bloggers who had been contacted by officials after criticizing the government, Zygar suggested that self-censorship online would begin to parallel the self-censorship in much of the traditional mass media: "The same thing happened to television, as we all remember. There was no presidential decree to abolish good television and replace it with bad. It all happened very slowly, gradually, of its own accord—mainly through the efforts of the television employees themselves. Live political talk shows vanished. Real news vanished. But a new production genre was born—absolutely unknown in world television practice—when 'an official reports to the president, and the president tells the official off'"(NP). Zygar did note that the Russian online generation tends to be much younger and is unlikely to have the attitude of older citizens who "remember what fear is in their bones" and the "internet . . . is inhabited by a different 'unwhipped' generation." At the same time, Zygar worried that this lack of fear had inculcated political apathy rather than political engagement: "They aren't scared of the Soviet system, because they never saw it. But for them the internet is not a collective agitator or collective organizer. It's unlikely to line them up and send them off to action. For them it's a collective kitchen, where they can come and talk about life. They can hear the latest political joke or gossip. They can talk about girls (or boys). And of course, they can complain." Thus, Zygar argued that the internet gives people voice, so that they feel the ability to complain: "Your only hope is that people will read your posts. And this is even more important than justice." Zygar's work would appear to parallel the understanding of the Russian state, in that a large amount of dissidence and a wide range of free speech was tolerated in the online sphere prior to the end of 2011. As a result, the state was content to allow, and even foster, discussion in the online sphere to maintain an illusion of a civic space, "because the main goal of any state is to keep people mumbling in the kitchen for as long as possible" (Zygar, NP). The conundrum is whether the protests in late 2011 and 2012 were political "mumbling" or something more fundamentally challenging to the state.

A Russian Internet Case Study: Alexey Navalny and His Anti-Corruption Campaign

In what ways does the greater scope and scale of information change the Russian media sphere? There are two particularly significant ways in which the internet could alter the Russian media environment. First, the traditional mass media could be forced to alter to address a broader range of issues in a more timely manner in order to compete for audience with the internet. Alternatively, sources in the online sphere could begin to overshadow the traditional mass media. Even if the Russian mass media, particularly the powerful and influential central television networks, fail to cover controversial issues such as corruption, people can turn to the Russian internet for influential information sources. However, it was difficult to find evidence that either of these phenomena had taken place before the end of 2011, although there was some confirmation of a fundamental shift in attention from television to online sources amongst the younger generation (discussed in Chapter 3). Central media outlets such as the state-run First Channel and state-owned All-Russia State Television and Radio Company respond more to top-down messages and self-censorship on issues critical to the current Russian president and administration than to audience demand. As a result, where a U.S. or British media outlet would likely respond to news broken in the online sphere, there is little evidence of a significant shift in framing and agenda-setting in most of the traditional mass media due to the broader coverage of political news on Runet. And while it is clear that Russian online users—particularly those who blog regularly—are employing a wider range of sources for information, there was little evidence before the end of 2011 that it was changing the political sphere in Russia.

How media framing was affected by the online sphere and protests in 2011–12 will be discussed in Chapter 7. However, this chapter considers the longer view, weighing whether there had been development of authoritative online sources—with links to critical issues—prior to the more explosive events of December 2011. This question can be addressed through the lens of a particularly pervasive social and political issue that attracted much interest but little sustained coverage during Putin and Medvedev's combined terms of presidency from 1999 to 2012: corruption and bribery. There is ample evidence that Runet offers the Russian citizen a far broader range of information in particular on this subject (Etling et al., 2010). For example, Navalny's national campaign against corruption in Russia would be impossible to imagine without the presence of the online sphere. Navalny, a former member of the relatively liberal Yabloko party, uses his minority shareholder position in large, state-controlled enterprises such as Gazprom and Rosneft to search for evidence of corruption and bribery. The Russian internet serves this purpose in a variety of ways. Navalny employs the internet as a traditional media outlet, publishing his views on his blog and disseminating information via his website (rospil.info). However, it is more than his opinion and summaries that he publicizes: In the tradition of WikiLeaks, he also publishes documentation of alleged corruption and solicits others to upload their own evidence. Navalny has amassed a significant following in the Russian blogosphere as well as relatively high visibility in the traditional mass media. Aside from those who read and even link to his blogs, his investigations and prose have been a significant part of the discussion of corruption and bribery, issues that are rarely addressed in a meaningful way in the mainstream media. Nor does Navalny lead a "virtual" existence. His activities have attracted the interest of the mainstream Russian media, the international media, and—unsurprisingly—Russian officials themselves. He was under investigation by the Russian government even before his participation in the December 2011 demonstrations against the regime.

The case of Navalny and his attempts to expose evidence of corruption at large state enterprises via Runet could suggest different things in the study of online political communication in non-free states. First, it is evidence that the online sphere does provide an outlet for citizen journalism that is fundamentally different from the pre-internet age. Despite the lack of a formal job as a journalist, Navalny is able to transmit news and information to a relatively large audience. More significantly, he serves simultaneously as a figurehead and a rallying point for the debate about a topic that is not discussed in a meaningful way in the mainstream media. Indeed, there is evidence that bribery is a huge problem in Russia, from corrupt local officials to a closed circle of oligarchic elites that divided the spoils of Soviet enterprise to create staggering personal wealth. Despite many years of rhetoric against corruption by Putin and Medvedev, there is little confidence on the part of the population that there is any meaningful progress against the widespread practice on all levels of Russian public life.[12] Navalny's website addresses this concern at the top of his website (rospil.info):

Why do we need this?

Because pensioners, doctors, teachers are on the brink of survival while the crooks in power are buying another villa, yacht or the Devil knows what.

This is our money.

This is for normal medical care. For high-quality education. This is a road on which you can ride. It's clean streets. This is an opportunity for all of us to live better.[13]

Navalny's activities transformed quite visibly from the online sphere to street protest in December 2011, as he was a key speaker and rallying point in demonstrations of tens of thousands of Russians against vote falsification in the Duma elections on December 4. Aside from Navalny's own activities online, concerns over election irregularities were highlighted by highly detailed documentation of falsification (including videos) that were countered by continued official denial, including the rather improbable report from the Russian government in February 2012 that the videos showing voting falsification had mostly themselves been doctored to cast the most negative light on the voting process.[14] Navalny was arrested, along with others, at a December 2011 demonstration in Moscow and spent 15 days in prison. His case was highlighted in some Russian and international media, along with the rising role and popularity of his online campaign against corruption, with the arrest lending further credence to him as a serious opponent to the Kremlin.[15] While in many ways this looks like a classic case of the struggle for free speech, it is important to consider it against the Russian backdrop, which is articulated well by a comment from a Russian citizen reported in BBC report. Zakhar Prilepin, a writer based in Nizhny Novgorod, said it wasn't the broader idea of media freedom that sparked his political concern, but rather a sense that Putin was failing to deliver politically: "I'm not worried about freedom of speech. My main concern is the gap between Putin's rhetoric and his actions. He projects the image of a strong leader, capable of standing up to the East and the West, but in practice he's a weak politician."[16] Sites on the internet such as rospil.info have highlighted just how wide the gap between rhetoric and reality can be in Russia.

Can Navalny and the online community that he has fostered effect change in the Russian political system through communicating issues and aggregating interests? The most visible effect of his blog and website up until December 2011 was attention from officials, which culminated in a lawsuit against him in 2011, although there was the resignation of one official in the wake of documents suggesting corruption. Despite efforts to publicize documentation to prove bribery, there have not been any significant repercussions for the large state enterprises. Rather, the state has been able to identify and track one of its most persistent critics due to Navalny's online presence. What is much harder to gauge is the effect that the dissemination and discussion of official documents that appear to show misdeeds might have on the Russian population. Are Russian citizens enlightened or politically engaged through the online information and interaction? Do they emerge as more empowered citizens or will the eventual fate of Navalny have the effect of inculcating online self-censorship and caution, reinforcing the state's asymmetric power over citizens in Russia? Alternatively, have the past few years and the evidence of online social entrepreneurship via Navalny and others served as a training ground for Russian citizens and Russian democracy movements alike, fostering the personal interest as well as the participation in projects such as the crowd-sourced Golos electoral violation map in late 2011? Confusingly, the Navalny case offers evidence for *both* the argument for the internet as a support to democracy and as a tool for repression. The goal of this section was to place cases such as Navalny's online campaign against corruption within a national context in order to create a better way of thinking about the meaning of this evidence. In a broader way, this book is attempting to place this case study within a more useful theoretical framework so that academics and policy-makers can understand the significance of online movements in the larger context of democratization.

The point is not whether one person such as Alexey Navalny is able—albeit at significant personal risk—to publicize documentation on corruption in Russia and eventually play an important role in organizing protest demonstrations over alleged vote rigging by the United Russia party. The point is whether there can be dozens, hundreds, or even tens of thousands of such people in Russia who will come to view it as politics as usual to share information via the online sphere. From the cyber-pessimist camp, we have the argument that not only does the internet tend to fragment society as people pursue relatively narrow interests in the online sphere, but corporations and governments can then use the data trails left behind to manipulate or even punish individuals. At the same time, there is compelling evidence that information and aggregation in the online sphere can lead to social and political change, ranging from the online campaign in the 2008 Obama election to protests in Egypt's Tahrir Square in early 2011 to the Moscow marches in late 2011. But how can we understand the role that the internet has played or could potentially play in change in non-free states such as Russia? Currently, we are left with the same paradox from the glasnost era in the Soviet Union. There is an enormous amount of information available to the Russian public, but there are significant barriers to translating social capital into political change because of a lack of robust political parties or other political institutions. At the same time, the Russian media sphere has not developed as a Fourth Estate. Rather, most media outlets remain political players in service to elites rather than political watchdogs with a broader interest in democratic values. However, there is now enough evidence as well as online research methodologies that can allow us to identify and measure critical elements of possible democratization in the online sphere. The next step, in the following chapter, is to understand the nature of the internet community—and the dynamic relationship between the online audience and the internet in Russia. This book will return to a discussion of Navalny, protests, elections, and media manipulation in its final chapter.

3

One Nation, Two Audiences

Internet Use and the Media Sphere in Russia

By 2011, the growth in internet use had fundamentally changed the media audience in Russia. As the use of the internet rose rapidly, particularly among the younger generation, there was compelling evidence that the long dominance of state-run television had come to an end for a significant number of Russians. While rising internet use has consequences in terms of audience and attention in all countries, in Russia it is particularly important because of the central societal role played by state television in Russia and the Soviet Union. While regimes have shifted and even collapsed, central state television has remained a trusted political touchstone for the Russian public. As a result, Russian television has been a key political tool, very carefully developed and controlled to shape public opinion. As internet use rises, particularly among the youngest Russian citizens, the state will lose its central ability to manipulate key political information via television.

Evidence presented in this chapter suggests that "internet" citizens are more cynical and demanding of the state than "television" citizens in Russia. In addition, this chapter presents a range of evidence about the size and nature of the internet audience in Russia against the background of studies of the Russian audience in general. At issue is the attempt to show how quantitative change in media use will signal challenges—and opportunities—for citizens and states alike. Much as in Egypt, however, it may be that the Russian government has relied too heavily on the traditional dominance of state-led television and its confidence in promulgating policies to the public. The same tactics are unlikely to succeed in the internet age, as the very different way in which the internet delivers information and connects users does not fit readily into the Russian media system of journalistic self-censorship and adherence to pro-Kremlin frames.

The single most compelling point about the Russian internet audience is the speed at which it has grown in recent years. Outstripping growth in virtually every country in Europe, Russia's online population was the second-largest in Europe after Germany by 2011 and penetration rates were fast approaching half of the population. While the penetration rate remained low compared with other developed countries, the sheer scale of the uptake of ICTs in Russia over a very short period of time suggests that the political effect of the internet may also have grown very rapidly. As Chapter 2 argues, there is more evidence that Runet has fit into an existing Russian media system of controlled self-censorship and political journalism rather than created a new political communication sphere. This chapter examines and charts the growth of the internet audience, comparing it with other post-Soviet countries to see if there is evidence that the sheer quantity of people online can drive political change. In particular, the chapter draws on a highly detailed report on the Russian internet produced by the Russian government in 2011 as well as data from a 2010 survey of 2,017 Russian citizens. From this evidence, it would appear that the internet audience changes qualitatively as it increases quantitatively.

How has the Russian audience changed? What emerges from these sources is compelling evidence that internet use appears to be linked to more skepticism and less support for the Russian regime. At the same time, a range of studies show the emergence of an "internet generation" in Russia, not only due to high levels of internet penetration among Russian youth, but also due to the fact that internet use is spreading fast and wide among Russians under the age of 40. Given that this skepticism appears to grow with heavy internet use—even when other socioeconomic variables are weighed in the balance—it would suggest that the rapid growth in internet use could signal a significant challenge to the communication strategy of the current Russian regime as its approach relies heavily on the dominance of state-run television. The broader issue to consider is whether there are particular features of an online audience, including size, attitude, behavior, or pace of growth, that could predict its contribution to democratization.

Russian Internet Usage

From 2000 to 2010, the number of Russians online grew twenty-fold, reaching 59.7 million users or 43 percent of the population by the end of 2010 (see Figure 3.1: Internet Use in Russia, 2000–2010). This growth not only outstripped virtually anywhere in Western Europe (aside from countries such as Bosnia-Herzegovina that started from a tiny base in 2001), but also meant that Russia added far more in sheer numbers than other post-Soviet countries with high internet growth in the same period (notably Ukraine, Belarus, and Moldova). While still lagging far behind internet giants such as China (477 million online by March 2011) and the United States (245 million online), Russia very

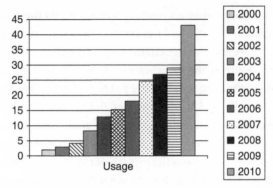

Figure 3.1 Internet Use in Russia, 2000–2010. Source: World Telecommunication/ICT Indicators Database, compiled by the International Telecommunications Union. This database uses figures reported by countries. The Russian figures for 2010 are for those aged 16–74 and are from the Ministry of Telecommunications and Mass Communication of the Russian Federation. The 2009 figure is reported as those under 74 and is from the Russian State Statistics Committee (Goskomstat). The figure for 2008 is an estimate from the International Telecommunications Union. The 2007 figure is from the Ministry of Telecommunications. The database does not give a source for the other years. See http://data.un.org/Data.aspx?d=ITU&f=ind1Code%3aI99H (last accessed February 27, 2012).

rapidly developed a commanding presence in the European online world. This also has contributed to the growth of the Russian language online, as Russian became one of the top 10 languages used in the online sphere by 2011 (albeit it ranked ninth overall).[1]

What has driven this rapid and widespread adoption of the internet in Russia? There have been several important factors contributing to the growth: a significant rise in income for Russians in the past decade; a spread of internet usage from urban elites to a much wider base; government policy that has encouraged the use of ICTs; a lack of overtly repressive state controls on the Russian internet; an attractive range of Russian internet platforms and websites for users that play to a strong cultural interest in reflective discussion and networking among friends; the development of mobile internet that is augmented by the extremely widespread use of mobile telephones in Russia; as well as a well-educated and attentive media audience. In particular, a detailed report from the Russian Federal Agency on the Press and Mass Communication (2011) gives extensive details on a range of studies providing illumination into key information and trends of Russian internet content and audience. As discussed below, some of the evidence is surprising or at times counterintuitive. However, both data from the Russian agency report as well as findings from a 2010 survey of Russians suggest that the Russian online audience has not only grown significantly in size, but has developed several features that would signal the beginning of the Russian internet's ability to possibly function as an effective forum for democracy.

Cooper (2008) argues that the uptake of ICTs is related to wealth. As incomes rise for citizens, they are more likely to have the disposable income to pay for online access, a cost that has continued to fall particularly with the rise of the mobile internet. Although Cooper found a few years ago that Russia's internet use actually lagged behind its economic growth and status, the country's population has since made up for lost time. The Russian agency report provides a more detailed picture of the distribution of internet use within the country, particularly noting its spread from the main cities into the smaller towns, villages, and countryside. Indeed, from the winter of 2009–10 to the winter of 2010–11, growth in internet penetration in Russian villages (*syela*) exploded, showing a 47 percent growth rate in a single year by increasing from 19 percent to 28 percent internet penetration. There was growth in Russian internet use throughout the country—from 22 percent in towns of 100,000 to 500,000 residents to a more modest 4 percent in the relatively saturated Moscow internet market—but the advance in the countryside was phenomenal (Russian Federal Agency, 2011).

As the Russian agency report points out, the growth in internet use away from the urban centers suggests another significant market expansion for ICTs. This could explain why growth of internet penetration in Russia has exceeded the expectations of many analysts. The recent growth of internet use in relatively rural areas means that more than a third of internet users live in small towns and villages, a fundamental shift from the dominance of the urban elite as internet users in Russia. However, there are significant regional variations in internet use in Russia, with 51 percent internet use in the northwestern region, 42 percent in the central region, 38 percent in the Urals, 34 percent in the Volga region, 34 percent in Siberia, 33 percent in the Caucasian region, and just 30 percent in the relatively economically depressed Far East (Russian Federal Agency on the Press and Mass Communication, 2011, p. 8). Thus, while no other regions have reached the high level of internet use found in Moscow and St. Petersburg at 65 percent and 70 percent respectively, the online audience does not yet represent an even national sample. As usage rises more quickly in small hamlets and in outlying areas, the nature of the audience is bound to change as well. In particular, it will mean a rising percentage of users who do not share the political and economic views of the powerful central cities in European Russia, views that have generally reflected more enthusiasm for Western-style markets.

The communications agency report remained optimistic that the growth of internet use will continue in waves, as communities that differ in size and location join the online world. The report notes that while the growth in the size of online population has stagnated in countries such as Portugal, this is unlikely to happen in Russia (p. 15). The report argues that as Russia has a wide distribution of relatively highly educated individuals who work in small cities and towns, these individuals are still joining the Russian online audience. The report predicts continued strong growth for several years: "It is possible that the 'fracture' that corresponds to a sharp drop in the rate of growth (as in Western Europe) . . . will not have to be observed in Russia as the points of increase gradually displace one another. At the end of the internet boom in the capitals and towns of more than a million population, there is a growth in small cities. Even now more than a third of internet users live in small cities and villages" leaving significant room for growth (p. 15, author's translation). Overall, studies have left the communications agency convinced that by the end of 2014, there will be 80 million people (or 71 percent of the population aged 18 or over) online in Russia and virtually all Russians from the age of 12 to 40 will be online. This would bring the overall usage into line with countries such as the United States and the United Kingdom.

At the same time that there are more internet users in Russia, the users are online more frequently, according to data from the Russian Public Opinion Foundation included in the communications agency report. The number of daily internet users had increased from just 34 percent of users in the winter of 2003–04 to 72 percent of internet users by the winter of 2010–11. What is particularly surprising is that many Russians are carrying out a lot of online activity with relatively low-tech phones. Twenty-two million Russians access the internet by phone, but smartphones with augmented internet function are still used by only about 8 percent of the population (p. 38). The communications agency reported data from studies to reveal what Russians do most online: online search (75 percent of non-mobile internet users); reading the news (51 percent); participating in social networking (50 percent); sending e-mail (49 percent); downloading and listening to music (45 percent); looking at photographs (42 percent); and downloading and viewing video (38 percent). Unsurprisingly given that they are generally not using smartphones and have fairly limited functionality, Russian mobile internet users engage in fewer activities except for sending messages (22 percent of Russian mobile internet users send messages compared with 18 percent of traditional internet users).

As in other countries, youth is a very strong predictor of internet use in Russia, although studies consulted by the communications agency suggest that internet use is poised to reach almost complete saturation for the Russian population for citizens all the way up to the age of 40. So far, however, the age-based digital divide in Russia remains stark. While 84 percent of those aged 12 through 17 use the internet, only 8 percent of those over the age of 55 are online (Russian Federal Agency, p. 11). The usage declines consistently across age groups. The report points out that while recent growth has been fueled by a greater adoption of the internet by older users, the older generation will continue to be less involved in the online world in Russia. Following current trends, the communications agency report predicts that virtually *all* Russians from the age of 12 to

45 will be online by the autumn of 2014. The report also forecasts internet usage saturation rates of 99 percent for 12- to 17-year-olds and 97 percent for those between 18 and 45. For the older age groups, while usage will reach 76 percent for those between age 45 and 54, the report predicts that the oldest segment of society will only reach 24 percent internet saturation by late 2014.[2]

The Internet's Challenge to Russian Television

For media scholars, what is particularly interesting about these measurements and predicted trends in internet use is the inevitable changes it will bring to the way in which people consume news. This is of paramount political importance in Russia, where state-run television has held extraordinary power since the end of the Soviet era and from the foundation of the Russian Federation in 1991 (Mickiewicz, 1980, 1988, 1997; Oates, 2006). Soviet television was developed as the key link between the ruling Communist Party of the Soviet Union and the populace. Although it was essentially a top-down propaganda organ, it was one that found great resonance and affection with the Soviet population. As a result, it was used as a powerful source in the transition from Soviet to Russian political elites (Mickiewicz, 1997) as well as deployed as a way of marginalizing and vilifying the Kremlin's political opponents in the young Russian Federation, particularly during elections (Oates 2006, 2007).

Despite obvious bias and manipulation, the Russian audience reports loyalty and fondness for their state-run television, especially First Channel. This might seem paradoxical, in that Russian media audiences are particularly attentive and attuned to political nuance (Mickiewicz, 2008; Oates, 2006). However, as Russian focus group participants commented in 2000 and 2004, their expectation of Russian television is that it should encourage an orderly and predictable state of affairs rather than foster a broad debate about society's direction (Oates, 2006). After the social, political, and economic shocks of the late 1980s and early 1990s, much of the Russian audience was suspicious of a broad media debate and not attracted to critical news coverage. Rather, the media should lead the nation, not follow the wishes of various factions in society. As a result, it is not surprising that many Russians found particular value in Soviet media, which fits the notion of top-down communication, over the more chaotic media system in the late Soviet era and early days of the Russian Federation (Oates, 2006).

It is hard to overestimate how much television, particularly the state-run programs on Channel 1, has dominated both the Russian media and political landscape. In a 2003–04 survey, national television was the most popular media outlet, with 95 percent viewership (82 percent of the respondents watching it routinely and an additional 13 percent watching it occasionally).[3] Local television was only slightly less popular than national television. Both national and local newspapers were markedly less popular.[4] Additional questions on the survey about how the respondents gathered political information also amplified the importance of television: 62 percent said they received news about politics every day from television, compared with 28 percent from radio and just 14 percent from newspapers. State television news dominated: 75 percent of the respondents said they watched Channel 1's *Vremya* nightly news regularly and 62 percent watched Channel 2's *Vesti* regularly. Only 38 percent reported watching the main commercial station's news (NTV's *Sevodnya*) regularly.

While it is relatively easy to measure the consumption of media, it is much harder to gauge the influence of the mass media on political life. As noted before in this book and as a general tenet of the study of political communication, the presence of the correlation between personal political beliefs and the bias of a particular media outlet does not prove causation. In other words, one does not know whether the audience selects media based on preexisting preferences or to what degree preexisting perceptions change (or consolidate) due to exposure to a particular point of view via the media. To make matters more complicated, it also is hard to balance the effect of the media via long-term acculturation to particular values and beliefs over time—a sort of cumulative "drip" effect—with how the media is particularly influential in times of political crisis and change. This may mean that how the media cover events, frame news, and set the news agenda during war, riots, terrorist acts, contentious elections, or other times that challenge the civic status quo may be particularly important in terms of understanding media's power in society. Thus, when thinking about the internet as a source of information that supplements or could even supplant the traditional mass media, it is important to consider both the internet's role in everyday information provision as well as its function during times of political crisis.

Overall, Russians trust their mass media more than most other political institutions. During the more chaotic period about 10 years ago in the Russian Federation, 36 percent of Russians placed trust in state television and 29 percent in commercial television, according to a survey of 2,000 Russians in 2001.[5] This compared with much lower levels of trust in a range of national institutions, including the judiciary, the police, parliament, and political parties (although trust in the presidency was high and remained so for a long time). Indeed, there is both indirect and direct evidence that the media, particularly television, matters a great deal to a large number of voters in Russia. The indirect evidence is that many Russian voters still make up their minds at a relatively late point in the electoral process, such as during the 2003 Duma elections. According to the 2003–04 survey, only about 59 percent of voters had made up their minds by September 2003. About 21 percent settled on a choice in the following months, but 11 percent left the choice until the last week of the elections, and 4 percent reported that they actually decided on the day of the election itself. It is unlikely that someone leaning toward the Communist Party, for example, would be persuaded to change his mind completely and vote for a relatively liberal, market-oriented party due to clever campaigning. But the high level of swing in the vote suggests that marketing techniques via the mass media were particularly important when there were relatively close choices among parties.

If so many Russian voters are waiting that long to make up their minds, are the media influencing them during that time? The evidence would suggest that the media, particularly state television, have quite a strong influence in elections: 40 percent of the respondents in the 2003–04 survey claimed that national state television was the most important source of information for their vote choice in the Duma elections. This was quite distinct from the responses relating to commercial television. Although watched relatively widely by the population at the time, commercial television was cited by just 1 percent of the respondents in the survey as the most important source for their vote choice. It should be noted that Russian voters *claim* a degree of independence from media sources: 32 percent said that they did not rely on anything but their "own thoughts" in making their vote choice in the 2003 parliamentary elections. They also were most likely to cite themselves as the most "helpful" factor in making their vote choice, 41 percent saying that their own experience helped them to a significant extent. Indeed, more respondents reported that they found the mass media confusing than those that reported it as helpful. While 8 percent of the respondents claimed that the media had confused them during the elections, only 5 percent of the respondents reported that the media had helped them to change their minds before the elections. A far larger number of the respondents (25 percent) said that the media had no effect at all on their vote.

But what does all this mean almost 10 years later, as Russia faced its first parliamentary and presidential elections with a significant online audience in late 2011 and 2012? On the eve of these elections, information in the communications agency report suggested there had been a fundamental shift in the way in which the Russian media audience consumed news. More significantly, it appeared that the dominance of state-run television in Russia was coming to an end. As the Russian agency report noted, media consumption is not exclusive, with the habit of surfing the internet and watching television at the same time particularly prevalent. Davis (2009) makes the point that the introduction of a new media platform does not completely replace the audience for the previous media form—i.e., the introduction of television did not stop people from reading newspapers. He argues it is more useful to think of audiences as overlapping or augmented by a range of different media types (p. 190).

The Russian agency report gave a very detailed picture of the Russian media audience, including statistics on the pattern of media use throughout the day.

When analyzing the contemporary Russian media audience aged 12 to 54, research by Taylor Nelson Sofres (TNS) in July 2010 found that radio listening dominates until about 5 pm daily, peaking at about 30 percent of the audience at noon (Russian Federal Agency, p. 16). From early evening, television viewing started to rise and peaked about 10 pm with more than 35 percent of the audience. Internet usage was more consistent during the day, rising to about 15 percent of the audience at 10 am and holding steady until about 10:30 at night. Internet usage overtook radio usage from the early evening, although it never rose above television usage (p. 16). However, the TNS data reported by the communications agency makes it clear that the internet was more prominent for newer generations of Russians, particularly those aged 12 to 17. For this group, the internet marginally outstripped television use for most of the day, with television only rising above the internet to capture about 25 percent of the age group from about 9 pm to 10 pm in the evening (the main edition of *Vremya* is aired at 9 pm, although the report did not say what the people were watching).

In a further investigation of media preferences of the Russian audience for those aged 12 to 54, TNS found that First Channel still dominates, with 40.5 percent viewership daily and 72.3 percent viewership weekly (Russian Federal Agency, see Table 3.1: Top 10 Media Preferences for Russians Aged 12–54). However, in comparison with the 82 percent viewership of television (with Channel 1[6] as the most popular media outlet) reported about 10 years ago, this suggests a significant decline in media dominance for the state-run First Channel. For those aged 12 to 54, the five most popular media outlets were

Table 3.1 **Top 10 Media Preferences for Russians Aged 12–54**

Outlet	Type	Daily average (in percentages)	Weekly average (in percentages)
First Channel	State-run TV	40.5	72.3
Rossiya-1	State TV	35.3	68.5
NTV	Commercial TV	34.0	65.9
STS	Commercial TV	33.2	64.8
TNT	Commercial TV	29.9	59.4
Yandex	Search engine	29.3	47.7
Mail.Ru	Online mail portal	25.8	44.0
Ren	Commercial TV	25.8	56.3
Vkontake.ru	Social-networking site	24.0	35.7
Evropa Plus	Commercial radio	22.1	48.1

Source: Russian Federal Agency on the Press and Mass Communication, 2011, p. 17.

television stations, but the search engine Yandex and the portal Mail.ru at sixth and seventh place respectively outranked a range of traditional media outlets including commercial REN TV (eighth place), Europa Plus Radio (tenth), Russian Radio (eleventh), and Moscow City channel TV-Center (thirteenth). VKontakte, the social-networking site, ranked as the ninth most popular outlet amongst those aged 12 to 54 (See Table 3.1). However, while television still tops the charts for a fairly wide age range, an internet source is the *most* popular media choice for those aged 12 to 34 years (see Table 3.2: Top 10 Media Preferences for Russians Aged 12–34). According to the TNS study reported by the Russian agency, the younger Russian generation placed Yandex and VKontakte as their first and second media choices respectively (p. 17). First Channel only ranked in third place. The tendency was even more marked for the younger cohort: Those aged 12 to 17 ranked VKontakte as their favorite media source, although commercial STS television was their second choice. Yandex was their third most favored source, while Mail.ru ranked sixth (see Table 3.3: Top 10 Media Preferences for Russians Aged 12–17). First Channel was fairly far down the list, in eighth place for this younger cohort of the media audience. While part of this may be due to age-related preferences for lighter entertainment, it does suggest that state-run television is not engaging with the youngest generation. By the time these young viewers are ready for more serious news programs and analysis, it is not clear they would abandon their preference for the internet and turn to state-run television as generations before them have done in Russia.

Table 3.2 **Top 10 Media Preferences for Russians Aged 12–34**

Outlet	Type	Daily average (in percentages)	Weekly average (in percentages)
Yandex	Search engine	35.4	56.5
VKontake.ru	Social-networking site	34.2	49.0
First Channel	State-run TV	33.7	66.6
STS	Commercial TV	32.5	63.6
TNT	Commercial TV	31.2	60.1
Mail.Ru	Online mail portal	30.3	52.0
Evropa Plus	Commercial radio	28.3	56.9
Rossiya-1	State TV	27.4	61.5
NTV	Commercial TV	26.6	59.5
Russkoe Radio	State radio	23.2	50.2

Source: Russian Federal Agency on the Press and Mass Communication, 2011, p. 17.

Table 3.3 **Top 10 Media Preferences for Russians Aged 12–17**

Outlet	Type	Daily average (in percentages)	Weekly average (in percentages)
VKontake.ru	Social-networking site	44.3	58.3
STS	Commercial TV	36.3	68.1
Yandex.ru	Search engine	35.1	55.4
TNT	Commercial TV	32.6	62.0
Evropa Plus	Commercial radio	32.5	59.0
Mail.Ru	Online mail portal	29.2	50.3
Russkoe Radio	State radio	26.0	47.8
First Channel	State-run TV	24.2	55.9
Love Radio	Commercial radio	21.4	41.2
Humor FM	Commercial radio	18.9	36.5

Source: Russian Federal Agency on the Press and Mass Communication, 2011, p. 18.

The figures above would suggest that the pervasive ability of state-run television to set and maintain the political agenda in Russia for generations has shifted fundamentally for the youngest Russians. Overall, there is now a divided media market in Russia, with the scales tipping month by month toward the internet. Only 17 percent of regular television viewers are aged between 12 and 24, 33 percent between 25 and 44, 19 percent between 45 and 54, and 31 percent—almost a third of the total audience—is over the age of 55 (Russian Federal Agency, p. 18). By contrast, more than a third of the internet audience (36 percent) is between the age of 12 and 24, 49 percent is between 25 and 44, 12 percent is between 45 and 54, and just 5 percent of the internet audience is 55 or older.

Online Activity in Runet: General Audience

As the Russian communications agency report notes, internet and television use is not mutually exclusive. People can watch and surf at the same time. However, it would suggest that in order to maintain a majority audience with television broadcasting, the Russian government needs to replicate the Channel 1 loyalty and influence in the internet age. However, one thing that Russians do *not* appear to be doing is watching television news—or really that much video in general—on line (although this contradicts the Berkman report cited in Chapter 2 to a degree).

After search and using web portals, the most popular activity on Runet is social networking. Here there is no Facebook Generation; if anything, one would call it a VKontakte Generation. TNS estimated that by the end of 2010, 28.5 million Russians had tried social-networking—and a lot of them liked it. They calculated that 22.7 million Russians use VKontakte every month, 18.3 million use it every week, and 12.5 million use it every day (p. 51). Odnoklassniki and Mail.ru/Moi Mir [My World] are also popular, but Facebook and Twitter much less so. While Facebook still attracted 10.2 million users monthly, according to TNS, it only had 400,000 users on a daily basis in Russia. Thus, VKontakte clearly dominated in terms of regular social networkers in Russia. It is also interesting to note that Twitter remained relatively unpopular in 2010, although analysts at the Berkman Institute predicted this was set to change (Etling et al., 2010, p. 12). The Russian platform LiveJournal also dominated in blogging, with 14.4 million monthly users, 6.9 million weekly users, and 2.1 million daily users in 2010.

There is plenty of news to discuss on Runet in social-networking sites and on blogs. According to figures from Yandex News in January 2011, there are more than 50,000 pieces of news published in Russian every business day (Russian Federal Agency, p. 52). Most of the news production was domestic, with two-thirds of the stories created by Russian publishers. Another 22 percent were from Ukrainian sources (and Ukraine supplies a large internet audience to Runet due to the large Russian-speaking and Russian-oriented segment of the population in Ukraine) and about 9 percent were from other former Soviet countries. Almost 80 percent of the news came from 20 percent of the prominent news publishers. The most prolific producer of online news items was the newspaper *Komsomolskaya Pravda*, which published on average 900 news items every business day, according to the Yandex News data. ComScore estimated the monthly audience for online Russian news at 40 million. About 25 million of the users were from Russia and about 12 million were from Europe (Russian Federal Agency, p. 52).[7]

However, despite the wide range of news and sources, LiveInternet.ru estimated that the Russian online audience received "information produced by a narrow circle of publishers" (Russian Federal Agency, p. 52, author's translation). The most in-depth news (defined as being the longest in terms of word count) was published on the sites of weekly magazines, while the shortest stories were found on the sites of television channels and radio stations. Surprisingly, the study reported that multimedia news sites were quite rare, with only 39 percent featuring image and only 1 to 2 percent with audio and video. While the report showed that television websites were offering video clips, only about 20 percent of news items on television sites included video. While there was at least some video fare there, it is clear that television networks were failing to make up for losing audience share by creating a compelling online product that played to the strength of television. This could explain why the websites of major television networks failed to draw in a mass audience as people moved progressively more online, unlike the way in which the BBC has developed an extensive and well-regarded online presence to maintain audience share in a changing media environment.[8] Overall, the communications agency report found that media outlets did not post as many news items per day as media outlets in neighboring post-Soviet countries—an average of 13 items a day in Russia, compared with 22 per day by Ukrainian media outlets, and 21 per day in the Caucasian and Baltic countries.

So how do Russians look for news online? If their online behavior followed the patterns of Russian news gathering observed during Soviet and post-Soviet times, we would expect the Russian online audience to have a favorite news source but be ready to compare. In earlier surveys and in focus groups, Russians have reported that they often will watch two or even three television news programs from different sources in a single day (Oates, 2006). For example, when internet penetration was about 2 percent in Russia (see Figure 3.1), Russians were actively engaged in trying to glean information particularly from television.

The 2001 survey found that, much as in the Soviet period, Russian viewers often switched among channels in order to gather information. Almost a quarter (21 percent) of those surveyed in 2001 claimed that they watched more than one news program a day on the same channel—and 22 percent claimed that they *always* watched more than one news program a day on different channels. An additional 45 percent of the respondents pursued both of these news-monitoring strategies on occasion. Although newspaper readership was lower than the use of broadcast media, it is still relatively high in global terms. In the 2001 survey, 58 percent of the respondents claimed to read local newspapers several times a week or more, while 36 percent read national newspapers at the same rate. The statistics show that this was an audience that sought news actively and energetically. Given the high levels of consumption of each type of media outlet (state television, commercial television, radio, national newspapers, local newspapers), it was clear that some people were paying attention to a range of media.

The communications agency report did not find the same sort of commitment to sampling a range of online sources as reported in the survey of Russians about traditional media use more than a decade ago. Rather, 38 percent of traffic to online media sites comes as a user goes directly to a particular URL. Another 17.5 percent comes from search. Thus, while search is the most popular activity on Runet, it is clear that people are only searching for *news* a fraction of the time. Other traffic to online media sites comes through news aggregators (9 percent), other media websites (9 percent), web portals such as Mail.Ru (8 percent), traffic aggregation sites (6.5 percent), and banner ads (5 percent) (p. 58). It is particularly interesting to note the way in which the online news sphere in Runet is divided into different segments, with very few web links among the major sources of news (Russian Federal Agency, pp. 56–57). Instead of a networked community of news organizations, it is clear that news websites would tend to isolate users, with virtually no interlinking of news websites. Major news websites appear to serve more as tunnels into narrow selections of news from single producers rather than opportunities to garner more news from a range of sources.

This channelization is particularly apparent from the web link analysis of Russian news sources in the communications agency report (pages 56 and 57). The news agency RIA/Novosti dominated as an information source for 36 other news outlets, overshadowing the use of Interfax as a source (11 links to other media sources) and ITAR-TASS (five links). The communications agency notes that material from RIA/Novosti and the Russian news agency RBK was copied by more than 800 other publications in October 2010. The web link analysis presented by the communications agency also showed very few links into major information providers and almost no links between information providers. This would suggest that there are relatively narrow information channels on Runet. In particular, it should be noted that the television networks are especially isolated, with only one link to Vesti.ru (the website of the main news program on state-owned Channel 2). Curiously, First Channel does not appear on this analysis. There are very few links to foreign media.

In terms of information provided from government sources, the Russian agency report found that government agencies in Russia were posting an average of three to six items daily. While this is much lower than news organizations, it still provides about 30 percent of the daily news updates just because of the sheer number of Russian government agencies. Further study of the content of the messages (discussed to a degree in Chapters 5 and 6) and comparison to E-Governance in other countries would be needed to give a better assessment of online government communication in Russia. However, it is worthwhile to note that the internet gives Russians exponentially more direct information from government sources than ever before in their history given that there has been no culture of government openness or even communication in the past. If it appears that Russians are fairly narrow in their *consumption* of news, it can be argued that they are relatively broad in their *discussion* of the news in the online sphere.

As noted in the report from the Berkman Center for Internet & Society at Harvard University, Russia has a vibrant blogosphere (Etling et al., 2010). This is an important aspect of the Russian online sphere that is not covered by the 2011 government agency report. Prominent bloggers on political issues will not dominate in the general online sphere, even if they are particularly influential within certain online communities. However, if the presence and activities of blogs and collaborative online spaces can change the parameters of political debate in small ways at first, it gives the potential of more widespread influence over time. An Internews report (2011) identified a "fifth estate" in the Russian internet as the rise of effective online campaigning reaching critical mass. In particular, the report highlighted important advances in online information, collaboration, and action in activities such as the "little Blue Buckets" campaign in April 2010 and the Help Map project during the Russian wildfires in 2010. The Blue Buckets protest highlighted citizen anger over state officials who use the blue, flashing lights on their vehicles to drive recklessly. In protest, drivers fitted their cars with mock blue lights in the form of small blue buckets, a demonstration that was organized and coordinated by bloggers. Another online initiative that developed from discontent into direct action was the Help Map project (www.Russian-Fires.ru) that allowed individuals to both seek and offer help in the online sphere on a collaborative map (echoed by the Golos electoral violation map in late 2011) as the state response to the crisis faltered. This effectively shifted responsibility (and authority) from the government to individuals, an important step in inculcating political capital. The Internews report also highlighted the activities of prominent Russian bloggers, including Navalny and Marina Litvinovich, identifying a consistent development of the capacity of the internet to become more inclusive and professional in information provision and social aggregation over the past few years.

Internet, Media Use, and Political Attitudes: 2010 National Survey

While the Berkman report found that Russian bloggers were fairly open about linking to a wide range of online sources, what further evidence is there that the Russian blogosphere has developed a robust set of well-defined online spaces to debate real change and opposition in Russian society? Although much of the activity would be considered more social than political, there is clear evidence that the internet expands the public sphere of the Russian audience. In part, this is due to the far greater range of information sources than have ever before been available to the Russian public, despite the fact that the communications agency report shows that Russian online news sources tend to channel the audience into relatively narrow information spaces. However, the facts that Russian television does not have a parallel dominance in the online sphere and that the younger audience shows more interest in online, rather than traditional, media could signal a fundamental shift in the loyalty and attention of key segments of the Russian news audience.

This part of the book uses data from a 2010 survey of 2,017 Russians to further explore the nature of the internet audience. In particular, this section is interested in what individual-level data can tell us about internet users in Russia.

This section analyzes how socioeconomic factors such as age, education, and wealth predict internet use in Russia. In addition, the broad range of attitudinal questions in the survey on human rights and the state of democracy in Russia allow for a relatively detailed examination of how internet users may differ from the general population in attitudes toward the liberalization of Russian society. Through this data, we can examine evidence for the idea that the internet could indeed be a transformative public sphere (Brandenburg, 2006) for the Russian audience, one that is only set to expand with the explosion of internet use in the country. The 2010 survey is part of a longitudinal series of surveys examining Russian attitudes to civil society and other issues over the years (see White, 2011 for an overview of the results). In 2010, the survey included a single question on internet use: "How often do you go on line (*obrashchaetes' k internetu*)?," with the options of "regularly," "sometimes," "seldom," and "never" (*regulyarno, inogda, redko,* and *nikogda*). The results tally relatively well with figures from the 2011 Russian agency report and the International Telecommunications Union (January 31, 2011): 23 percent of the respondents reported that they went online routinely, 16.3 percent sometimes, 14.1 percent seldom, and 46.5 percent claimed they had never gone online (see Figure 3.2: Media Use in Russia).

Theories of the digital divide (Norris, 2001) suggest that internet use is asymmetric both within and between countries. Within countries, socioeconomic characteristics including income and education have been noted to be particularly important in predicting internet use. In some countries, women have lagged behind men in the use of the internet, although the link between gender use and the level of ICT engagement has diminished over time in many countries. In Russia, a key cleavage is between urban and rural inhabitants,

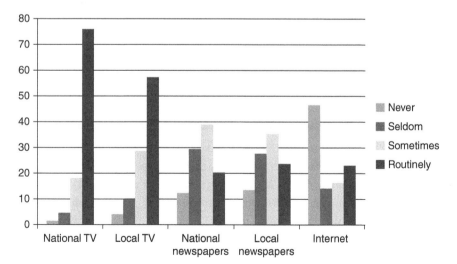

Figure 3.2 Media Use in Russia. Source: 2010 survey.

with urban dwellers having greater access to technology. In addition, a range of surveys since the collapse of the Soviet Union in 1991 have shown more support for liberal values in the cities, with rural areas demonstrating more support for the communists and less market-oriented, pro-Western views (Oates, 2006). This is augmented by the particular political systems and values found within Moscow and St. Petersburg, with Moscow tending to support pro-Kremlin parties in a type of "inside the Beltway" political syndrome and St. Petersburg often exhibiting a deliberate independence from Moscow politics with a more liberal outlook. With reference to both comparative theories about the digital divide as well as specific trends in Russian politics, this analysis looks first at the correlation of internet use with gender, age, education, income, and population density.[9] In addition, as the Russian communications agency report noted the unusually high internet penetration in Moscow and St. Petersburg, the effect of residence in the two major Russian cities is analyzed.

In a bivariate correlation analysis, the single most important of these factors in predicting internet use is youth (See Table 3.4: Bivariate Correlation Analysis of Factors Predicting Internet Use in Russia). Figures from the 2010 survey show that age is strongly and significantly negatively correlated with increasing internet use. This is the only significant negative correlation in the analysis: Education, income, and rising population density are all strongly and positively correlated with internet use (although youth is an even stronger predictor). Being male is a weak, but significant, predictor of internet use in Russia. Living in Moscow and St. Petersburg is also positively correlated with higher internet use, but the effect is almost twice as strong for Moscow (despite a higher average penetration rate in St. Petersburg reported by the Russian communications agency). Overall, residence in Moscow and St. Petersburg is a weaker predictor of internet use than urban density in general as measured by living in a city with 200,000 or more residents.

All things being equal, what did this survey find as the most important predicator of internet use if the strongest predictors of youth, education, income, and higher population density are taken into account? Unsurprisingly given that all of these factors had strong correlations in bivariate analysis, regression analysis also shows these factors to have a significant effect on internet use (see Table 3.5: Regression Analysis of Internet Use in Russia). The four factors explain almost a quarter of variance in use. Youth is still the dominant predictor of internet use in Russia in this model, with education, income, and population density each predicting internet use with less strength. It is interesting to note that when factors are held to be equal in the regression model, education is a somewhat stronger predictor than income for internet use. The socioeconomic predicators of internet use are not particularly surprising, although it is interesting that residence in Moscow and St. Petersburg no longer confers a strong advantage in access to the

Table 3.4 **Bivariate Correlation Analysis of Factors Predicting Internet Use in Russia**

		Internet use
Male	Pearson Correlation	.067**
	Sig. (2-tailed)	.003
	N	1980
Age (low to high)	Pearson Correlation	-.473**
	Sig. (2-tailed)	.000
	N	1980
Education (low to high)	Pearson Correlation	.280**
	Sig. (2-tailed)	.000
	N	1980
Income (low to high)	Pearson Correlation	.245**
	Sig. (2-tailed)	.000
	N	1023
Population density (low to high)	Pearson Correlation	.209**
	Sig. (2-tailed)	.000
	N	1980

Correlations

		Internet use	Moscow	St. Petersburg
Internet use (none to high)	Pearson Correlation	1	.165**	.095**
	Sig. (2-tailed)		.000	.000
	N	1980	1980	1980
Muscovite	Pearson Correlation	.165**	1	-.057*
	Sig. (2-tailed)	.000		.010
	N	1980	2017	2017
St. Petersburg resident	Pearson Correlation	.095**	-.057*	1
	Sig. (2-tailed)	.000	.000	
	N	1980	2017	2017

* Correlation is significant at the 0.05 level (2-tailed).
** Correlation is significant at the 0.01 level (2-tailed).

Source: 2010 survey.

Table 3.5 **Regression Analysis of Internet Use in Russia**

Model		Unstandardized Coefficients		Standardized Coefficients		
		B	Std. Error	Beta	t	Sig.
1	(Constant)	1.362	.168		8.088	.000
	Age	-.034	.003	-.352	-12.909	.000
	Education	.153	.021	.204	7.383	.000
	Income	.112	.022	.149	5.221	.000
	Population density	.320	.070	.130	4.578	.000

a. Dependent Variable: Internet use

Adjusted r-square = .249, standard error = 1.050

Source: 2010 survey.

online sphere. Indeed, this is a point underlined by the communications agency report in pointing out that the most significant waves of growth in internet usage are in areas far from the dominant cities in Russia's western region.

Is the internet pulling people away from the traditional mass media in Russia? Evidence from the communications agency report would suggest this is the case, especially for younger Russians. However, the 2010 survey indicated that television still dominated the Russian audience in terms of sheer viewership across the population. It is not surprising that a correlation analysis finds that older age is strongly associated with watching national television and less strongly associated (although still statistically significant) with watching local television. The communications agency report points out that internet use and television use are by no means mutually exclusive and, indeed, it is not uncommon to watch television and surf the internet at the same time. However, is the internet ultimately pulling people away from television and hence undermining the particular dominance of state-run television in the Russian media market? If so, we would expect to see a negative correlation between internet use and television viewing. Indeed, there is a weak, negative correlation between internet use and viewing of national television in the 2010 survey data (see Table 3.6: Correlation between Television Viewing and Internet Use). However, this may be an artifact of the lower television viewership among the younger population. A regression analysis with television viewing as the dependent variable shows that when the factors of age, education, income, urban density, and rising internet use are taken into consideration, internet use is no longer a significant predictor of watching television less. Older age is a strong positive prediction of interest in watching national television, although higher income is an even stronger predictor and

Table 3.6 **Correlation between Television Viewing and Internet Use**

	Correlations		
		Frequency of watching national television	*Internet use*
Frequency of watching national TV	Pearson Correlation	1	-.052*
	Sig. (2-tailed)		.020
	N	2011	1978
Internet use	Pearson Correlation	-.052*	1
	Sig. (2-tailed)	.020	
	N	1978	1980

*. Correlation is significant at the 0.05 level (2-tailed).

Source: 2010 survey.

overall the predicative strength of the variables is weak given the low r-square score (see Table 3.7: Regression Analysis for Factors Predicting Television Viewing).

If the internet isn't really crowding out use of other media, what is it doing? In an initial analysis, we now turn to an examination of internet use in general vis-à-vis attitudes toward democracy and a range of civil rights in Russia. The correlations were rarely significant. However, when the internet users were segmented and the analysis focused on those claiming regular internet use,

Table 3.7 **Regression Analysis for Factors Predicting Television Viewing**

		Coefficients[a]				
Model		*Unstandardized Coefficients*		*Standardized Coefficients*		
		B	*Std. Error*	*Beta*	*t*	*Sig.*
1	(Constant)	3.277	.107		30.518	.000
	Age	.006	.002	.109	3.248	.001
	Education	-.018	.013	-.045	-1.386	.166
	Higher income	.052	.013	.127	3.874	.000
	More urban	.077	.044	.057	1.760	.079
	Internet use	.008	.019	.015	.424	.671

a. Dependent Variable: Frequency of watching national television
b. Adjusted r-square = .028

Source: 2010 survey.

interesting patterns about attitudes emerged from the survey data. In a correlation analysis, it was clear that regular internet users are more positive about respect for human rights, freedom of speech, the ability to join organizations, and the chance to participate in public life in Russia (see Table 3.8: Bivariate Analysis of Attitudes of Regular Internet Users in Russia). All of this suggests that the Habermasian idea of a public sphere may be taking hold, but it is also clear that regular internet users were somewhat more cynical than non-regular users about certain aspects of Russian society (see Table 3.9: Correlation Analysis of Regular Internet Use with Confidence in Russian Institutions). Although regular internet use did not appear to affect confidence in the Russian courts, political parties, the police, trade unions, the church, the president, or commercial television, it did appear to have a negative effect on confidence in the following institutions: the Russian armed forces, parliament, state television, regional government, and national government. The only positive relationship appears to be a greater confidence in commercial enterprises amongst regular internet users in Russia.

Table 3.8 **Bivariate Analysis of Attitudes of Regular Internet Users in Russia**

		Regular internet use
Respect for human rights	Pearson Correlation	.063**
	Sig. (2-tailed)	.006
	N	1923
Support for non-communist system	Pearson Correlation	-.185**
	Sig. (2-tailed)	.000
	N	1709
Freedom of speech easier	Pearson Correlation	.091**
	Sig. (2-tailed)	.000
	N	1912
Easier to join organizations	Pearson Correlation	.133**
	Sig. (2-tailed)	.000
	N	1864
Easier to participate in public life	Pearson Correlation	.087**
	Sig. (2-tailed)	.000
	N	1879
	N	1980

** Correlation is significant at the 0.01 level (2-tailed).
* Correlation is significant at the 0.05 level (2-tailed).

Source: 2010 survey.

Table 3.9 **Correlation Analysis of Regular Internet Use with Confidence in Russian Institutions**

		Internet use
	N	1980
Court	Pearson Correlation	-.039
	Sig. (2-tailed)	.093
	N	1874
Political Parties	Pearson Correlation	-.044
	Sig. (2-tailed)	.058
	N	1882
Police	Pearson Correlation	-.034
	Sig. (2-tailed)	.034
	N	1926
Armed forces	Pearson Correlation	-.078[**]
	Sig. (2-tailed)	.001
	N	1897
Parliament	Pearson Correlation	-.075[**]
	Sig. (2-tailed)	.001
	N	1897
The church	Pearson Correlation	-.037
	Sig. (2-tailed)	.114
	N	1837
Trade unions	Pearson Correlation	.005
	Sig. (2-tailed)	.846
	N	1791
President	Pearson Correlation	-.033
	Sig. (2-tailed)	.145
	N	1922
Commercial enterprises	Pearson Correlation	.060[**]
	Sig. (2-tailed)	.010
	N	1867
State television	Pearson Correlation	-.066[**]
	Sig. (2-tailed)	.004
	N	1934

Table 3.9 (continued)

		Internet use
	N	1980
Commercial television	Pearson Correlation	-.003
	Sig. (2-tailed)	.884
	N	1886
National government	Pearson Correlation	-.094**
	Sig. (2-tailed)	.000
	N	1913
Regional government	Pearson Correlation	-.075**
	Sig. (2-tailed)	.001
	N	1934

Source: 2010 survey.

These results are interesting in that they could suggest that the greater level of information and communication in the online sphere serves to foster dissatisfaction with political institutions in a non-free state. Coupled with this dissatisfaction, however, are some hints that regular internet users may feel more political empowerment than those who are not online on a regular basis. Regular internet usage was positively (albeit fairly weakly) correlated with the conviction that people can influence the central government (the bivariate correlation is .046, significant at the 0.05 level). This is not overwhelming proof of the effect of the virtual public sphere online, but it is at least some indication that online citizens may feel both more a sense of dissatisfaction and empowerment that is not as strong for those who are not online regularly. Indeed, being a regular internet user was strongly and positively correlated with agreement for the statement that "people should have the opportunity to speak out" (.081 correlation, which is significant at the 0.01 level with a significance score of .000).

Still, the 2010 survey highlights how few Russians take part in civic organizations in general (a finding consistent over several waves of similar surveys, see White, 2011). For example, only 1.8 percent, or 36, of the respondents reported being members of political parties and a mere 46 people (2.3 percent of the respondents) claimed to be members of neighborhood associations. The membership is slightly higher for trade unions (186 people or 9.2 percent), but this is still arguably quite low for a former communist country in which trade unions were large, if not particularly powerful, institutions. In addition, respondents reported low levels of political activity: only 3.3 percent said they had participated in a demonstration; 2.7 percent said they had signed a petition or written to a newspaper; and only 1.2 percent (24 people) said they had participated in a strike. Somewhat more (4.5 percent) had consulted with an elected official.

Despite a lack of formal activity in civil society, however, some respondents at least reported an interest in politics (see Table 3.10: Interest in Politics: Full Sample and Regular Internet Users). About 5 percent of all the survey respondents claimed to be "very interested" in politics, 35.9 percent were interested in general, 42.8 percent were not very interested, and only 16.5 percent were not interested at all. There was little difference for regular internet users and no significant correlation between interest in politics and regular internet use. Thus, while internet users would appear to be both more politically cynical as well as at times more liberal, they do not seem to show much political consciousness that would set them apart from the general population on the specific question of political interest. Although the percentages for participating in these political acts were slightly higher for regular internet users, the numbers of political activity overall were too small to show significance (and there is no significance shown in a bivariate correlation).

Finally, is there evidence that regular internet users felt differently about politicians and vote choice than the population as a whole? President Medvedev was not finding much favor among regular internet users in 2010. Regular internet use was negatively correlated with voting for Medvedev in the 2008 elections (a correlation of -.066, significant at the 0.01 level with a significance score

Table 3.10 **Interest in Politics: Full Sample and Regular Internet Users**

| | | Regular internet user | | |
		No	Yes	Total
Interest in Politics	1 Very interested	75	20	95
		5.0%	4.4%	4.8%
	2 Interested in general	533	171	704
		35.4%	37.7%	35.9%
	3 Not very interested	642	196	838
		42.6%	43.3%	42.8%
	4 Not interested at all	257	66	323
		17.1%	14.6%	16.5%
Total		1507	453	1960
		100.0%	100.0%	100.0%

Source: 2010 survey.

of .005). However, was this just an echo of the general characteristics of regular internet voters, which may dovetail with a lack of support for presidents? Or is there an identifiable internet "effect" that would show that the regular use of the internet is indeed a significant factor in predicting past (and possible future) support for Russian presidents? Earlier studies have shown a strong correlation (including when other factors are held constant in ordinary-least-squared regression analysis) between watching state television and voting for the Kremlin-backed presidential candidate (White and Oates, 2003). Thus, a regression analysis measuring the effect of regular internet use on the 2008 vote for Medvedev should include the preference for state television as well as key socioeconomic factors that have been shown to affect vote choice in Russia (Oates, 1998; Rose, White, and McAllister, 1996; Colton, 2000; Rose and Munro, 2002). The analysis shows that regular internet use *was* a significant predictor of not voting for Medvedev in 2008 (see Table 3.11: Regression Analysis for Predicting Vote for Medvedev). However, a preference for *Vremya* was a stronger, positive predictor, suggesting that television news still trumps the internet in terms of electoral influence. In addition, it was clear from the regression analysis that Medvedev had the female vote, as being male was significantly and negatively correlated with failing to vote for this president. The rest of the factors (income, dwelling place, and age) were not significant in this model.

Table 3.11 **Regression Analysis for Predicting Vote for Medvedev**

Model		Coefficients[a]				
		Unstandardized Coefficients		Standardized Coefficients		
		B	Std. Error	Beta	t	Sig.
1	(Constant)	.562	.047		11.926	.000
	Income (low to high)	.021	.011	.073	1.913	.056
	Male	-.109	.031	-.117	-3.500	.000
	Muscovite	-.001	.070	-.040	-1.079	.281
	Older age	.022	.075	.000	-.014	.989
	Population density	.22	.033	.023	.666	.505
	Prefer Vremya news	.140	.035	.129	4.002	.000
	Regular internet user	-.081	.037	-.074	-2.198	.028

a. Dependent variable: Vote for Medvedev
b. Adjusted r-square: .029

Source: 2010 survey.

The Next Generation: Online Activity and Young People in Russia

The Russian communications agency report, which has a decidedly cyber-optimistic tone, stressed the importance of computer training in schools, linking the provision of "access to the network" by schools to continuing to reduce those who do not use the internet by an estimated 12 percent a year (p. 15).[10] After that, continued use will "depend on the interest and wishes of each Russian. Growth is not just about the quantity of megabytes per second, but the various services for both young and old to use" (p. 15, author's translation). Despite the talk of older people here, it is clear from the research reported by the communications agency that Russian youth are particularly wired into the internet. The report noted that 66 percent of boys and 69 percent of girls from the age of 9 to 16 were online in Russia every day or almost every day (p. 19). The percentage grew from 54 percent for ages 11 to 12, 76 percent for 13–14, to 80 percent for 15–16. Most of them were going online via their own computer (58 percent) while the rest used mobile internet (but some used both). Up to 30 percent of young Russians spent three hours a day or more online. According to a study by EU Kids Online in Russia, Russian youth went online for a wide range of activities: 80 percent went online for homework, 78 percent for social networking, 68 percent to play games, 64 percent to download films/music, 61 percent to send e-mail, 59 percent to send messages, 53 percent to post content, 48 percent to read news, 31 percent to chat, and just 12 percent to use blogging sites (see Figure 3.3: Activities of Russian Kids Online). The survey was not

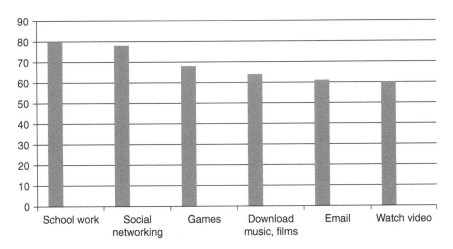

Figure 3.3 Activities of Russian Kids Online. Source: EU Kids Online, Russia survey, as reported in the communications agency report, p. 19.

clear on whether the young users were reading or writing blogs. Overall, it was clear that the internet is a central social tool for young people in Russia. It is less clear that it is a political tool, although as Owen (2006) points out, the line between social and political activity is far less distinct in the online sphere than traditional perceptions of political activity such as campaigning or voting. For example, aspects of important topics for young people such as education or military service have links to key political questions regarding government funding and conscription (for further discussion on the link between social and political issues on line, see Chapters 6 and 7). Of particular note is the relative decline of e-mail and the importance of social networking. While one can use social-networking sites to send individual messages, it is both the deliberate and inadvertent many-to-many communication that enhances the speed and intensity of online discussion. Given that 35 percent of young users have between 10 and 50 friends on social-networking sites and 14 percent have between 100 and 300, there is clear potential for extensive networking (Russian Federal Agency, p. 19).

The Internet in the Former Soviet Union

There is a very divergent rate of internet penetration and growth in the 15 former Soviet states. Russia, Belarus, and Ukraine are frequently compared in terms of political communication, particularly as these three former Soviet states share linguistic and political characteristics. In terms of politics, Belarus has developed a more authoritarian regime than Russia, fostering a system centered on the charismatic personality of President Alexander Lukashenko and characterized by Soviet-style repression of dissidents. In addition, the economy in Belarus has not enjoyed the oil and natural resource wealth of Russia. Russia, while more liberal and tolerant than Belarus, still ranks poorly both in terms of democratization and freedom of information. Unlike Russia and Belarus, Ukraine has weathered a stormy transition from the Soviet power base through the Orange Revolution, a successful challenge to a rigged election, and the eventual election of Viktor Yushchenko as president in 2005. While Ukrainian political observers note that Yushchenko was not a particularly effective president, Ukraine ranks far higher on markers of democratization, openness, and freedom than Russia or Belarus (Freedom House, 2011a). Interestingly, Ukraine has the lowest internet penetration of the three, measured at just 33.7 percent in 2011 by Internet World Stats (see Table 3.12: Internet Penetration Rates and Freedom Rankings in Former Soviet Countries).

Cooper would argue that post-Soviet internet penetration is a factor of economic development. Indeed, a correlation analysis between internet penetration rate and GDP per capita finds a strong correlation between income and

Table 3.12 **Internet Penetration Rates and Freedom Rankings in Former Soviet Countries**

Country	Internet penetration (%) (2011)	Political rating (lower is more free) (2010)	Press rating (lower is more free) (2010)	Press freedom category (2010)
Russia	43	5.5	81	Not free
Ukraine	33.9	3.0	53	Partly free
Belarus	46.3	6.5	92	Not free
Moldova	30.9	3.0	65	Not free
Lithuania	59.5	1.0	21	Free
Latvia	68.2	2.0	26	Free
Estonia	75.7	1.0	17	Free
Armenia	47.1	5.0	66	Not free
Azerbaijan	44.1	5.5	79	Not free
Georgia	28.3	3.5	59	Partly free
Kazakhstan	34.1	5.5	78	Not free
Kyrgyzstan	39.3	5.0	73	Not free
Turkmenistan	1.6	7.0	95	Not free
Tajikistan	9.2	5.5	78	Not free
Uzbekistan	26.8	7.0	92	Not free
AVERAGE	39.2	4.4	65	

Source: Internet penetration rate is from World Internet Stats (http://www.internetworldstats. com/stats.htm). Press rating and press freedom categories are from Freedom House, see its *Freedom of the Press 2010* report, available online at http://www.freedomhouse.org/template. cfm?page=16.

internet use in the former Soviet Union (.742 or 74.2 percent). While Belarus has a marginally higher internet penetration rate (46.3 percent compared with 43 percent for Russia), citizens in Belarus have far fewer political freedoms either online or offline (Freedom House, 2011b; Morozov, 2011). The linkage of wealth to internet use tends to hold across the region, with some interesting exceptions (See Table 3.13: Internet Penetration, Growth, and GDP per Capita in Former Soviet States, 2011). On average, the former Soviet states have an internet penetration rate of 39.2 percent and an average gross domestic product per capita of $5,651 USD. However, there are huge variations, from the impoverished Central Asian state of Tajikistan to the relatively wealthy countries in the European region of the former Soviet Union. While the Baltic countries of Estonia, Latvia, and Lithuania enjoy the benefits of an orientation toward the

Table 3.13 **Internet Penetration, Growth, and GDP per Capita in Former Soviet States, 2011**

Country	Population	Internet users	Internet penetration	Growth (2000 and 2011)	GDP per capita (USD)
Russia	138,739,892	59,700,000	43%	1,826%	$10,437
Ukraine	45,134,707	15,300,000	33.9%	7,550%	$3,000
Belarus	9,577,552	4,436,800	46.3%	2,365%	$5,800
Moldova	4,314,377	1,333,000	30.9%	5,232%	$1,630
Lithuania	3,535,547	2,103,471	59.5%	835%	$11,043
Latvia	2,204,708	1,503,400	68.2%	902%	$10,695
Estonia	1,282,963	971,700	75.7%	165%	$14,836
Armenia	2,967,975	1,396,550	47.1%	4,555%	$2,846
Azerbaijan	8,372,373	3,689,000	44.1%	30,672%	$6,008
Georgia	4,585,874	1,300,000	28.3%	6,400%	$2,658
Kazakhstan	15,522,373	5,300,000	34.1%	7,471%	$8,883
Kyrgyzstan	5,587,443	2,194,400	39.3%	4,153%	$864
Turkmenistan	4,997,503	80,400	1.6%	3,920%	$3,939
Tajikistan	7,627,200	700,000	9.2%	34,900%	$741
Uzbekistan	28,128,600	7,550,000	26.8%	100,567%	$1,380
AVERAGE			39.2%	14,101%	$5,651
Average excluding Tajikistan and Uzbekistan				5,070%	

Source: Internet and population statistics are from Internet World Stats at http://www. internetworldstats.com/stats.htm (which uses population data from the U.S. Census Bureau). Figures on gross domestic product per capita are from the International Monetary Fund (www.imf. rg).

European market and membership in the European Union, Russia, Ukraine, and Kazakhstan profit from wealth in natural resources such as oil. Armenia and Kyrgyzstan show unusually high rates of internet use despite relatively low gross domestic product (see Table 3.13). On the other hand, internet penetration is extraordinarily low in Turkmenistan given its level of economic development. This makes it clear that both market and governance factors play a role: people in Armenia and Kyrgyzstan are finding ways to get online despite a general lack of wealth while the highly repressive regime (not GDP) would appear to be limiting internet access in Tajikistan.

Overall, internet freedom lags in many parts of the post-Soviet region, according to reports by Freedom House (2011a, 2011b). Freedom House, which describes itself as "an independent watchdog organization that supports the expansion of freedom around the world,"[11] provides an annual ranking of how countries have performed in terms of political and media freedom. In particular, Freedom House has charted the decline of media freedom in Russia and other post-Soviet states. Much of the region, which was ranked as fairly free in the early 1990s, has since mostly become "not free" in the annual assessment of media freedom. Unsurprisingly, the political ratings also performed by the organization have shown a decline in civil liberties as many post-Soviet regimes developed as well.

It is through the Freedom House rankings that the divergence across both regions and individual countries in the former Soviet Union become clear. The Baltic states, with Estonia possessing particularly strong rankings in political and media freedom, are all rated as "free." This compares favorably with rankings for the United States and the United Kingdom, who are both rated as having free media systems (the United States was tied for 24th place and the United Kingdom for 26th place in the 2010 rankings). Russia and Belarus are both ranked as not free, which illuminates some of the problems of the rankings. Although Russia has significant challenges to media freedom, as outlined in Chapters 2 and 4, Belarus is a notably more repressive regime (Morozov). Despite a relatively low internet penetration on the western side of the former Soviet Union, Ukraine scores markedly better in media freedom, as does Georgia. Both of these countries have undergone color "revolutions" that led to relatively peaceful transitions between two competing political blocs. As a result, the media have not been dominated so thoroughly by a relatively narrow set of political elites who have never ceded control over the regime, as in Russia and Belarus.

Aside from the Baltic states, Georgia, and Ukraine, the outlook for media freedom is relatively grim in the former Soviet Union. The Central Asian countries have an especially poor track record of media freedom, including the thwarting of democratic movement in Kyrgyzstan. On the other hand, there has been no democratic movement at all in Turkmenistan, with such widespread human rights abuses and media control that it placed above only North Korea in the Freedom House rankings for media freedom in 2010. However, despite the variations in both internet penetration and media freedom across the post-Soviet region, there still remains a positive correlation between internet penetration and media freedom. In a bivariate correlation analysis comparing the percentage of internet penetration with the Freedom House scores for media freedom, there is a strong negative correlation. As the Freedom House scores increase to indicate more problems with media freedom, the negative correlation shows that the trend is for media rights abuses to decrease as levels of internet penetration rise within countries.

However, a more detailed knowledge of different cases across the post-Soviet sphere and beyond suggests that online activity cannot safeguard or promote media freedom. One of the problems is with the direction of any internet 'effect'—in other words, people may seek out and use the internet due to other democratizing conditions, thus making internet use merely correlated with greater freedom rather than a cause of democratization. Indeed, in a study of 28 countries in Africa and Asia, Nisbet et al. (2012) found that the measurement of internet penetration in a country did not predict greater citizen commitment to democratic governance. Rather, the scholars found that there was a need to look at individual patterns of internet use, which were useful in predicting support for democratization. This research shows the importance of looking beyond the overall availability of the internet in a country and examining how individuals use this communication tool.

In addition, the discussion in this chapter did not take into account the effect of the speed of growth in online activity, which would appear to be a promising way to measure the ability of the public to challenge authority in non-free states. The next chapter (Chapter 4) will consider how state policy and control of the internet and its audience may constrain the promise of online engagement. In particular, Chapter 4 will use more detailed information from internet freedom rankings devised by Freedom House and used to measure online freedom in Russia, Azerbaijan, Belarus, Estonia, Georgia, and Kazakhstan.

Conclusions

An examination of the internet audience fuses the categories of content and community in the 5C model of content, community, catalyst, control, and co-optation outlined in Chapter 1. The nature of online content is almost infinite, as there are few limits or filters in the online sphere in Russia. Users have the ability to use content from virtually any site around the world. However, as the studies in the communications agency report suggest, Russians are being channeled into a relatively narrow set of news sources online. Thus, the broad potential of content is constrained by the online community. People tend to stay within relatively small communities in the online sphere, often seeming to reinforce, rather than challenge, their information set. That being said, the preference of younger people for the internet over state television suggests a fundamental shift in the information "high ground" in Russia. State-run television has long served as a critical tool for opinion formation by the Russian (and former Soviet) political elites. Even if the internet audience is not particularly entrepreneurial about seeking out new information online, their lack of attention to state-run television—and perhaps lack of interest in it—signals a significant shift in political communication in Russia. When fused with a catalyzing event, such as a contentious election or further economic shocks, it seems much less likely that state-run television will be able to continue to set the dominant news agenda and control political outcomes to the same degree in Russia.

A NOTE ON INTERNET USE AND THE DECEMBER 2011 PROTESTS

What were the effects of internet use on the widespread protests in the Russian winter of 2011–12? Sam Greene at the Center for New Media and Society at the New Economic School in Moscow provided an analysis of a street survey at one of the major protests in Moscow in December 2011 (Greene, January 18, 2012). The Levada Center interviewed 791 of the protestors at the rally on December 24 on Sakharov Avenue in Moscow.[12] While estimates of the numbers varied wildly between 30,000 and 120,000 (Greene, 2012), the meeting was one of the largest protests in post-Soviet history. The street survey asked the protestors a range of questions about their media use, political orientation, and motivation for joining the protest. As Greene notes, there was no overwhelming evidence of the use of the internet as a mobilizing tool. Thirty-seven percent of those surveyed did say that they regularly discussed issues related to the Duma elections in online social networks or other internet forums; another 31 percent said that they periodically took part in such debates; and 32 percent said they had never done so. Overall, there was little socioeconomic and attitudinal difference between those who took part in the online debates with those who did not. However, those who were engaged in online discussion were "considerably more likely to support less traditional political and opposition leaders, including anti-corruption activist Alexey Navalny, television personality Leonid Parfenov and billionaire playboy Mikhail Prokhorov, while offliners retain greater affinity for liberal economist Grigory Yavlinsky and the Communist Party" (Greene, NP). Thus, while both online debaters and those who did not engage politically in the online sphere showed up for the protestors, their political choices were somewhat different. Clearly, an alternative political sphere with different leadership has emerged in the Russian online sphere.

The Levada survey did show that those engaged in online debates were more likely to be habitual protestors—at least in the beginning of protest waves. Overall, more than half of those interviewed on December 24th on Sakharov Avenue had also taken part in a December 10th protest on Bolotnaya Square in Moscow and about 22 percent were at an illegal Moscow protest on December 5th. However, Greene's analysis shows that those who were engaged online were somewhat more likely to protest: 25 percent of onliners took part in the December 5th protest, versus 17 percent of offliners, and 67 percent of onliners came out on December 10th versus 48 percent of offliners. However, Greene notes that the effect of internet engagement appears to have declined over time, suggesting that the fact that the protests could no longer be ignored by the traditional mass media (especially television) led to a "mainstreaming" of the protest activities. Perhaps most intriguing is data from the Levada survey that shows that "offliners" were more likely to go to protests as individuals while "onliners" were more likely to go as part of a group (Greene). The point that Greene takes from the data is that it is misleading to talk about "virtual" protests or to attempt to separate the idea of "off-line" and "on-line" recruitment. The sphere of politics in Russia (and elsewhere) is embedded within Russian media outlets and political institutions. However, the nature and speed of online communication promise to bring significant change to those factors in Russian society.

4

Internet Control in Russia

As much as the internet might at times appear to be a global information space, there is compelling evidence that states play a significant role in shaping and constraining the democratizing potential of the online sphere within national boundaries. Chapter 3 found that the Russian online audience is growing incredibly quickly in terms of both size and depth of activity, with the younger generation switching its attention from traditional media to new media. Yet while online content and online audiences have formed with great rapidity in Russia, it is critical to consider the role of national online control and co-optation. Building on the discussion of global versus national factors in internet control, this chapter will examine and analyze specific Russian government policy toward the internet.

Overall, the Russian Federation has exhibited a somewhat divided approach. While the government clearly promotes the use of the internet for social and economic development, it also uses the internet as an additional political tool for control and co-optation. The central question is whether the Russian government can follow the same pattern with the internet as it has for the traditional mass media, allowing diversity to flourish to a degree while ultimately using media as instruments for state power rather than as tools for democratization. At the same time, problems with the protection of free speech in the media and for individual journalists have resonated into issues for the online sphere. On the eve of the December 2011 protests, did the Russian state appear to treat the online sphere as a legitimate threat to power that needed to be controlled? Or did the control of the internet parallel a general lack of respect for free speech, journalism, and the rights of citizens that pervade Russian society? Finally—and most intriguingly—is there evidence that Runet managed to retain some unique democratizing potential within a non-free media system in ways that fostered the range and power of anti-state protests that began in late 2011?

Russian Internet Freedom in Post-Soviet Context

As noted earlier in the book, the Russian Federation scores poorly in media freedom in rankings by organizations such as Freedom House. In addition to general media rankings, Freedom House began providing internet freedom reports and rankings for a selection of countries (including Russia and some other post-Soviet countries) in 2009. The assessments are based on three categories for the online sphere in each country: obstacles to internet access, limits on its content, and violations of internet user rights (Freedom House, 2011a). Obstacles to access include structural and economic barriers, as well as governmental efforts to block online applications and technologies. Problems with access also include legal, regulatory, and ownership controls over internet and mobile phone providers. The category for limits on content addresses the filtering and blocking of websites; other means of censorship and self-censorship; manipulation of content; the diversity of online news media; as well as the use of digital media for social and political activism. The analysis of the violation of user rights "measures legal protections and restrictions on online activity; surveillance; privacy; and repercussions for online activity, such as legal prosecution, imprisonment, physical attacks, or other forms of harassment" (Freedom House, 2011a, p. 1). The total of the scores go up to 100 points (see Table 4.1: Freedom on the Net Scores for Post-Soviet States, US, and UK) with the higher score being assigned as violations to internet freedom increase.

Table 4.1 **Freedom on the Net Scores for Post-Soviet States, US, and UK**

Country	Net freedom status	Net freedom total	Obstacles to access score (0–25)	Limits on content score (0–35)	Violations of user rights score (0–40)
Estonia	Free	10	2	2	6
Georgia	Partly Free	35	12	10	13
Azerbaijan	Partly Free	48	15	15	18
Russia	Partly Free	52	12	17	23
Kazakhstan	Partly Free	55	16	22	17
Belarus	Not Free	69	19	23	27
United States	Free	13	4	2	7
United Kingdom	Free	25	1	8	16

Source: Freedom House, 2011b. Note that higher scores indicate more challenges to media freedom.

The Russian internet ranks as partly free and appears in the middle of the other five post-Soviet countries (Estonia, Georgia, Azerbaijan, Kazakhstan, and Belarus) ranked for internet freedom by Freedom House in 2011. However, it should be noted that Russia's Freedom House score for internet freedom is better than its score for overall media freedom, which is set at "not free" (see Table 3.12). This is evidence that Russia does not enforce as much compliance from all online content as it does from central media outlets such as state television. However, there also are indications that a relatively relaxed approach to policing the internet in Russia already is undergoing a change.

Certainly, the 2011 internet report by Freedom House found much cause for concern about diminishing online freedom in Russia. To be fair, it should be noted that the organization found reasons for concern in a range of countries, including a rather high score for violation of user rights in the United States (see Table 4.1). In addition, the organization relies heavily on experts— rather than more objective means of collecting evidence—to determine scores. Under this system, Russia scored 12 out of 25 for obstacles to access, 17 out of 25 for limits on content, and 23 out of 40 for violations of user rights for an overall score of 52. Russia is identified by Freedom House as one of the five countries most "at risk" of slipping further into a controlled and censored online sphere, with a "notable decline" in internet freedom since scoring 49 in 2009 (Freedom House, 2011b pp. 9-10, note that higher scores indicate more violations of media freedom). In particular, the 2011 *Freedom on the Net* report highlighted the tension between a "partly free" internet and a "not free" media environment in Russia (which parallels the same division found in Egypt in late 2010). The Freedom House report predicted that as the internet became a space for broader political news and discussion, it would fall under increasing surveillance and threat to match the Russian state's broader repression of media freedom (p. 17). The Freedom House analysis suggests that countries such as Russia with mid-range internet freedom scores and rising internet penetration can possibly develop more open internet spheres (p. 18). However, given the evidence collected by Freedom House in terms of internet access, content, and user rights, the report predicted a continuing trend of increasing online repression in Russia. Specifically, the report was concerned that "Russia's last relatively uncensored platform for public debate" could come under threat (p. 27). Although conditions for access had improved, other facets of online freedom had deteriorated. In particular, evidence of technical blocking as well as "tactics for proactively manipulated conversations in the online sphere were refined" (p. 27). The Freedom House report found at least 25 cases of blogger harassment in 2009 and 2010, including 11 arrests. The report noted that several newspaper websites experienced cyber attacks, "typically in connection with articles that could seriously influence offline events" (p. 27). In addition, at least 16 blogs sustained hacking attacks during the time period, according to the report.

The detailed Freedom House report on the Russian internet found distinctive challenges to internet freedom across the three categories of access, content, and user rights. However, in two of the three most critical categories, Runet did not show evidence of internet oppression: Web 2.0 applications were not blocked and there was no "substantial" political censorship (p. 269). However, bloggers and/or online users have been arrested (and served prison time), which means that Russia failed in one of the three critical categories of internet freedom as identified by Freedom House. In terms of access, the Russian affection for mobile phones and information technology marks a huge difference from the lack of personal communication infrastructure in the Soviet Union. As the Freedom House report notes, there has been substantial, if uneven, development across the vast country in terms of communication infrastructure. The Freedom House report cited a Taylor Nelson Sofres (TNS) report that most Russians (94 percent) do not need to seek out the internet in cafes or other public spaces as they are able to access the internet either from home or the workplace.[1] As noted in reports by both the Russian Federal Agency on the Press and Mass Communication (2011) and Freedom House, Russian schools are now generally connected to the internet as well.

While the Freedom House report was concerned about a lack of transparency in communication company ownership, this is a widespread issue for Russian enterprises in general. Although the transparency and ultimate control of communications enterprises is problematic, they have delivered a range of affordable communication technologies to a wide swathe of the Russian population. Five access providers (including the state-owned Svyazinvest) controlled more than two-thirds of the broadband market as of February 2010 (Freedom House 2011, p. 217). Meanwhile, three major operators control 83 percent of the mobile-phone market. As a result, the majority of digital communication is controlled via a small number of enterprises, which increases the state's ability to manage access. This is a concern for Freedom House as participation in the communications industry "usually depends on political connections and the tacit approval of regional authorities" and "reflects an element of corruption that is widespread in the telecommunications sector and other parts of the Russian economy" (p. 271). This is not a surprising finding, in that corruption in Russian enterprises is so pervasive.[2] Although there is ample evidence of selective censorship, tracking, and punishment for posting material online, there is no "comprehensive, centralized filtering system" for Runet (p. 271). Examples of specific cases of internet repression will be discussed below.

The issues relating to internet freedom vary a great deal in the five other post-Soviet countries assessed as part of the 2011 Freedom House internet report.

In fact, Estonia was ranked as having the freest online sphere in the entire study of 37 countries, scoring slightly better in internet freedom than the United States (Table 4.1). Freedom House found virtually no issues of access, content limits, or problems with internet user rights in Estonia. Georgia was challenged across all three categories, as was Azerbaijan to a slightly greater degree (although both were judged as having somewhat more free online spheres than Russia). However, Georgia was assessed to be improving, while Azerbaijan's performance was not seen to be getting better. Uptake of the internet in Georgia also had grown sharply, partly in response to lower prices (p. 142). It should be noted that the main improvement from the earlier report was a dearth of the type of censorship that marked the Georgian-Russian conflict in 2008, in which many Russian websites were blocked. Freedom House analyzed Azerbaijan for the first time in 2011, finding the country one of four along with Venezuela, Jordan, and Rwanda assessed for the 2011 internet freedom report in which there were "initial signs of politically motivated internet controls" (p. 2). These signs included politicized censorship that violated user rights, although there were only a handful of cases reported in Azerbaijan despite the country's general lack of media freedom and free speech.

As is often the case due to the similar political experience of Russia and Kazakhstan in the post-Soviet era, the situation in Kazakhstan appeared in many ways to echo the Russian state of affairs for internet policy. While officials in Kazakhstan wish to develop the internet as a modernization tool for Central Asia, they also seek to control it (Freedom House 2011, p. 214). Thus, while the Kazakhstan government has enhanced the telecommunications sector and promoted internet use, the state has at the same time made even stronger attempts than Russia to control the democratizing potential of citizen online communication (p. 214). In particular, the Kazakhstan government has restricted online criticism of longtime president Nursultan Nazarbayev. While there have been isolated incidents of a lack of tolerance for criticism of Russian President and Prime Minister Vladimir Putin (see below), there were no high-profile cases of arrest for insulting Russian President Dmitri Medvedev in Runet reported by Freedom House.

Finally, Belarus scores very poorly indeed in internet freedom in the Freedom House study, which is unsurprising in that the more aggressive censorship and control by authorities in Belarus have made headlines for years. Unlike the isolated incidents of internet censorship, monitoring, and control found in Kazakhstan and Russia, Belarus has proactively used the internet to monitor, detect, control, and arrest political dissidents (Morozov, 2011). In particular, the government carried out denial-of-service attacks against opposition websites after the December 2010 elections, which were widely seen to be rigged, according to the Freedom House report. The Belarus government even carried out a highly

public web deception on its citizens, using the large, state-owned internet service provider to redirect "users from independent media sites to nearly identical
clones that provided misleading information, such as the incorrect location of a
planned opposition rally" (Freedom House, 2011, p. 6).

The relevant question is whether the array of internet regimes in six former
Soviet states represents a particular spectrum of use, a continuum through
which states would seem to travel from relatively free to progressively more
restrictive internet regimes over time (or possibly vice-versa, although evidence for this is weak). For example, will Russia inevitably add more types of
"post-Soviet" controls to its relatively mild attacks on individual web users and
its manipulation of the internet to become more like Kazakhstan or even Belarus? The evidence suggests that Russia is taking the path toward more, rather
than less, control of the online sphere. While it is unlikely that countries would
pursue exactly the same tactics—and Russia does not have the level of leadership "cult" that is found for President Alexander Lukashenko in Belarus or
Nazarbayev in Kazakhstan—it is still worrying that the trend in Russia is more
toward online control and less toward online freedom. This is not inevitable
for the post-Soviet world, as the excellent record of online freedom in Estonia
and the improvements in online freedom in Georgia from 2009 to 2011 suggest. However, on balance, the evidence would imply that Russia, Azerbaijan,
Kazakhstan, and Belarus share particular tendencies toward the use of the internet as a tool for the government rather than as an instrument for citizen
empowerment.

Case Study of Russia and ICTs

While the Freedom House report was able to identify broad trends and highlight issues within the three important indicators of internet access, content, and
user rights, it is important to analyze Runet more closely within the Russian context. In other words, what evidence is there to suggest that Russian state policy
can successfully control the online sphere? How do laws relating to the internet
and the experience of managing the online world parallel Russia's effective top-
down management of media and politics in general in the first decade of the
twenty-first century? In some ways, there are compelling parallels between
Russian internet management and how the Russian state has used political communication as an outlet for the state rather than as a voice for the people. On the
other hand, the Russian government must deal with facets of the internet that
are new and change with great speed. Will the Russian governance style be able
to tame the internet, or will the internet be able to fundamentally reshape the
relationship between the elites and the public? What developments in Russian

control and co-optation of Runet give evidence for either side of this argument?[3] This discussion serves as background for understanding the environment in which the state was significantly challenged via the online sphere in the protests in late 2011 and 2012.

LEGAL ENVIRONMENT FOR THE RUSSIAN INTERNET

Constitutional Law and Resolution 16

The development of internet law in Russia has grown more slowly than the use of the internet. This is exacerbated by legal issues relating to mass communication in general in Russia. While a characterization of the law is that it favors the use of online information for the benefit of the state rather than for the good of the citizen, Richter (2011) argues that the 2010 Russian Supreme Court Resolution 16, which sets out limits on state control of freedom of expression, significantly advances protection for online communication by citizens and combats some state excesses in governance of the online sphere.[4] However, this is against the confusing wealth of laws to protect freedom of speech coupled with evidence of a lack of respect for free speech in Russia.

Some of the fundamental legal protection for free media in Russia includes Article 29 of the 1993 Russian Constitution that specifically guarantees "freedom of ideas and speech" as well as expressly gives Russian citizens the right to "freely look for, receive, transmit, produce, and distribute information by any legal way." In addition, freedom of mass communication "shall be guaranteed" and censorship is banned by the constitution. There is provision in the constitution that should protect the privacy of internet users, in that Article 24 (Part 1) forbids the collection, storage, use, and dissemination of information about the private lives of individuals without their consent. In addition, Article 2 stipulates that the state is obligated to recognize, observe, and protect the "rights and freedoms of Man and citizen." While no society tolerates absolute free speech when it is deemed to threaten state security,[5] the liberal values expressed in the Russian constitution do not offer practical protection to journalists or citizens. The Russian constitution could not be described as an authoritative document with legal force in Russia. Rather, much like the Soviet constitutions that came before it also claiming freedom of speech for citizens, it is recognition of values without the strength of law. Journalists, citizens, internet service providers, and internet users all face a political environment with somewhat arbitrary attacks on freedom of speech. This leaves them all with little confidence that the rights outlined in the constitution are protected in any meaningful way, although Richter argues that the Russian Supreme Court Resolution 16 (On the Judicial Practice Related to the Statute of the Russian Federation 'On the Mass Media') attempted to redress this imbalance in 2010. According to Richter, the resolution "sets out the important political and legal principle that the freedom to express opinions and views and the freedom of mass information are the foundations for developing a modern society and a democratic state," meaning that "courts should take this principle into consideration in all cases in which this freedom is challenged" (p. 4).

Almost a decade ago and years before Resolution 16, Alexander recognized in 2003 both the paradox and the opportunity of the internet for Russia. The novel features of the internet, which Alexander identified through its five characteristics of interactivity, multiplicity, architecture, cost, and timing, all provided challenges to the way in which the Russian state had controlled information through traditional media outlets. As a result, "the original proliferation of the Internet at first encountered an unprepared government that dealt with the new medium not much differently from its Soviet tradition in national media and technology regulation" (Alexander, p. 5). This meant that the government's first attempts included some direct censorship, but the internet "escaped tight regulation as the government was initially unprepared for the challenge" (p. 5). He identified the first wave of Russian internet policy-making (throughout the 1990s) as "characterized by legislation closely resembling Soviet tendencies of state bureaucratic oversight, at cost both to free growth of the industry and practical efficacy of executive policy-making" (p. 9). Alexander credited the first succession of Putin as president in 2000 with an improvement in the Russian state's ability to regulate the internet. However, Alexander notes that the Russian government was quick to realize that it was not just control, but co-optation, that was the key challenge for Runet.

If the Russian constitution does not function as the legal definition for internet rights, what does? As with media law in general, the development of internet law in Russia has been patchy. The Russian law as of mid-2011 omitted basic internet-related definitions and was mostly regulated via indirect legislation across a range of issues.[6] Regulation of the internet in Russia fell under both constitutional and federal laws, which constructed the general framework for citizens' rights and role of information in the society. Regulation of the internet also was controlled by the laws related to mass media and national security issues (including anti-terrorism laws). Finally, the online sphere was regulated by laws relating to electronic commerce.

Richter identifies the passage of Resolution Number 16 "On the Judicial Practice Related to the Statute of the Russian Federation 'On the Mass Media'" on June 15, 2010, by the Supreme Court of the Russian Federation as a landmark event in Russian media law as well as for regulation of the internet. The resolution, the result of a widespread consultation on media law, clarified several important points in Russian law to generally improve the protection for freedom of speech online (Richter). Notably, the resolution makes reference to "international covenants that regulate freedom of expression and freedom of mass information" to make them binding for the Russian Federation (p. 9). Both the ideal in looking toward international norms as well as the practicalities of the law, which give more protection to online communication, are at odds with the notion of a Russian state that seeks to control the internet for its own ends.

Richter, a noted Russian media law scholar, identified several areas in which the resolution addressed media freedom in a range of situations. The resolution clarified that while websites could choose to register as media outlets to gain accreditation, they were not obliged to do so. As a result, websites are not subject to the same requirements in terms of editorial responsibility as traditional mass media. This ability to choose—in effect creating a parallel media sphere— is surprisingly liberal for a state that has pursued relatively strict controls in much of its media sphere. This could be interpreted as an important step in acknowledging that people have the right to disseminate information online without being subject to mass-media regulation.[7] By the same token, the resolution states that video content can be distributed online without a broadcasting license, which again removes a very effective way for the state to control online content. An additional liberal aspect to the Supreme Court's resolution is the finding that websites cannot be held responsible for comments made by users in unmoderated forums, removing a significant threat for those who host open forums online. Rather than creating a climate of fear in hosting unmoderated forums, the resolution "took the more liberal view" that the "editorial offices" of these websites were liable for comments that broke the law (i.e., extremism, libel) only if the website officials receive an official state complaint that the "content of a communication presents an abuse of freedom of the mass media" and should officials fail to deal with this . . . the "offending material has to be subsequently found illegal by a court for the complaint to be upheld" (Richter 2011, p. 13). While the Supreme Court could have used arguments such as the need to control extremist or even terrorist speech, it took the more liberal position to protect unmoderated speech on forums by drawing a parallel with live broadcasts in that it is impossible to control what people say in advance.

One of the most interesting parts of the Supreme Court resolution is the way in which it criticizes and attempts to limit the ability of Russian state telecommunication agency (Roskomnadzor[8]) to demand the deletion of online materials. The tension between the court resolution and the practices of Roskomnadzor in demanding the deletion of online material is an interesting example of conflicting legal norms within a non-free state. Richter (p. 13) notes that the head of Roskomnadzor issued Order No. 420 to approve "Rules for addressing requests concerning the prohibition of abuse of the freedom of mass media by material sent to the mass media and disseminated through information telecommunication networks, Internet included" shortly after Supreme Court Resolution 16 was issued in 2010. During the drafting of the Supreme Court resolution, representatives of Roskomnadzor had objected strongly to allowing websites registered as media outlets to avoid being held responsible for unmoderated forum content (Richter, p. 13): "Their position was based on the argument that registration as a mass media outlet assigns the editorial office of an Internet site certain responsibilities. Among such responsibilities, the basic one is editing the information disseminated by the media outlet." In other words, Roskomnadzor was worried that the resolution allowed a "loophole" for websites to claim no responsibility for undesirable forum content (from a state point of view) such as extremist views or pornography that could flourish under the guise of "user" comment. Roskomnadzor rules instructed its officials to prepare reports along with the screenshots of the offending material, with a demand that offending material be removed within 24 hours (Richter). According to Richter's analysis of Russian internet policy, this system has been used by Roskomnadzor "on a number of occasions" (p. 13). Supreme Court Resolution 16, however, notes there is no law to force compliance within 24 hours and "there is no obligation for a mass media outlet to indicate its e-mail address on its website, to check its e-mails every day, or to have a facsimile device" (Richter, p. 13). In other words, the Roskomnadzor rules do not meet the spirit or the letter of the Supreme Court resolution. This example highlights the lack of a unified state policy on internet control in Russia.

In addition to protecting the rights of websites to have unmoderated forums and responses online without fear of prosecution, the majority of the editorial group for the constitutional resolution felt that defamation could be dealt with within the online sphere itself. Those who felt themselves to be defamed in the online sphere "should make use of their right to a refutation of the defamatory statements in the same fora and chats" (Richter, p. 14). This weakens an argument that one could sue for defamation or a lack of a right to reply due to user-generated content. The Russian Supreme Court resolution even supports satirical and humorous content by referencing Article 10 of the European Convention of Human Rights in allowing for a wide degree of exaggeration and even provocation. These genres are "now considered permissible in the media and shall not serve as grounds for liability in defamation lawsuits," according to Richter (p. 21). Overall, Richter found the provisions of the resolution suggest that "courts shall not establish circumstances that will actually limit the right to freedom of expression, including the freedom of opinion and the freedom to obtain and to disseminate information and ideas without any interference by public authorities" (p. 19), although his conclusions that this resolution "allows Russian media to engage in socially responsible journalism without being threatened by illegal pressure in the courtroom, extreme demands by state bodies and excessive bureaucratic procedures" is arguably too sweeping given the significant challenges that still face journalists in Russia (see Chapter 2). As with the constitution in general, it is clear that the theory of law and the daily practice by bureaucrats can vary significantly in the media sphere. Yet the resolution and the lack of sweeping controls for the Russian internet are significant.

Technical Controls on Runet

As in many societies, internet policy in Russia moved over time from the technical and economic aspects to issues of societal surveillance. While early internet law was developed for commercial reasons, such as the internet law on electronic signatures and trademark, the Electronic Russia program (*Federal'naya tselevaya programma "Electronnaya Rossiya"*) from 2002–10 was designed with a broader provision in mind, including the optimization of public services via the online sphere. The federal law "On Provision of Access to Information about Activity of State Organs and Local Government Authorities" was part of this E-Russia program and appeared to encourage E-Governance. In particular, the law was oriented toward government-to-business and government-to-government internet service, with a view to the economic benefits greater online communication could produce. This law gave citizens of the Russian Federation a right to the prompt receipt of information about the activity of state and local authorities as well as information about government and self-regulated organizations via the internet. The law mentions which information should be allocated on their web pages. The law also designates the internet an official medium that serves the public by linking government and society.

The later wave of Russian internet policy included the controversial SORM and SORM-2 directives, which required that all Russian internet service providers had to provide monitoring of internet content at their own cost for the Federal Security Service (FSB).[9] Alexander noted the early rise of online media and political websites, including the use of websites for propaganda wars against Kremlin opponents in the 1999 and 2000 elections. However, more recent studies (March, 2006; Oates, 2010) suggest that the political content linked to opposition parties or groups remained relatively weak and underdeveloped when compared with Western groups (discussed in more depth in Chapter 5). While Alexander noted that political content could provide a serious challenge to Russian state control (p. 11), in fact there was little evidence of Russian opposition political groups making effective use of the internet in the almost 10 years since Alexander's study. By the same token, there was relatively little presence of a Russian opposition in general, much less online, prior to the end of 2011.

Even as laws were developing relating to the internet, there remained a lack of clarity about some fundamental principles. One of the key problems is a dearth of legal definitions of central terms such as internet, website, spam, domain name, and so on in Russian law, despite an attempt in 2008 to pass a law developed by the inter-parliamentary assembly of the Commonweath of Independent States on these issues. What *was* passed into law is the ability of the state to collect and use virtually all online information about citizens, with the added burden that Russian internet service providers must bear the cost and responsibility for the collection of the information. One of the most important and controversial parts of Russian legislation related to regulation of the internet is SORM, which stands for System for Operational-Investigative Activities in Russian.[10] It allows the Federal Security Service (FSB) "to conduct real-time monitoring of every e-mail message, credit card transaction and web page sent or received in Russia" (Tracey, 1999). As SORM is not so much internet regulation as a means of using the internet to monitor communication, it is often criticized by human rights organizations, citizens, and political forces that promote liberal values. SORM was created on the basis of the Communication Law and the Law on Operational Investigation. SORM-1 provided government bodies with access to the content of telephone communications without citizens' consent. SORM-2 extended this by enabling access to information transmitted via the internet. The aim of SORM is to provide technical support for investigations, particularly to enable collection of information passed and accepted by specific people in electronic communication.[11] SORM enables state investigative bodies to have access to the information transmitted via electronic means of communication[12], although there is no stipulation of special equipment for the investigative activities.[13] SORM allows for the collection of information including the time of the service provision, location of the information transmitter, network addresses and names of users, and information passed or accepted by a user (i.e., content).[14] The latest update of the decree as of 2011 also required redirection of the information to the control center of the body that will carry out the investigative activities. Thus, with introduction of SORM, any type of electronic information in the territory of the Russian Federation can be accessed, recorded, and used in investigations by civil or military security services.

This means that Russian internet service providers are compelled to aid the state in violation of Article 24 of the Russian constitution, although both the Russian government and Russian internet service providers could argue that by using an ISP, an individual has given consent for his or her information to be collected, stored, and used by the government.[15] This is an ongoing global concern for all governments, many of whom actively mine both public and private internet data to detect terrorists, child pornographers, and other criminals. Thus, the issue of privacy and online rights remain unclear in a range of societies. However, the access to ISP data granted to the Russian security services by the SORM legislation gives sweeping powers to the government to violate privacy and use personal, online communication as a way of detecting, tracking, and punishing not just criminals but opponents to national or local regimes as well. However, as noted in the Freedom House reports, this potential for control does not appear to be deployed in a consistent, unified way.

The operation of SORM raises some troubling questions about the lack of privacy online in Russia, although technically users are somewhat protected as any information collected without court permission cannot be used in legal cases. However, the SORM rules are only one way that the Russian government can access data from the online sphere. There is also the Information Security Doctrine, which was passed in 2000 soon after the second wave of SORM decrees. Unlike SORM, this doctrine does not specifically refer to the internet; rather, it deals with all threats to national security from the information sphere. Among other issues, it stresses the importance of the domestic production of information technologies, development of information security technologies, strengthening of national mass media, licensing of organizations in the information security area, and the certification of information security equipment. The doctrine gives the principal role for information protection security to organs of the state, including the legislative and executive bodies. As Alexander (2003) points out, the doctrine welds governance of the internet with core state security issues: "The doctrine grounds media policy in general, and Internet policy in particular, in the core 'national security' concerns of the state" (p. 15). Alexander notes that the Information Security Doctrine is particularly significant for three reasons: (1) it endows the government with right not only to interfere, but to actually engineer development of the internet; (2) it sharply defines the limits of the rights of individuals and groups to use the internet; and (3) it pushes the government to proactively extend its control over Runet (p. 15). This is balanced by the 2010 Supreme Court resolution discussed above, but it would seem that a resolution establishing some norms of internet freedom is not as powerful as state security legislation enabling wide-scale collection and monitoring of online activity.

In addition to the broad tenets found in the Information Security Doctrine, internet content also is controlled through more recent anti-extremism law in Russia. Adopted in 2007, this legislation modified the existing law on state investigation of extremist activity[16] by allowing the monitoring of electronic, telephone, and postal communication of people who are suspected or accused of committing a greater range of crimes. This change gave the authorities far broader powers to access private communications without the consent of the user (of telephone services, internet, mail, etc.). Depending on the definition of "extremism," the law gives the Russian government more power to use online information to monitor and build court cases against political opponents. However, attempts to legalize tapping of Skype were unsuccessful by mid-2011.[17] Mobile phone purchases are, however, regulated as they are in many countries: operators are required to collect passport details from people who buy SIM cards and keep the records for a period of three years after the end of any contracts.[18]

Advanced Cyber-Control: The Third Generation and "Networked Authoritarianism"

Almost 10 years ago, Alexander warned that the Russian state might develop an effective way to use the internet not as a tool for economic and political engagement, but as another method through which to strengthen state power. This idea is echoed by studies from the Berkman Center for Internet & Society at Harvard Law School (Deibert et al., 2009; Deibert et al., 2010). In the burgeoning field of internet policy research, analysts study how authoritarian states use the internet to manipulate domestic populations. Many analysts and scholars now argue that the greatest threat posed to civil society by the internet is not widespread internet blocking and content censorship obvious in states such as China (Deibert et al., 2010). Instead, scholars such as Deibert et al. now warn that "the *center of gravity* of practices aimed at managing cyberspace has shifted subtly from policies and practices aimed at denying access to content to methods that seek to *normalize* control and the exercise of power in cyberspace through a variety of means" (2010, p. 6, emphasis in original). This means that not only state agencies, but a wide range of internet service providers, could actually be aiding repressive regimes in their online strategy to misinform and manipulate the population.

There is certainly significant potential for repression under the SORM regulations in Russia, as Russian ISPs are obliged to collect and hand over information about users as well as the content that they create. It is an argument that Morozov persuasively makes from a more qualitative study across a range of countries (2011). Deibert et al. call this the "third generation" of internet control, an advance from first-generation control of blocking internet access and second-generation controls that were mostly linked to censorship. In the third generation of internet control, "the focus is less on *denying* access than successfully *competing* with potential threats through effective counter-information campaigns that overwhelm, discredit, or demoralize opponents" (2010, p. 27, emphasis in original). The third generation of internet control allows states to deploy the internet in a carefully choreographed manner that simultaneously promotes state interests through propaganda; discredits opponents via information campaigns or strategic take-downs of internet sites at critical political moments; and enables selective intimidation or arrest of cyber-dissidents. At the same time, repressive states set up systems to coerce or encourage citizens to stay within national domains or types of websites in the online world, further promoting the distortion of information while state officials harvest online interactions to gain nuanced information on political actions and orientations of individuals. Thus, the provision of high-speed internet access in schools could be perceived as wiring young citizens into propaganda and tracking their behavior rather than providing them access to global sources of information.

MacKinnon (2011) describes a similar phenomenon, which she labels "networked authoritarianism," in China. She argues that networked authoritarianism is complex yet effective state internet policy that allows states to take advantage of the economic efficiencies of the spread of online information. Perhaps even more significantly, networked authoritarianism allows the state to capitalize on the political communication potential of the internet to consolidate the state's central position in civil society. In networked authoritarianism, the state can and will use hard methods such as blocking opposition websites; shifting through content with software to find existing and potential political threats; identifying individuals through ISP information; charging political opponents with a range of online crimes, including breach of national security; and making examples of certain cases of online defiance of the state in order to inculcate self-censorship, repression, and fear. All of this is useful for a repressive state, but it is essentially using the internet to carry out "repression as usual." At the same time, the state can use what MacKinnon calls "astroturfing" (p. 41), a term that unfavorably contrasts the idea of grassroots politics with the planting of ideas by paid online commentators posing as citizens to "steer" online conversations in China. There, people are paid to write favorable posts about their employers in online chat rooms, social-networking sites, blogs, and the comment sections in news websites (p. 41).

While the internet is an excellent tool for both the identification of political opponents and the dissemination of propaganda, this use of the internet for repressive means does not represent an entrepreneurial step-change in political communication. As noted by the Soviet and authoritarian models of the press described by Siebert et al. (1963) almost 50 years ago, states have long understood the significance of the mass media for political control. However, when a tradition of communication repression can be combined with proactive measures, the internet can deliver as a particularly effective communication tool for state power. Specifically, the state can co-opt popular bloggers to conduct smear campaigns against political opponents; use search-engine optimization to point people away from popular opposition pages to well-designed government sources of information; and employ social-networking and microblogging services such as Twitter to deliver attractive, pro-state messages (what many would call propaganda). In these ways, the internet becomes a formidable instrument through which non-free regimes can consolidate their power. As leaders in Egypt learned, it is not wise to ignore the speed and power of the internet, particularly the way in which information and organization can spread in social networks. However, if repressive governments could figure out reliable ways not just to stop, but to actually co-opt those networks, the internet could represent a fundamentally more powerful tool for them.

Morozov forcefully makes the point that the internet provides many opportunities for repression. Using a range of examples from across the region, he points out that the internet affords the government in post-Soviet states the ability to quickly find, and even arrest, dissidents. Thus, the power of networks often works against dissidents, in a way that would not have been possible in the pre-internet days in which it was far harder for government officials to penetrate networks of dissent. Morozov also sounds a warning about the fundamental misunderstanding of the power of the internet in the hands of the state between Western protestors and their colleagues in non-free states. While protestors in democracies may urge people in authoritarian countries to go online to aggregate their interests, many protestors in these places may not realize the danger of the visibility of the online world. As a result, cyber-optimists can put individuals in non-free states at risk in new and particularly dangerous ways.

It is clear that governments in states such as China and Russia seem relatively convinced that the information flow in the online world can be harnessed to state interests, although they approach internet policy and regulation in very different ways. However, neither the Chinese nor the Russians may have sufficiently considered the transformative effect on citizens when they are empowered even in small ways via the online sphere. MacKinnon points out that the Chinese state certainly mitigates against the benefits of any transformative experience by arresting and imprisoning individuals who challenge the state online. While there is some evidence of this in Russia (discussed below), it is far less systematic and widespread than in China. One Russian NGO that tracks violations of internet freedom identified 111 separate threats to online freedom in Russia, including two murders and three assaults linked to internet activity (Agora Human Rights Association, 2011, p. 1, see Table 4.2: Threats to Internet Freedom in Russia, 2008–11). In addition, the Agora Human Rights Association found 25 civil lawsuits linked to internet control; 22 proposals to regulate the internet; 22 criminal prosecutions; 14 cyber-attacks; nine cases of limitation of access; six cases of administrative pressure; and other threats. Some of these specific threats and others will be discussed in more detail below, but it is interesting to note that the Agora Human Rights Association reported a growing trend toward more controlling incidents by mid-2011, with 23 in the first four months of 2011 alone. On the other hand, violence linked to internet communication—murders and assaults—is relatively isolated and had not occurred in the year leading up to mid-2011, according to the organization's report.

Table 4.2 **Threats to Internet Freedom in Russia, 2008–11**

Threats	Year				Total types of threat
	2008	*2009*	*2010*	*First 4 months of 2011*	
Proposals to regulate the internet	6	7	5	4	22
Murders	1	1	-	-	2
Assaults	1	1	1	-	3
Criminal prosecution	1	10	8	3	22
Civil actions/lawsuits	1	8	10	6	25
Administrative pressure	2	1	2	1	6
Limitation on access	-	6	2	1	9
Cyber attacks	6	2	1	5	14
Other dangers	-	1	4	3	8
TOTAL	18	37	33	23	111

Source: Agora Human Rights Association 2011, p. 1.

User Rights: Online Journalists and Online Citizens in Russia

The analysis by Freedom House of media and internet freedom in Russia highlights that, by mid-2011, there was more freedom online than in the traditional media sphere. This section looks at the treatment of both online journalists and online citizens in Runet, attempting to find patterns and trajectories of their treatment. Do online journalists suffer from the same issues of a lack of independence from political elites, commercial pressures, and dearth of protection from legal and even physical attacks when they attempt to cover controversial stories? At the same time, do citizens who use the internet for political communication suffer the same repression? Was the situation getting worse for online journalists, online citizens, or both by 2011?

User Rights in Russia

Anyone who expresses their opinion about the current governance of the Russian Federation (including in direct, sarcastic, ironic, verbal, or visual forms) is at risk of legal liability. In Russia, both journalists and citizens can be sued for their online activity. While this is true in countries around the world, the Russian government has a fairly powerful ability to detect and punish internet users. In part, this is due to the legislation (discussed above) that favors the needs of the government over the needs of citizens in terms of policing the online sphere. There are three central ways in which users are restricted in the posting of online content, all of which are discussed in more detail through the evidence below. First, journalists can be constrained in the online sphere for liability for the non-observance of their rights and duties, including the violation of the rules about the disclosure of state secrets (Law on the Mass Media, 1991, Article 5). In addition, those who post content online can be accused under the broad terms of the 2006 Russian federal law on countering extremism. Finally, citizens of the Russian Federation also may bear legal responsibility for their comments on texts and audiovisual information distributed online under the terms of Decree No. 420 on ICT information dissemination by Roskomnadzor, although this is balanced by the statements in Resolution 16 as discussed above.

PROSECUTION FOR ONLINE JOURNALISM OR RELAYING OFFICIAL INFORMATION

The Agora Human Rights Association compiled a list of prosecutions against online journalists between January 2008 and April 2011. On September 18, 2009, the editor-in-chief of the online publication *Novyi Focus (New Focus)* was charged by Abakana police under Article 282 (for defamation by accusing someone of being involved in a serious crime). The *Novyi Focus* editor, Mikhail Afanasyev, was charged in relation to an article that claimed those running a local hydroelectric station had failed to protect people following an accident at the station in August 2009. Although the charges against the editor were eventually dropped, the Agora association reported that Afanasyev was badly beaten (discussed below in a section about violence against online journalists). The Agora association also reported that the journalist and blogger Irek Murtazin was sentenced to 21 months in prison in November 2009. Murtazin, the former press secretary of Tatarstan Republic President Mintimer Shaimiev, was convicted of defamation and incitement to hatred against representatives of authorities. He was released after serving more than a year in a prison camp (Agora Human Rights Association).

In December 2009, a student at the Medical Institute in Saratov was arrested after he reposted a news item about the spread of a respiratory illness that had appeared on the city's information portal (Agora Human Rights Association). The re-publication of the item by Ivan Peregorodiev caused panic and the student was charged with knowingly disseminating false information. According to Agora, this was the first case in which a Russian blogger was arrested for merely reprinting news derived from a public source. News dissemination aside, the Agora report indicates that the use of the law in relation to internet content can also challenge the definition of what is art and what is politics. In December 2010 a criminal investigation was launched into the activities of Novosibirsk artist Artem Loskutov, known for artistic demonstrations in the defense of the right to free assembly. The artist was accused of insulting a representative of the authorities by depicting a policeman as a demon on his website. Loskutov claimed he was a victim of a police harassment and was illegally seized and searched, which resulted in his conviction of possession of marijuana in March 2010 and a fine of 20,000 rubles (approximately $600 USD).[19] In 2012, he was convicted of religious disrespect and fined 2,000 rubles (approximately $60 USD) for displaying icons with themes from Pussy Riot, the Moscow female punk rock band whose members were arrested and imprisoned in 2012 for a church performance that mocked the Russian government.

A review of the documented cases in which people have been accused by the security services of violating Russian law in the online sphere suggest the reasons fall into three broad categories: (1) fomenting of hatred for the Russian military and police; (2) contempt of government officials, including Vladimir Putin; and (3) state-defined extremist activity.

In terms of fomenting hatred for the military and the police, Savva Terentyev in Komi was reported as having made internet history in Russia for being the first person in the country arrested for making a blog post.[20] Along with the case of Dmitri Soloviev and Alexander Domrachev, Terentyev's case provides evidence that derogatory comments online about the Russian military or police can lead to serious consequences.[21] Terentyev was sentenced to a year of corrective labor in 2008 after his post expressing his hatred of the Russian police was interpreted as agitation of hatred against a societal "group" (i.e., the police). Soloviev, an activist in the Russian youth movement Oborona (Defense), criticized the Russian government and the FSB on LiveJournal for anti-Semitism; the unwillingness to recognize Nikolai II and his family as victims of political repression; and the failure to admit to crimes committed by the Soviet government in not providing medical treatment for some citizens.[22] A case was brought against him, but it was closed after three years due to lack of evidence. As an 18-year-old, Domrachev was arrested in February 2011 for the creation of an anti-police group on the social-networking site VKontakte. All of these internet users could be said to have violated Russian law.[23] What is perhaps puzzling is the selection of these particular individuals to prosecute, given that it is hard to find qualitative differences between their posts and much of the content that is readily available on Runet. However, a targeted strategy of limited but high-profile arrests is sufficient to inculcate norms of self-censorship, which are more efficient, economical, and socially acceptable than a heavy-handed regime of content examination and prosecution. It is also noteworthy that these cases are generally taking place outside of Moscow, and further study is needed on the approach by regional elites to internet policing and policy. These are cases that have been highlighted by NGOs and the media—no doubt there are further cases throughout Russia.

Issues of online contempt for government officials include cases in both St. Petersburg and Kovrovo in which two young men were accused of contempt for government officials because they discussed online the imaginary murder of their governors.[24] However, it is important to note that politicians as well as ordinary citizens can be accused of online contempt in Russia. In 2007, the Russian politician Viktor Alksnis (using the online name v_alksnis) quarreled with another LiveJournal blogger registered as "tarlith." Alksnis began legal action against the other blogger, who appeared to be the politician Timofey Sheviakov.[25] It is significant that online contempt of Putin is a particular category that attracts legal action from the Russian government (in contrast to the United States, in which status as a public figure means people have far greater license to publically comment on or ridicule a president). In 2005, a young member of the National Bolshevik Party named Andrei Skovorodnikov was sentenced to six months of correctional work and destruction of his computer for the creation of a web page carrying offensive information about Putin.[26] A year later, a radical nationalist named Aleksandr (his last name was withheld from press reports) was sentenced to a year in a correctional colony, as materials he distributed online were deemed to foment international conflict and dishonor Putin. Among the material he published online was a graphically manipulated picture of Putin, depicting the president as a skinhead.[27] Aside from arresting individuals for using image-manipulation software to create and disseminate doctored photos of leaders, Russian security services also arrest journalists for doing this as well. In 2006, the editor of the online newspaper *Kursiv* was fined (40,000 rubles or about $1,440 USD in 2011 exchange rates) for publishing an article entitled "Putin as the phallic symbol of Russia."[28] In a case that could be attributed to limitations on comments about Putin or limitations on the media more broadly, the St. Petersburg-based Sobaka.ru (Dog.ru) had to withdraw from printed circulation a copy of its published version with a caricature of Putin as a somewhat sad-looking bear on its cover in August 2007. Undaunted, the publication claimed the attention from the incident was a "PR coup."[29]

In terms of state-defined extremist activity as a trigger for internet control, those who express radical nationalist views or Nazi views are among those often accused of online extremism in Russia. One group that has come to the attention of authorities is the National Bolshevik Party. In 2006, 21-year-old Konstantin Strokolsky was sentenced to two years of parole for publishing an article entitled "The most constructive party," which discussed the National Bolsheviks from Kemerovo.[30] Another individual was sentenced to two years of imprisonment for anti-Semitism after his website published his intention to create a new city for Slavic people only.[31] In 2009, criminal action was brought against a 21-year-old woman for publishing a street "textbook" that detailed how to fight against people of other races.[32] In the same year, a group of young bloggers in Bashkortostan were accused of extremism and inciting ethnic hatred for publishing an excerpt from Airat Dilmukhametov's book *Wars Against the Bastards [Voiny protiv ugluidkov]*.[33] Although expert testimony did not identify any extremism in the text, members of the group were sentenced to up to six years of imprisonment in a penal colony.[34] It should be noted that the men were active opponents to the Bashkir government and the blogs criticized the Bashkortostan leader (Agora Human Rights Association). This evidence suggests that while the law is deployed against those identified as radical nationalists such as the above cases of those linked to the National Bolshevik Party (which is officially recognized by the Russian government as an extremist group and has been banned since 2007), the same law can be used against groups that could be better defined as political opponents (such as the group in Bashkortostan).

Court cases aside, there is evidence that websites can be blocked due to extremist content. For example, local government officials in the Russian Far East ordered the blockage of YouTube and four other websites by claiming they contained extremist materials.[35] One of the main reasons to close the websites was due to the presence of excerpts from Hitler's *Mein Kampf* as well as a YouTube nationalist video called *Russia for Russians*.[36] In a similar case involving extremist material, access to the website for Kronos was blocked in 2009. Apparently this website also provided quotations from *Mein Kampf* as well as criticized the governor of the St. Petersburg region.

All of the above categories suggest that a citizen can be arrested and prosecuted for quoting material from other parts of the web or expressing thoughts and opinions in a personal blog. In particular, it would seem that citizens can get in trouble not only for creating caricatures of Putin, but for uploading and disseminating them as well. While it is clear that some of this material would be considered unacceptable in a range of states, there is evidence that some of the cases are politically motivated (particularly in the instance of the Bashkortostan bloggers, although study of the blog content would be needed). Aggressive complaints about state government could also be dangerous—although there must be thousands of negative comments about the Russian government on Runet daily—but if one can be prosecuted successfully for criticizing the police as a "societal group," it would seem that the barrier to prosecution is quite low.

THE CONTAGION EFFECT?: VIOLENCE AGAINST ONLINE JOURNALISTS

As discussed in Chapter 2, one of the most disturbing issues surrounding Russian journalism is the number of assaults and murders of the journalists themselves. It is clear that this violence has migrated from the offline to the online media, which is unsurprising given the lack of protection (legal and practical) for journalists in general in Russia. The Agora Human Rights Association has identified two murders and three serious assaults for people whose work was "directly related to their exercise of freedom on the Internet" (Agora Human Rights Association, p. 3). According to Agora, the owner of the ingushetiya.ru website was shot and killed on August 31, 2008, during an unlawful arrest by police. Magomed Yevloev's website had taken a critical position toward the Ingushetian authorities, according to the Agora association. The violence related to this website continued after Yevloev's death. Maksharip Aushev, a member of the Expert Council of the Russian Human Rights took over the website but was killed on October 25, 2009, on a street in Nalchik. Agora also reported that Valery Savinkov, the editor-in-chief of the Bankfax news agency, was attacked in Barnaul (Siberia) on January 31, 2008. Savinkov, who received a blow to the head, survived. The Russian Federal Agency for Communications and Cultural Heritage had secured a court order to shut down Bankfax on the grounds of extremism (although Agora does not provide any evidence linking the violence to state officials). On September 9, 2009, the editor of the internet journal *Novyi Focus* Afanasyev (discussed above in the legal sanctions section) was badly beaten in the wake of his investigation of safety violations that led to a tragic accident at a local hydroelectric station. The Moscow journalist Oleg Kashin was "brutally beaten" in Moscow on the night of November 5, 2010, near his home, and "one interpretation of the attack much discussed in the media, linked the assault to publications by Kashin in his personal blog" (Agora, p. 3).

Conclusions

The Russian novelist Leo Tolstoy once wrote that "Happy families are all alike; every unhappy family is unhappy in its own way."[37] This parallels a perspective about how states regulate the internet: While analysts can readily see the difference between the liberal regulation of the internet in places such as the United States and the overt repression of cyber-dissidents in China, it is even more important to perceive the various types and levels of state media control of the internet. This chapter has outlined a range of ways in which the internet is controlled by the Russian state. Overall, indicators from international observers such as Freedom House suggest that Russia is not only failing to provide a free online sphere, but repression is increasing over time. This is balanced by the more optimistic interpretation of Supreme Court Resolution No. 16 offered by Richter, who has been an observer of Russian media law for decades. While the internet still remains more free than the traditional mass media in Russia, there is evidence that there is a convergence between the two, with the internet coming to parallel the more repressive norms of the offline media relatively quickly. International comparisons aside, there is compelling evidence from the wide range of laws that have been deployed to control, rather than foster, freedom of speech in the online sphere. In particular through the SORM regulations, the Russian state has extremely broad powers to mine the internet to detect anti-state activity. While a range of states—including the United States—use online data for purposes of state security, the law in Russia gives a very asymmetric amount of power to the state. Without proper oversight, which is certainly not available to Russian citizens and exacerbated by the lack of an independent judiciary, this power is open to abuse, particularly in terms of using data collection to detect and punish political opponents. Through the cases of people who have been arrested and even imprisoned due to posting (or reposting) of online content, it is clear that the state can interpret these powers quite broadly. While some cases can clearly be seen to be fomenting hatred or violence, in others it would appear fairly evident that it was political, rather than security, motivations that led to the arrest of the individuals who were posting content. Whereas the arrest of citizens for cyber-dissidence is still relatively rare in Russia, even a handful of high-profile arrests can generate an atmosphere of fear and self-censorship.

While it is fairly disturbing that the lack of support for freedom of speech in traditional media has translated into regulation for the online sphere, it is even more worrying that the violence against Russian journalists continues with violence against online content providers. The cases identified by the Agora Human Rights Association show that the relative anonymity and flexibility of the internet cannot protect individuals against the high levels of crime and corruption in Russian society. In terms of internet control, it would appear that national norms work at subverting the democratizing potential of the online sphere in Russia. This leaves us with the question of how effective these controls operated for the Russian state in the crisis of late 2011, which will be discussed against the background of content, community, catalyst, control, and co-optation in the final chapter of this book.

5

Russian Parties Online

While the internet is often studied as a way to augment democratic institutions, what role can the internet play in democratization if there are no robust democratic institutions to effect the change suggested—or demanded—by informed, engaged, or even outraged citizens? In other words, if parties are failing to foster democracy in Russia, does it make any difference what they do online? How much will the historic and societal role of political parties dictate how parties capitalize on information opportunities offered by the online sphere? What do new and evolving communication technologies and behaviors of the online audience offer political parties in systems in which parties have failed to inculcate democratic norms? Alternatively, will the online sphere change particular *aspects* of party communication asymmetrically, for example by allowing nationalist parties to have a disproportionate effect on political discourse or by forcing dominant political parties to become more inclusive and transparent?

How can one measure, analyze, and explain the similarities and differences in the ways in which Russian political parties are using the internet? This study examines these issues through an analysis of web usage by four major Russian political parties that held seats in the lower house of the Russian parliament in mid-2011: United Russia, the Communist Party of the Russian Federation, the Liberal-Democratic Party of Russia, and A Just Russia. Using content analysis of party websites, a review of how parties use web communication tools, a discussion of public attitudes toward political parties in Russia, and web link analysis, this chapter suggests new ways of understanding the democratizing potential of the online sphere in the absence of robust democratic institutions. What this analysis reveals is that Russian parties online in mid-2011 tended to mirror the parties offline, reflecting but not augmenting their political power. Each political party used the information potential of the online sphere in a different way, from further wielding of state and party power for United Russia to providing a voice for protest on the Communist Party website. Overall, the findings suggest that a broad theory about the success or failure of political parties online to democratize societies may miss important nuances about the ways in which parties in non-free states can communicate their particular party "brands" and provide relatively small spaces of political contestation that are not available in the mainstream media.

Political Parties and the Online Sphere

The internet would appear to offer a range of ways to help political parties fulfill their optimal function of translating the wishes of the electorate into policy. The communicative tools of the online sphere allow for parties to provide much more information about their organization, history, structure, values, ideology, and policies. If parties are elected into office or form part of the government, they also can provide more policy information with far greater detail to a broader range of citizens. The interactive capabilities of the online sphere make it possible to discuss policies in depth and use crowd-sourcing as ways to foster ideas for political engagement. Parties that are still attempting to win seats can provide voters with nuanced arguments and have the ability to form reasoned (and possibly appealing) arguments without struggling to win the attention of the mass media or paying for expensive advertising, as in the U.S. electoral system. The internet should lower costs at the same time it lowers barriers, helping parties to campaign for support, recruit members or volunteers, and avoid media bias or framing that could be detrimental to their fortunes. The advent of social networking and other many-to-many networking tools should allow political ideas and actions to flourish, piggybacking on preexisting online social networks.

Studies of how parties use the online sphere, however, suggest that any sort of cyber-utopian era for political parties is very far from realization (Norris, 2003). Attention has been drawn to the use of the internet in campaigns in the United States, particularly during presidential elections (Anstead and Chadwick, 2008). However, the United States is rather exceptional in this case, as elections are centered more on candidates than political parties. Thus, while lessons can be drawn in particular from the synergy between Barack Obama's use of Web 2.0, the rise of the internet as a central source of political information, and the particular youth appeal of his candidacy, it is not necessarily a lesson that can be translated into different political environments.

The fundamental work for studying online communication by political parties in comparative perspective has its roots in Gibson and Ward (2000), who established a cross-national tool for analyzing central features of political party websites (also see Gibson et al., 2003; Gibson, 2010). The scheme assigns points for features of websites in the categories of information provision, resource generation, internal networking, external networking, participation, campaigning, and delivery (encompassing a "glitz" factor, access, navigability, freshness, and visibility). Studies using the Gibson and Ward scheme have found that while parties are becoming increasingly sophisticated in their online use, this use varies by country and between parties. While this is countered by a study by Foot et al. (2010), who found cross-national similarities in different types of parties that used the internet, this work also discovered that the adoption of online tools in political party organization and communication is not fully realized in many cases. Beyond the measurement of how parties may use the internet is concern with how the audience might choose to engage with online parties. A study by Lusoli and Ward found that while British parties were creating more elaborate websites with impressive amounts of information resources, the audience was not particularly interested.[1] This parallels findings by others who have studied the online political sphere, with Hindman (2009) suggesting that the online hierarchies of information do not promote political information out-side of the mainstream and Davis (2009) finding that those who do discuss poli-tics in blogs tend to stay in relatively self-contained groups. In addition, there does not appear to be compelling evidence that the online sphere fundamentally changes the level of openness or transparency in party organizations.

A study of Russian political parties online in 2003 found that the parties were taking little advantage of the opportunities offered by online communication (March, 2004, 2006). This was not surprising, not only due to the relatively weak development of Russian parties (discussed below), but also because of the low penetration of the internet in Russia almost a decade ago (less than 10 percent of the population, according to March, which parallels Russian internet audi-ence figures discussed in Chapter 3). However, there are two quite significant factors relating to the internet and political parties in Russia that would suggest a fundamental shift of the role of online communication for parties since the 2003 study by March. First, as discussed in Chapter 3, Russia has experienced very rapid growth in the online audience in the past 10 years. Second and more significantly, the penetration rate is far higher among younger Russians, paralleling the levels of use in the West (Russian Federal Agency on the Press and Mass Communication, 2011). By 2011, Russia was showing the signs of having an unusually active and engaged online population. Could political parties capitalize on this growing online audience to fundamentally change the nature of party communication?

Russian Parties: Democratic by Design, but Not by Function

The modern structure of the Russian political party system was created by the 1993 Russian Constitution. The constitution mandates a party-based democracy, with a bicameral legislature (the Duma as the lower house and the

Federation Council as the upper house of the Russian Federative Assembly) and a particularly strong presidency. Political parties were designed along liberal principles in the new constitution, although the actual practice of Russian politics has not fostered a democratic environment (White, Rose, and McAllister, 1996; Colton, 2000; Hutcheson, 2003; White, Wyman, and Oates, 1997; Rose and Munro, 2002; Smyth, 2006; Smyth, Lowry, and Wilkening, 2007; Gel'man, 2008; Reuter and Remington, 2009; Slider, 2010; Sakwa, 2011; White, 2011). The constitution guarantees the right of citizens to form parties freely, for parties to raise funds and organize and—perhaps most critically—the right for parties to receive free time and fair media coverage in elections.[2] For Duma elections, the electoral system was designed to balance the power of national parties with local politics: Half of the 450 seats were elected through a national party list system, while half were elected via single-member constituencies. In the constituency races, it was possible to run with or without party affiliation.

Since the passage of the Russian constitution nearly two decades ago, the Russian government has amended and limited the ability of parties to form from the grass roots and win election in parliament. Most notably, the government introduced complex rules on national party registration that involved collecting signatures of support nationwide;[3] eliminated single-member constituency elections; and raised the distribution of party-list seats from those parties that get at least 5 percent of the national party list vote to those that receive 7 percent or more.[4] These rules aside, the reality of Russian party politics and elections has little to do with the institutional design for parties in the 1993 constitution. Aside from the end of national elections to the upper house, the constitutional guarantees were ignored or even amended by the Russian government to guard against their opponents gaining office. In the early Duma elections of 1993 and 1995, pro-Kremlin parties failed to win significant shares of the vote despite massive state resources and sycophantic television coverage on state-run television (Oates, 2006). In particular, the nationalists and the communists thrived in the new system, respectively winning the largest number of Duma party-list seats in 1993 and 1995. The Communist Party of the Russian Federation also had a strong showing in 1999.

The Kremlin has responded to the popularity of communist and nationalist parties in several ways, including by significantly increasing media propaganda against relatively successful opposition parties; co-opting the popular nationalist party as well as incorporating stronger nationalist messages into the pro-government parties; and changing the electoral rules to favor the fortunes of pro-government parties that could be better controlled through national party-list elections (Oates, 2006; Gel'man, 2008; White, 2011). United Russia now overwhelmingly dominates the media (particularly during elections) as

well as holds a majority of the seats in the Duma. Vladimir Putin was leader of
the United Russia party as prime minister from 2008 to 2012 and ran as the
party presidential candidate in 2012. In addition, former Russian President
Dmitri Medvedev was visibly aligned with the party. It is particularly apparent
that the media, especially the influential state-run television First Channel,
have been used to undermine, rather than support, party development (Oates,
2006). Television and key journalists have been utilized to spread negative
propaganda about the opposition (some of it both dubious and personal)
while flooding the airwaves with constant coverage of pro-Kremlin parties and
supporters (Oates, 2006; European Institute for the Media 1994, February
1996, September 1996, March 2000, August 2000; OSCE/ODHIR, June 2,
2004, January 27, 2004).

The Russian Disdain for Political Parties

It is not fair, however, to blame the pro-Kremlin bias for its own parties completely for the general failure of parties to foster democratic culture in Russia.
From the collapse of the Soviet Union onward, Russian citizens have shown
little enthusiasm for political parties as effective and trusted political institutions (White, 2011; White, Rose, and McAllister, 1997; Rose and Munro,
2002; Colton, 2000). In a 2010 survey of 2,017 Russians, trust in political
parties ranked the lowest on a list of 13 political institutions in the country.[5]
Thus, parties face an uphill battle in a society that does not generally perceive
them as particularly worthwhile. Even with the greater information resource
provision offered by the online sphere, it is hard to reach an electorate in
which 41 percent of the population claimed no specific political orientation in
the 2010 survey and 79 percent claimed they did not support any particular
political party. The dislike of political parties also must be weighed against the
general popularity of the office of the president and the specific enthusiasm
for Putin, who had consistently outranked any other Russian leader (including
President Medvedev in 2010) in opinion polls by the time he stood for his
third election in 2012. Thus, it would seem more likely that the power of
online information provision and aggregation would be more successful for
political leaders, who already were winning more respect and confidence from
the public than political parties. It would be logical to be concerned that the
internet could further the popularity and credibility gap between charismatic
leaders and parties, aiding the former at the expense of the latter. There have
been a large number of weak parties in Russia—in the 1999 elections alone
there were more than 40 on the ballot—but only a few have endured for more
than one election.

Parties in the Russian Duma, 2007–2011

By 2007, the effects of stricter regulation of party registration were apparent as only 11 parties made it onto the party-list ballot. Four of these parties won more than 7 percent of the vote in order to gain seats in the Duma: United Russia (64.1 percent of the vote and 315 seats), the Communist Party of the Russian Federation (11.6 percent and 57 seats), the Liberal-Democratic Party of Russia (8.2 percent and 40 seats), and A Just Russia (7.8 percent and 38 seats).[6] These are four very different parties, not only in terms of ideology, but also in terms of structure and leadership. Indeed, even to call all four of them "parties" is somewhat misleading.

United Russia is the party of the government and often referred to as the "party of power." Although federal law technically prohibits the asymmetric allocation of state resources for parties, there is little actual distinction between the federal elites and the United Russia party. Putin's popularity and prestige historically outranked that of the United Russia party. United Russia is often called a party of power in that it reflects—rather than creates—the power of the leader himself. Hence, the party has relied to a degree on his favor in order to stay in power, rather than the opposite situation in states such as the United Kingdom in which the leader can be deselected by party members. In a distant second is the Communist Duma "fraction," as Russian parliamentary blocs are known, which still maintains some opposition to the government. In particular, the Communists have maintained a relatively stable ideological stance (softening from a return to the Soviet system, but still measurably more favorable of redistributive politics than other main parties; see Oates 2006). The CPRF has a clearly hierarchical leadership status, party bylaws, regular party congresses, and well-established party media such as communist newspapers. CPRF leader Gennady Zyuganov has been in post since the collapse of the Soviet Union and has provided steady, if not deeply charismatic, leadership to the party.

While United Russia could be described as a party of power and the CPRF as a party in the more traditional sense, the Liberal Democrats are a personality party centered on the flamboyant and popular Vladimir Zhirinovsky. Zhirinovsky, who has been known to call for all news announcers to be blond and blue-eyed as well as the return of Alaska to Russia, has headed this nationalist party that has been elected to the Duma since 1993. The party does particularly well at marketing itself as a pro-Russian, anti-Western, xenophobic party of opposition to the more centrist party of power. However, the Liberal Democrats and its members of the Duma tend not to openly oppose the government on key issues (Shekhovtsov, 2011) and Zhirinovsky served as vice chair of the fifth Duma (2007–11) itself. A Just Russia, formed from a coalition of several parties and groups, had a prominent leader in the form of veteran

Russian politician Sergei Mironov. The party was considered to be somewhat left of the centrist United Russia. Although the party also was created by political elites as a type of loyal opposition, it later distanced itself from United Russia and was providing a noticeably more socialist ideology in its party documents online in mid-2011.

Russian Parties Online: Information and Resource Provision

An analysis of the websites of the four parties in August 2011 using the Gibson and Ward scheme for cross-national coding of political party websites showed few differences. The four parties were remarkably similar in measurements of information provision, resource generation, and participation. More differences were found in examining how party websites used Web 2.0 and other features such as social-networking sites, blogs, RSS, forums, and so on, which will be discussed in more detail below (see Table 5.1: Web Communication Tools Linked from Russian Party Websites).

Table 5.1 **Web Communication Tools Linked from Russian Party Websites**

Feature	Score			
	United Russia	*CPRF*	*LDPR*	*Just Russia*
VKontake [Russian social-networking site]	1	0*	0	0
Facebook	1	0*	1	0
Twitter link from website	1	0*	1	0
Video "channel" (YouTube or other)	1	1	1	1 (internal)
RSS feed	1	1	0	0
E-mail direct link	1	0	0	1**
E-mail via portal	0	0	1	1**

continued

Table 5.1 (continued)

Feature	Score			
	United Russia	*CPRF*	*LDPR*	*Just Russia*
Public forum linked to web page	0	1 (can see comments without registering, but must register to post)	0	1**
Private forum linked to web page	1 (need to register to see comments)	0	0	1**
LiveJournal link	0	0	1	0
Other blog link	0	0	1	1**
Other (list)	0	1 (Yandex)	3 (Formspring, Infox, Echo of Moscow.)	1 (Q&A forum)**
TOTAL	7	4	9	0 from main website, 6 from partner website

* There are links to "share" news items and so on on a range of social-media sites, includng Twitter, VKontakte, Odnoklassniki, Facebook, MoiMir (MyWorld) and LiveJournal. But there are no links to specific CPRF areas within these platforms.

** All provided via a "partner" link to Just Russia Online at http://www.spravedlivo-online.ru/.

Source: Author's research in August 2011.

Case Studies of Russian Parties Online

UNITED RUSSIA

For United Russia, the key question was whether its website served the government or the party. In mid-2011, how much did the party website reveal about the nature of a "party of power" (as opposed to a "party of the people") in the post-Soviet context? Was there a particular promotion of either Putin (as party leader) or Medvedev (as president) on the party website? Was one or the other framed as the more effective leader on the eve of the December 2011 Duma elections and March 2012 presidential contest?[7] Aside from the information provision measured in the Gibson and Ward scheme, was there compelling evidence of interaction and access to the party on the part of possible supporters or the broader electorate?

In fact, the United Russia website demonstrated the lack of distance between the ruling administration and the party. Indeed, at times it was difficult to assess the pages as those of a political party rather than those of a state administration. The pages included a wide range of information that one would expect from a party website, including the organizational history, structure, values, ideology, policies, and party documents such as the party manifesto. The website had extensive information on the leaders of the party, including a page[8] with profiles of 62 party leaders. However, the website did not excessively focus on Putin or give the impression that United Russia was just a following around Putin. Nor was there excessive framing of Medvedev to underline United Russia as the "party of power." Indeed, the home page itself had mug shots of 10 different leaders with links to articles about them and their activities or comments. The link with the Kremlin was not through personality politics; rather, it was through a focus on government work. The United Russia website devoted much attention to government projects, including links and photos at the bottom of the home page to highlight 24 state initiatives such as constructing swimming pools, building roads, modernizing education, opening sports complexes, undertaking health projects, and so on. While it is appropriate for incumbents to highlight ongoing or successful initiatives on their websites, here it was practically impossible to tell the difference between the role of the party and the role of the state.[9] As the dominant party in parliament, with the clear support of both President Medvedev and the powerful Putin, the party website made it obvious that there was no meaningful distance between the state and the United Russia party. This would suggest that the internet is more a reflection of the political status quo than an engine for political change or renewal in Russian political party life.

In one way, however, the United Russia website differed markedly from its Western counterparts by a *lack* of focus on the upcoming Duma elections in December 2011. Compared with the heavy focus on campaigns in Western websites close to polling day, there were signs that United Russia had not integrated campaign information across the website. In the "party" section that linked from the top of the home page,[10] the discussion around elections linked back to the 2007 Duma race (with ample reference to "President Putin"). There was a link to "Elections 2011" in the center of the home page,[11] but it did not feature any obvious party platform or slate of candidates. Rather, it linked to a series of news stories about party activities, including primary races for the United Russia party list in the regions. There were no election results or statistics on the United Russia website. Interestingly, there *was* an entire section on "opponents" in the elections, which featured negative news stories about Communists and other contenders. This fits into the "white" and "black" propaganda traditions in Russian elections, in which parties of power broadcast an enormous amount of positive news (infrastructure projects, citizen services, national achievements, effective leadership, etc.), along with as much negative or "black" information that they can find or create on opponents (Oates, 2006).[12] Another element of the United Russia website that jarred is the fact that the "links" page was empty.

Although there were gaps in information provision on the United Russia website, can a party really remain closed off from the public and still maintain a meaningful online presence? There was a great deal of information broadcast from the United Russia party website, including details on leaders as well as regional offices. This was much more information than was available a few short years ago in Russia. However, the details on the national leaders did not include any contact information, either via mail, telephone, e-mail, or personal website addresses on the United Russia website (although there were a range of more impersonal links to online communication tools across the top of the United Russia home page). There were icons for direct links to United Russia RSS feeds, Twitter, Facebook, VKontakte, a generic party e-mail address, and YouTube (in that order, see Table 5.1). There was also a link to a "private office" forum.[13]

If there was any web space in which there appeared to be political dialogue related to the party, it would seem to have been the Facebook page linked to United Russia through its home page.[14] However, while there were some intriguing discussions there (such as one about abolishing the upper house of the Russian parliament), the conversation was clearly among just a handful of people. Indeed, overall the official Facebook page of United Russia boasted just 327 members on August 16, 2011. The United Russia page on VKontakte had more than 10 times as many members (3,606 on the same date) but was plagued on August 17, 2011, with spam by a user named Artem Mazalov who continually posted : "This is a group of curs and thieves. Curse you!" This would suggest that there was not particularly good editing or monitoring of the page—positive from the point of view of democratic exchange, but perhaps suggestive that social networking was not seen as a particularly official or serious aspect of the party communication strategy.[15]

COMMUNIST PARTY OF THE RUSSIAN FEDERATION (CPRF)

The internet should give the Communist Party the ability to communicate with its relatively large constituency free from the neglect or negative framing it has received from most of the Russian mass media (Oates, 2006). Thus, one would expect the Communist Party to focus on its framing of society as a need for the rebirth of communism in Russia, with the use of Soviet-era images and language. At the same time, could the CPRF take advantage of Web 2.0 to spread the message or does the website reflect the older, less technological demographic of party support? Finally, how much of a leadership "cult" did the Communists pursue in the online sphere to counter the images of Putin so prominent throughout Russia?

An earlier analysis of the CPRF website in March 2010 showed a relatively cluttered Web 1.0 site with homage to Soviet imagery (Oates, 2010). This look remained essentially unchanged over the 18 months between the studies, although there were some updates. While the website lacked a leader "focus," it gave ample information on party history, organization, values, and ideology. The party shared with A Just Russia (discussed below) a particular interest in social welfare and socialist values, with party documents focusing on justice and equality viewed through a communist lens. The language and imagery were reminiscent of Soviet-era party documents, but modernized to have a more contemporary and humanistic feel.

What was perhaps most striking about the information provision of the website, however, was the presence of a series of links to party-controlled media as well as a lack of the use of external Web 2.0 platforms for party information dissemination and discussion (see Table 5.1). The CPRF had just four identifiable web communications tools. It would appear that the Communists were not attempting to harness the networking power of popular, public platforms in the Web 2.0 environment. Rather, the party was relying on a closed circle of party media (including its own web TV channel) for public communication. This reinforces the idea that the internet reflects, rather than transforms, party practices. While it is unsurprising that the CPRF would choose to foster its own relatively closed, controlled media environment after suffering from decades of neglect and aggressive attack in most of the mainstream Russian media, it is nonetheless not very promising for the future ability of the party to prosper beyond its aging support base.[16]

Thus, the CPRF website is perhaps more interesting for what features it lacked in mid-2011 rather than the features it had. In particular, it should be noted that Zyuganov did not have a separate "leader" section as did the leaders of United Russia, the LDPR, and A Just Russia. Zyuganov was prominent via a picture of the Communist leader clenching a socialist-style fist on the home page as well as throughout the videos on KPRF-TV (the online video channel linked from the CPRF home page, see http://kprf.tv/). However, the Communists avoided a heavy reliance on Zyuganov as a proxy for the party, although it was not clear whether this was due to party philosophy or because the steady Zyuganov lacks the on-screen flamboyance of a Zhirinovsky or a Putin. It is also somewhat an open question as to why the CPRF web page was not exploiting popular platforms such as LiveJournal or VKontakte.[17] The party did have a Twitter feed, but it essentially functioned as an RSS, with a large volume of posts (10,066) to a very small number of followers (517) as of August 2011. Was the CPRF avoiding linkages to popular internet platforms to maintain control over its party message? Or did the party fear that public social-networking pages or blogs could be attacked, in particular by well-funded and tech-savvy forces loyal to United Russia? Did it fear that the use of Web 2.0 would alienate its core constituency? The CPRF website did feature a fairly active forum, in which participants discussed political philosophy and issues. However, an analysis in 2010 showed that a relatively small number of individuals dominated in the forums and there was little evidence of persuasive interaction at work, i.e., it appeared to be party supporters "preaching to the converted" (Oates, 2010).

The most significant addition to the CPRF website between an earlier study in March 2010 (Oates, 2010) to August 2011 was the promotion of a section on protest (http://kprf.ru/actions/). By August 2011, this was a very large section, with 422 pages giving details of political protests since 2000. The pages were actively updated. In just three days (August 16–18, 2011), the protest section of the CPRF website included news on a protest by 256 families in Moscow waiting for their homes to be completed in a business deal gone bad; a protest from agrarian scientists over research; concerns that a Black Sea oil project by Russian oil giant Rosneft threatened the local environment; complaints about police interference in a demonstration in the Moscow region; a picket by pensioners who were left without support from their former state farm in Krasnodar Krai; campaigning for a referendum in Kaluga; reports on CPRF demonstrations on "20 years without the USSR" in the Novosibirsk region and Kurgan; and campaigning on a referendum in Magadan. This would give a very different idea of the breadth and depth of street protests across the country from the lack of coverage of such events in the traditional mass media in Russia. Of all the party websites in mid-2011, the Communist Party website appeared to have the greatest focus on actual political protest and action. Ironically, the party's *lack* of engagement with social-networking platforms noted above would seem to correlate with actual engagement in the real world. As highlighted in earlier work (Oates, 2010), the CPRF website would seem to be a place that carries alternative political news in general, although it appears unlikely this is attracting a broad audience.

The CPRF inherited the historic and emotional legacy of the CPSU, which gives it considerable strength as a political movement with the older generation. The sense of nostalgia for the Soviet "Great Power" finds resonance across age groups in Russia (Oates, 2006). Thus, it is not surprising that the CPRF website highlighted its affection for the Soviet Union in late August 2011 through the commemoration of the 20th anniversary of the 1991 coup that signaled the end of Soviet rule. Furthermore, the party retains symbols and formalities from its Soviet era, including rules for membership that echo the responsibilities of CPSU membership.[18] They were the only website of the four parties analyzed to list the obligations of party members, which included the necessity of expanding the influence of communist ideals; paying membership fees of 1 percent of income; participating in party activities, rallies, and pickets; distributing promotional materials; serving as election observers; and recruiting others to the party.

LIBERAL-DEMOCRATIC PARTY OF RUSSIA (LDPR)

The LDPR has two central features as a political party: populism and its colorful leader Zhirinovsky. An additional feature would be identified as survival skills, for the LDPR has held seats in the Russian Duma since its inception in 1993. With the Communist Party, it is the only political party to have survived five Duma elections and the consolidation of authority into the central party of power (now United Russia). Studies have shown that the LDPR, despite its combatant rhetoric during elections and in the media in general, tends to cooperate with the party of power. What does the party website reveal about this controversial, yet resilient nationalist party?

The LDPR website stood out from other Russian party websites for its more compelling ability to frame and present solutions to key Russian issues. The website had a different appearance from the sleeker, sparer United Russia or the glowing red, busier CPRF website. LDPR website had more of a Web 1.0 format, with the traditional party website appearance designed in the party colors of blue and gold. The party seal (with an eagle imposed over a map of Russia) featured at the top of the site, while there were the following series of links across the top of the page: News, Party, Leader, Power (*Vlast'*), LDPR Speaks, Youth, For the Mass Media, and Contacts. As with the United Russia website, there was also a "Join the Party" link located in the top right-hand corner of the home page. However, while the United Russia home page had a series of photos with different party leaders, the main photo on the LDPR home page showed Zhirinovsky, with his characteristic ironic expression, standing in front of a massed group of LDPR deputies. Zhirinovsky faced the camera head-on, while the deputies were mostly looking to the side. The impression of a general leading his troops was unmistakable.

In a parallel to the United Russia website, the LDPR website did not provide information on election results and did not feature obvious campaign materials on its website in mid-August 2011. It also linked to a youth organization, which for the LDPR was Youth Time at http://www.molvremya.ru/. LDPR chose different platforms for social networking than United Russia, with no link to

VKontakte from the LDPR home page. In addition, while United Russia opted for slightly less modern direct e-mail, the LDPR linked to an e-mail portal (блоги@mail.ru) that allowed party information/campaigning to be included along with e-mail communication. In addition, Zhirinovsky himself appeared to be responsive online via the Formspring site (http://www.formspring.me/) that allows individuals to pose questions directly to people such as political leaders. As of August 18, 2011, Zhirinovsky had provided substantive replies to individuals, the most recent being a response to a question about LDPR's concerns for invalids. However, there were only 17 questions and responses in total by that date on the Formspring site and it was impossible to say whether the questions were posed by actual citizens (as opposed to the party faithful). In addition, it is interesting to note that the LDPR had set up an open forum on the Formspring site. There was no open forum linked from the United Russia page, although the United Russia Facebook page was relatively lively, if sparsely used.

Overall, the web communication tool links from the LDPR page could be described as leader-centered, with a range of options to view Zhirinovsky, see his opinions, and even ask him questions (with links to the Echo of Moscow radio station website, infox.ru, as well as to Formspring). The LDPR home page also linked to a video site called LDPRtube (http://ldpr-tube.ru/). LDPRtube was distinctive from the more predictable video links to statements by party leaders or supporters or even traditional campaign films. Rather, the site featured home videos highlighting petty abuses by businesses, police, and other officials, with a discussion of how the party was investigating matters. This parallels the CPRF protest web page as a place to highlight citizen concerns or grievances.

There was ample information about LDPR party policies on its website. These policies could be described as nationalist, anti-American, pro-Slavic, and somewhat socialist in nature (in terms of giving benefits to low-income people, farmers, pensioners, etc.). The LDPR party program online (http://ldpr.ru/#party/Programme_LDPR) was divided into themes: LDPR shows the way; state-building; direction of the country and civil society; foreign policy; domestic policy; pressing questions; and the practical program of the LDPR. The party stated its purpose was to "resurrect the status of Russia to that of a Great Power [*Velikoi Derzhavy*]." There is an element of social conservatism that resonated throughout the program, particularly in suggesting the promotion of parenthood and taking issue with the high abortion rate in Russia. The program combined short, sharp statements about the need to bolster Russian businesses; to rebuild the former Soviet sphere of influence to counter the West; the need to extend the social welfare net; and other concrete issues. These were claims that would resonate well with much of the Russian electorate, including the statement that the current administration "protects the rich." Unlike the way in which United Russia highlighted particular projects, the LDPR focused on five priority policy areas on its website:[19] the "Russian question"; cultural policy; the fight against corruption; the fight against terrorism and extremism; and defense and security. This suggests that the LDPR is effective at identifying central concerns to Russian citizens and highlighting them in their program. However, at times this streamlining of ideas is lost in the details, which included a call for free public toilets and the idea that young fathers could be exempt from military service. The party program ends with the warning: ONLY LDPR or SUFFER FURTHER!!! (*TOL'KO LDPR ili TERPI DAL'SHE!!!*) Unlike the earnest and serious tone of the United Russia and CPRF websites, the phrasing on much of the LDPR website was more casual and "folksy." A good example of LDPR prose would be:

> *Staryi dom mozhno razobrat' tol'ko togda, kogda postroish' novyi. Starye bryuki mozhno ispolzovat' na tryapki, lish' kogda sosh'esh' ili kupish novye. Inache – golyi. I skol'ko my perevudali etikh golykh korolei, kotorye ne tol'ko sami ogolyalis', no i ogolyali obmanutyi ocherednymi ekonomicheskimi reformatsyami narod?*

> You can only tear down an old house when you've built a new one. You can use your old trousers for rags, but only if you've managed to sew or buy some new ones. Otherwise, you're naked. And how much have we seen so many of these naked kings, who have not only bared themselves, but because they've deceived others with so-called economic reforms, have left the people bare as well?

While the website has an array of information provision that would parallel any party site, including party history, structure, policies, news, and membership information, there were elements of the website that reflect the particular LDPR approach to Russian politics. The discussion of party policies was much more engaging and accessible than that found on the United Russia or CPRF websites. It is significant to note that Zhirinovsky did not attempt to frame himself as close to Medvedev or Putin, with little mention of either leader in the website. By the same token, the "leader" section that linked from the home page was (unsurprisingly) solely about Zhirinovsky. However, the "LDPR speaks" section also featured comments from two other LDPR deputies as well as from Zhirinovsky, so there was some voice for other party leaders. Perhaps the most unusual aspects of LDPR online was an entire section devoted to patriotic songs (http://ldpr. ru/#leader/Songs), in addition to a video of Zhirinovsky singing the LDPR "hymn."

Many of the statements about "Great Russia" and the "motherland" (*rodina*) might puzzle some political observers. However, one of the significant strengths of the LDPR that goes beyond the personal appeal of Zhirinovsky as a "man of the people" is the way in which the party is able to amplify the Soviet tradition into a powerful sense of pride in the contemporary Russian state (Oates, 2006). The LDPR has shown the ability to identify and articulate a brand of populist nationalism that other parties, including the parties of power, have sought to emulate after watching LDPR successes, particularly in 1993 (Oates, 1998). The internet allows the LDPR to build and expand on this brand of nationalism. In particular, the ability to broadcast nationalist messages without the limiting frame of the mass media—as well as the presence of audio and video online— give an advantage to a party with the ability to craft particularly resonant messages. However, these are messages that are not linked to very realistic policies or leaders beyond Zhirinovsky.

While there is debate on the extent to which the LDPR actually challenges the government, in any case it should be recognized that the party has successfully fostered its own support base and constituency. It has managed this with a dearth of serious coverage of political contenders from central television, although Zhirinovsky has been successful at garnering political coverage of his own. His showmanship and ability to provide provocative sound bites make him a staple on Russian television.[20] Despite Zhirinovsky's history of xenophobic and extreme nationalist rhetoric, there was relatively little evidence of this on the main party website. Thus, while there might be complaints that the Liberal-Democratic Party of Russia is not particularly "liberal" or "democratic" in its nationalist, pro-state stance, the very existence of a separate political party from United Russia and the party of power in general is important for the possibility of democracy. The internet gave the LDPR the ability to promote the necessity of fair elections in general, a topic that was still far from a central agenda in August 2011.

A JUST RUSSIA

A Just Russia is a party created as a reaction to other political forces rather than an independent political institution that arose from either bottom-up support from the electorate (as with the Communists and LDPR) or top-down forma- tion from the Kremlin (United Russia). Rather, A Just Russia in 2011 repre- sented a group of leaders and smaller parties that had joined in a coalition to create critical mass as an electoral bloc and just passed the 7 percent barrier for seat allocation in the Duma in 2007. Indeed, the website for A Just Russia in August 2011 appeared to reflect a political coalition rather than help to create a unified party profile. The website itself is perhaps closest in appearance to that of the Communist Party, with a rather crowded, Web 1.0 appearance. The page used yellow, red, and orange, giving it a very distinctive appearance from the crisper red, white, and blue of the United Russia page. Across the top of the page was a Soviet-style party icon, with two detailed photo-icons below linking to the Just Russia deputies. Also on the top of the fairly cluttered home page was a series of Soviet-style headshots of the party leaders. Uniquely among the central party websites in Russia, there was an "international" link situated prominently on the home page (the top right-hand corner). There were links to a site map, WAP, PDA, and RSS on the top of the home page, although the links to older ICT technologies and the dearth of links to Web 2.0 features made the party seem rather old fashioned in web terms. There was, however, a rolling news headline feed just below the mug shots, although only one headline was scrolling past on August 18, 2011, when the analysis was performed.

The Just Russia website could be considered distinctive in two ways to the three party websites discussed above. First, there was more concern and attention regarding the upcoming elections in a way that was missing from the websites of the more popular and established Duma parties. By mid-August 2011, Just Russia already had uploaded a full electoral program for the December 2011 Duma elections. In addition, it was clear that the party was concerned about being a target of negative campaigning, given that the party had long since fallen out with United Russia. Just Russia party leader Sergei Mironov warned his party's congress on August 18, 2011, that United Russia would wage a dirty (*gryaznaya*) campaign against Just Russia and her deputies.[21] In addition, the somewhat fragmented nature of the Just Russia party was obvious from the way in which the website featured party "partners," both through scrolling promotion across the bottom of the home page and via the "partners" link under "party."[22] There are 50 partners listed, who alternatively appeared on the bottom of the home page, including personal websites of some of the party leaders, a party forum site, Mironov's LiveJournal page, and links to groups such as the Russian Union for the Development of Healthy Children[23] as well as links to Rodina, another former political party.

Just Russia also was distinctive for delineating the rights of party members, as opposed to a focus on the responsibilities and terms of membership. In addition, Just Russia promoted use of home-grown web communication tools rather than links to large, branded Web 2.0 products such as Facebook, VKontakte, and Twitter. Indeed, analysis for this project could not find a Just Russia Twitter account at all and no major[24] Web 2.0 links were found in the coding on August 18, 2011. Rather, the social-media aspect of the party was organized via a Just Russia Online website at http://www.spravedlivo-online.ru/. While the website featured Web 2.0 tools such as forums and blogging, it would lead party supporters into an internet cul-de-sac of sorts, without the ability to exploit the huge networks from the major social-networking and blogging sites used by the general population of Russian voters. It would be interesting to know why the party leaders chose a type of exclusive online interaction space, as opposed to bringing discussion about the party and its activity to a far broader audience.

Website Traffic for Russian Political Parties

In an analysis of website traffic using Alexa statistics (www.alexa.com) in August 2011, it was clear that the United Russia website had much more traffic than the other three party websites. This is a distinct development from the older version of the United Russia website (www.edin.ru, now relabeled as http://old.er.ru/).[25] Alexa statistics revealed some interesting facts about the relative popularity of party websites in Russia. First, it should be noted that the United Russia party website was far more popular than the website devoted to the United Russia Duma fraction (www.er.duma.ru, defunct as of August 22, 2012). Neither website was particularly popular in general, but this parallels the relatively low use of political websites when compared with entertainment or commerce websites worldwide. On August 9, 2011, the United Russia site (er.ru) was ranked 2,621 in Russia, with 391 sites linking in according to Alexa. Much like the relative unpopularity of the Labour Party website in Britain (when compared with fringe parties such as the British National Party; see Oates, 2010), it is arguable that Russian citizens do not need to turn to the internet to get basic information about the United Russia party, policies, or personalities. The main media outlets, particularly state-run television, cover the ruling party and Putin as its leader extensively. Also, it is difficult to be too optimistic about the audience interest in the United Russia website when the most popular search term affiliated with the page was "the party of thieves and swindlers" (*partiya zhulikov i vorov*) on August 19, 2011, on the Russian search engine Yandex.[26] This also suggests that people might be somewhat pragmatic that what they find on the United Russia website would be more propaganda than useful insights into the running of the Russian state.

When compared with traffic to the United Russia website, it was clear that the Communist Party website attracted a similar amount of traffic over the same time period. Despite the Communists' relative lack of Duma seats or affiliation with the presidency, the Communist website was a relatively popular *party* website. This might be due to the dearth of coverage of this serious, long-term opposition movement in the traditional mass media in Russia. While the Communists may compete fairly equally on the Russian internet with United Russia—although as web statistics suggest, United Russia held its own and even generally outstripped the Communists in online popularity in the months before August 2011—the websites of the two remaining Duma parties discussed in this chapter did not even register in a comparison with United Russian over the six months prior to August 2011.[27]

Web Link Analysis of Russian Political Parties

The study of web links is able to provide a new layer to content analysis schemes by showing us how websites are located within the broader information sphere created by the internet. However, web link analysis using tools such as IssueCrawler (www.issuecrawler.net) was problematic for this group of party websites. In order to create a useful list of seed crawls, one needs to find outlinks from party web pages. As United Russia has very few outlinks, it was difficult to create a meaningful crawl. Attempts to provide a list of seed URLs that were party websites and major media websites also failed, with the media websites quickly overwhelming the party website links due to the far greater popularity of the media sites.

However, a web link analysis performed by Ali Fisher at Mappa Mundi for an earlier project (Oates and Fisher, 2011) that attempted to look at the political spectrum created by party and other websites showed an interesting online political "spectrum," albeit with a limited sample of political websites.[28] This analysis was particularly focused on the online informational architecture between United Russia and the CPRF as the best-known opposition group. The seed URLs included A Just Russia (spravedlivo.ru) as an elite-drive spin out from United Russia, two youth organizations linked to United Russia (Nashi or 'Ours' and Molgvardia or 'Youth Guard) as well as an opposition group campaigning for the right to free assembly promised in Article 31 of the Russian constitution (Strategy-31).[29] The inclusion of the youth groups and Strategy-31 was an attempt to see whether these groups overlapped with political parties.

The map of links showed that United Russia (er.ru) and the Communists (KPRF.ru) shared very different informational locations on the internet. This suggests that the structure of online material creates very distinctive information pathways for supporters of different political parties. This contrasts with the findings of the 2010 Berkman report on the political blogosphere in Russia that found blogs did not fall into oppositional camps, although Berkman looked at a wide range of blogs rather than a sample of party websites. However, it is interesting to note the differences, in that via an examination of the web presence of the central political parties (generated by their own web content) there would seem to be very distinctive online "camps" for United Russia and the CPRF. This would suggest that parties themselves, via their web page content and their web linkages, are not helping to create a "public sphere" for party politics in Russia in the Habermasian sense (Brandenburg, 2006). It is also interesting to note that the youth organizations, both linked to United Russia, were closer in terms of online geography to their related party. In addition, A Just Russia was located between United Russia and the CPRF, which would be expected of a party that began as a top-down party of power but then shifted toward a more populist, socialist focus in party documents. It is clear from the Just Russia website that the party no longer viewed itself as a friend or partner of United Russia as it braced for a propaganda attack from the party of power in the upcoming elections. Finally, it is significant to note that Strategy-31 was not well linked with any of the parties or groups mentioned. This would suggest that the problems of a lack of cooperation among opposition groups continued to pervade Russian party politics.

Conclusions

This chapter began with an attempt to measure whether the internet can bring fundamental change to parties in non-democratic states—or whether the internet itself is shaped by national party institutions. What this study of the content of four Russian political party websites has shown is that parties in this non-democratic context are using the internet in different manners. In many ways, this use reflects the historic development of the parties themselves. As the party of power, United Russia's website reflected government developments and further merged the state with the dominant party in the Russian Duma. The Communists used their website to promote their view of society and to publicize events, including social protests, which were typically ignored in the mainstream media. While the internet was just another channel for the dominance of communication by United Russia, the online sphere offered the Communists a more valuable communication tool because they were vilified or excluded to a large degree in the traditional mass media. The website of the LDPR reflected the idiosyncratic and leader-oriented nature of the party itself, with the emphasis on Zhirinovsky and policy presenting down-to-earth messages for the electorate. There was element of opposition here, though, through the videos that claim corruption or unfairness on the part of elites. Finally, the Just Russia website reflected the nature of the party itself, a coalition among a number of forces that faced the December 2011 elections with a justifiable degree of trepidation.

The examination of party websites addresses only one aspect of the Russian political communication sphere. In particular, this study has not provided an analysis of "second spaces" of political communication on social-networking and blogging sites in particular (although acknowledging how parties link to these platforms from their websites). In addition, there has not been a discussion of the lively Russian blogosphere itself, which does engage in political discussion (and political humor) to a large degree (Etling et al., 2010). However, this discussion has contributed to the ongoing study of the ability of the internet to contribute to communicative democracy in some important aspects. In addition to proof that the nature of political parties is reflected—rather than transformed—by the internet, this chapter also has suggested a new way of measuring web communication tools in comparative perspective. It has posited that web link analysis is an important aspect of thinking about the position of parties within the internet information space, an aspect that cannot be captured by content analysis or even web traffic reports alone. Finally, it is hoped that this chapter—in addition to adding to the study of the Russian internet in this book—has contributed to thinking about the broader role of the internet in democratization. The findings here suggest that while the internet offers opportunities for democratization via the establishment of a party system, they must be understood within the specific constraints of a national political system. This would suggest some important issues in democratization for states such as Egypt, in that both the new Egyptian government and the international community should not place too much reliance on the mere presence of political parties. Rather, it is critical that the parties function as a way to interpret the will of the people rather than as a tool for elite consolidation of power as the central power has operated in Russia.

6

Parents and Patients

Online Health and Fairness Campaigns in Russia

Unlike the dramatic events as the internet played a key role in organizing resistance to authoritarian rule in the Arab Spring, there was relatively little overt evidence that the internet was transforming the political sphere in Russia by mid-2011. There was more concern that powerful state entities such as the United Russia party would be able to adopt the internet as an additional tool in its top-down political agenda. There were a multitude of relatively small opposition groups and blogs, but none that seemed to provide significant political capital for unified opposition to the Kremlin. Many different political ideas and opinions were being mooted in the active Russian blogosphere, but most seemed to be broadcasting—rather than aggregating—opinions. However, there were cases that provided evidence that the internet was changing the fundamental nature of politics in the country by allowing citizens to articulate their grievances and successfully demand change in a particular aspect of Russian life: health care.

The successful campaigns analyzed in this chapter were linked to significant online involvement within a relatively narrow segment of the population, including parents of children with specific disabilities and dialysis patients. However, the experience of these movements showed that Russians could and did use the internet to aggregate interests and actions within certain specific parameters. The key question is whether once Russians learned that the internet could bring them justice on a small scale, did this make them willing and able to seek justice on a larger scale, both online and off? Despite the lack of a coherent opposition in Russia by mid-2011, the experience of the Arab Spring shows that the sheer speed and power of online information aggregation often empowers citizens in new ways unforeseen by leaders and foreign observers alike. What is at issue in this chapter is whether these relatively small-scale, successful ways of using the online sphere to challenge entrenched attitudes and power relationships were emblematic of the ways in which Russian citizens were empowering themselves in much broader ways. Were Russians becoming empowered "below the radar" of traditional political venues such as parties and mass demonstrations prior to the December 2011 protests?

This chapter will analyze two case studies that demonstrate successful online aggregation and action in Russia: children with genetic disabilities and provision of kidney dialysis. The treatment of children with genetic differences became particularly politicized, to a large degree via online activism in Russia, after a tabloid journalist suggested that children with disabilities could be killed at birth. The chapter looks at reaction to this controversy from websites linked to support for families of children with Down syndrome and a rarer genetic disability called mucopolysaccharidosis (MPS). In the case of MPS, the parents also were successful at compelling the Russian government to pay for very expensive drugs for their children, an activity that was linked to the online network later enraged by comments about euthanasia for infants with disabilities. The other case study analyzes the internet activity relating to the successful campaign to reestablish a facility for kidney dialysis, the closure of which had essentially condemned dialysis patients to a slow death. The case studies were chosen because they represented compelling evidence through user-generated and other online content that the internet had played a key role in successful campaigns to challenge state authorities and bring benefits to citizens.

Here it is reasonable to ask whether it would be more fruitful to study some of the larger political movements prior to the 2011–12 protests in Russia, including the demonstrations over the Khimki forest development near Moscow or the Strategy-31 protests that mobilized regular demonstrations against illegal repression of public meetings. In part, the decision to focus on the health-care issues was simply practical, in that reviews of web content relating to political causes such as Khimki and Strategy-31 did not generate grassroots comments in which people discussed the idea of rights. In addition, there was a theoretical reason, in that evidence from earlier studies (including Lonkila, 2008, and the Union of the Committee of Soldiers' Mothers of Russia) suggested that the most emotive issue of rights was often linked to family and health in Russia, a prism through which Russians appeared to be more willing and able to discuss their relationship to power structures in their society. The idea was that while elites might be quite comfortable talking about "post-modern" issues such as the environment, a more emotive and popular view of grassroots discussion could be found on websites dealing with health and family issues. Certainly, prior to the December 2011 protests, there was relatively little evidence of political outcomes from online discussion and aggregation. Yet evidence of small triumphs and political transformation could be found via these health discussions.

This chapter considers three types of evidence relating to health protests in Russia: (1) how online information and discussion frames personal health issues in politicized ways; (2) the measurable links between online engagement and offline activity such as protests, legal challenges, provision of services, or demonstrations; and (3) the role of online social entrepreneurs in creating internet capital that translates to offline action. The chapter employs online research tools including web link analysis to identify the location of significant online content; quantitative analysis of information provision on websites; and analysis of discourse among users. The research found that the internet can serve as a key conduit for encouraging both parents and patients to think of seeking help in political, rather than personal, terms. In particular, there would appear to be a strong element of "parental politics" and "patient politics," in that these groups were willing to challenge the Russian state when they felt it had failed in its duty to provide care for their children, themselves, or fellow citizens. Overall, this analysis provides compelling evidence of the way in which online political empowerment was occurring prior to the December 2011 protest.

The analysis for this chapter suggests that online political action can be better understood by looking for evidence of political discussions across a range of platforms and issues outside of standard party politics—and watching how these nascent political networks can be activated at surprising speed by the combination of catalyzing events and online social entrepreneurs. This chapter argues that the future of understanding the political role of the internet is in coming to know the online collective consciousness: The internet as a political force is not about particular websites, blog posts, social-networking groups, or specific bloggers per se, but about comprehending the way in which the internet fosters social consciousness that develops across, around, and among web platforms. This is particularly useful in understanding states such as Russia in which there were few effective democratic institutions or voices for the public in mainstream politics by 2011. It helps us to understand how citizens might have been "rewired" prior to the protests that began in December 2011. In addition, this strand of the research implements a methodology that can be used as a template for identifying and coding material relating to political action online in a range of contexts.

Health and Politics in Russia

Some of the most vocal complaints in Russia are linked to the problems of state provision of services in the post-Soviet era. The way in which Russian citizens struggle to obtain state benefits highlights the changed role of the state from the Soviet period, when it served as the central distribution point of all benefits, to the more chaotic and uncertain distribution of benefits in the Russian Federation. Many social and economic entitlements that were held during the Soviet period have been—or are perceived to have been—lost (Chandler, 2008). This has resulted in a need for citizens to work actively to claim entitlements and an increasing reliance on individual resources to access specific benefits or, more broadly put, to access what citizens deserve by right. This real or perceived loss of social and economic rights has resulted in a variety of strategies to secure access to these entitlements. In Turbine's (2007a) study of women's perceptions and access to human rights in Russia, women spoke in terms of the violation of "everyday rights," most of which focused on the loss of social and economic rights as a consequence of the increasing costs and the creeping privatization of key services including health care, education, and childcare.

While Turbine's additional study (2007b) showed there was a high level of awareness of the violation of everyday rights, there was less certainty as to how to access rights. A number of strategies were identified and often used in conjunction (i.e., mixing informal measures such as seeking advice from friends with formal approaches such as writing to local officials). These included many strategies that have already been well-documented in the literature on everyday welfare in the post-Soviet period, including the continuing use of informal networks, connections within key services, and direct appeals to the administration (Pickup and White, 2003; Salmi, 2003; Patico, 2002; Lonkila, 1997). Turbine found that internet use was one measure within a range of strategies that Russian women used in attempts to exercise their rights (2007b). For example, some respondents discussed using the internet to source information on a variety of issues including cases of unfair dismissal from the workplace, consumer rights, and citizenship status, as well as to share information and advice on internet forums. However, this use of the internet was embedded within a broader approach to seeking legal advice, mainly from friends with relevant training or formal legal consultations and cases. What this shows is that the internet was domesticated, to a degree, to fit the ongoing strategies and needs of the Russian population.

Case Studies

One of the issues to reach relative prominence in Russia in early 2010 was societal attitude and treatment of children born with disabilities, a discussion sparked by a tabloid newspaper article suggesting that parents should be able to kill these children at birth. The analysis of this movement focuses on Downside Up for support of families of children with Down syndrome as well as two websites relating to MPS, a genetic disorder that causes systematic cell destruction, disability, and premature death. In 2010 the groups differed online in terms of domestic web linkages, history, and format, yet across their web presence there was compelling evidence of politicization of health and disability issues. At the same time, some of the discussion about the issues suggests that the conceptualization of rights relating to people with disabilities was linked to post-Soviet notions of rights as protection of the vulnerable rather than the championing of humanity. However, a rising political voice—that of parents of vulnerable children—could be heard.

Down syndrome was chosen for the study as it is a common, well-recognized chromosomal deviation that occurs in approximately one in every 800 live births.[1] Individuals with Down syndrome have 47 chromosomes instead of the usual 46 and the condition causes developmental delays. While people with Down syndrome are often at risk from serious physical problems such as heart disease or celiac disease, they have a longer life expectancy and fewer severe medical problems than those with MPS. The rate of Down syndrome births would suggest that about 1,900 boys and girls are born with it every year in Russia. The second online community on Runet studied for this chapter is related to support and advocacy for families with children born with MPS, of which one variant is Hunter syndrome. According to the U.S. National MPS Society, MPS is caused by a genetic variation that is generally inherited through recessive genes. Individuals with MPS do not produce specific enzymes and are unable to flush toxins out of the body. MPS causes progressive damage in the body and a limited life expectancy, although the severity varies depending on the type of MPS. There is no cure, although enzyme replacement treatment continues to improve and offers significant help for the condition (www.mpssociety. org). Physical and mental challenges for people with MPS vary. The U.S. MPS Society estimates that one in 25,000 births in the United States results in some form of MPS. Although much rarer than Down syndrome, MPS advocacy was chosen for this study because of a catalytic event that illuminated an ongoing online campaign for the Russian government to pay for proper treatment for all children with Hunter syndrome, one type of MPS.

In December 2009, journalist Aleksandr Nikonov published an article ("Finish Them Off, So They Don't Suffer") in the Russian tabloid *Speed-Info*. The article argued that parents should be able to have the option of "post-natal abortion" to kill newborns diagnosed as having defects at birth. This article gained prominence in the national and international community when disability activists Snezhana Mitina (whose son has Hunter syndrome) and Svetlana Shtarkova (whose son was born with disabilities), filed a complaint with the Russian Union of Journalists against Nikonov and his paper.[2] The story was amplified by reporting from Radio Liberty, which hosted one of Shtarkova's blogs about her son on its Russian website. While the Union of Journalists did rule that Nikonov's article "bordered on extremism" and asked the tabloid to publish a rebuttal by Mitina and Shtarkova, the journalist himself was unapologetic.[3] Both of the mothers who brought the complaint to the Union of Journalists had been active online. While Shtarkova maintained several blogs about her three-year-old son, Mitina waged a successful, four-year campaign to get the Russian government to fund extremely expensive medication for Hunter syndrome children in Russia. In particular, Mitina used the internet to locate a sufficient number of families of children with Hunter syndrome to justify the provision of the treatment.[4] Mitina also had a blog and chaired an organization to champion the cause of those with Hunter syndrome.[5]

While the MPS and Down syndrome supporters' discussions were galvanized by the tabloid article suggesting euthanasia for newborns with genetic disabilities, a dialysis patient forum was catalyzed by the planned closure of a treatment ward. The First Clinical Hospital in Rostov-on-Don, a city of about a million people in European Russia, informed 11 dialysis patients on June 1, 2010, that they would no longer be able to receive treatment at the federal hospital. These patients were chosen for exclusion from treatment because they did not work in particular professions, such as transport, that were deemed to be of importance to the region. According to the hospital, the regional health ministry would no longer pay for the procedure and the hospital could not transfer funds from other budgets to cover the cost. Most of the action discussed in this description takes place on an online forum for patients with kidney problems, started by Moscow doctor Alexei Denisov.[6] As became clear immediately from the discussion—and subsequent coverage by the traditional mass media—the closure of the facility was not just an *inconvenience* for the 11 dialysis patients. They would be unable to get treatment at any other dialysis facility in the city as there was no space available. The posts made the point that the removal of the service would likely prove fatal to the patients, who refused to be put off with duplicitous arguments that they could survive with less regular dialysis or that the hospital could do nothing for them. In the course of the discussion about the 11 patients in Rostov-on-Don, it became clear that many dialysis patients across Russia were experiencing problems with both quantity and quality of dialysis treatment, with online reports from people who said relatives had died while waiting to start treatment or died because their treatment was inadequate.

Locating the Issue Discussion in Runet: Search Engines and Web Link Analysis

Once the case study is chosen, how does one find the relevant online community? The online content for this analysis was identified (with a combination of Yandex searches and web link analysis) after traditional media coverage had highlighted the location and central players in both the controversy surrounding children with genetic disabilities and the dialysis threat. Indeed, the discussion of the mass media coverage and links to it were part of the broader "content" of the forum. Once the user-generated content location was identified, native-language researchers coded the individual forum posts for a range of factors, including the mention of rights, benefits, the type of arguments put forward, and actions suggested (see Appendix for coding frame).

This research, carried out in July and August 2010, started by searching the name of the conditions (in Russian) on the most popular Russian search engine (Yandex.ru). The word searches were in Russian for Down syndrome (*Syndrom Dauna*) and mucopolysaccharidosis (*Mukopolisakharidoz*).[7] The project then used web link analysis from the top-ranked specific sites that were Russia-specific (i.e., not Wikipedia) to graphically map the flow of the internet traffic around the issues. In the case of Hunter syndrome, this was www.mpssociety.ru. For Down syndrome, this was www.downsideup.org (see Figure 6.1: Web Link Analysis for Downside Up).[8] Initially, the search for mucopolysaccharidosis (in Russian) returned www.mpssociety.ru (see Figure 6.2: Web Link Analysis for MPS Society). However, the qualitative analysis of www.mpssociety.ru showed that its homepage had become static since 2006, while Mitina was heavily involved in posting on the website's forum with very recent responses (some in August 2010). She was directing traffic to her own website on Hunter syndrome at www.mps-russia.org, so this also was included in the analysis (see Figure 6.3: Web Link Analysis for Hunter Syndrome Group). Mitina's site was one of the top returns in the Yandex search engine for the search Hunter syndrome in Russian, although her site did address the broader range of MPS.

As Bruns points out (2007, NP), web link analysis parallels the way in which search engines crawl the web to establish page ranking returns for searches. A web crawl is a very powerful tool that allows social scientists to follow the flow of links (and, by assumption, the movement of information and communication) across various locations in the online sphere. This gives an idea of a particular website's "level of centrality" (Bruns). The arrows distinguish between origins and destinations for web traffic. One would assume that proximity between nodes would suggest common causes, values, or beliefs. However, as Bruns points out, web link analysis can only show us the map, and not the actual traffic, along the routes. That being said, the map alone is particularly helpful in revealing the most common paths and directions relating to a particular issue (as defined by a search term and origins in an issue-related web space) online.

The web link map for Downside Up showed heavy linkages within Runet itself. The starting URL is downsideup.org, which listed itself as a non-commercial Russian organization and, despite the transliterated English name, is Russian-based. The organization "lends its support to families, states and non-profit

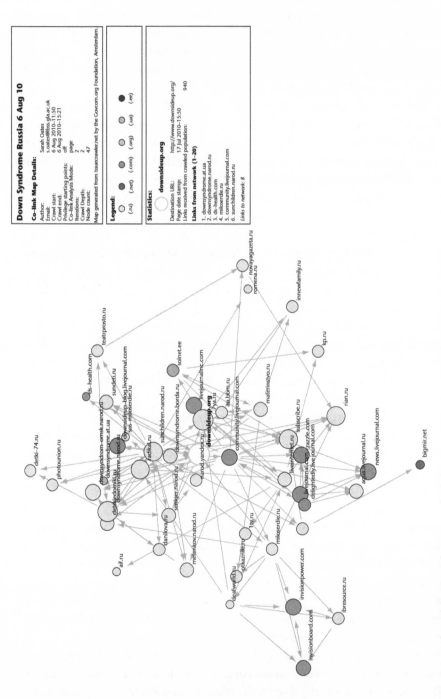

Down Syndrome Russia 6 Aug 10

Co-link Map Details:

Author:	Sarah Oates
Email:	s.oates@lbss.gla.ac.uk
Crawl start:	6 Aug 2010-11:50
Crawl end:	6 Aug 2010-15:21
Privilege starting points:	off
Co-link Analysis Mode:	page
Iterations:	2
Crawl Depth:	2
Node count:	47

Map generated from Issuecrawler.net by the Govcom.org Foundation, Amsterdam.

Legend:

(.ru)   (.net)   (.com)   (.org)   (.ua)   (.ee)

Statistics:

downsideup.org

Destination URL:	http://www.downsideup.org/
Page date stamp:	17 Jul 2010-15:50
Links received from crawled population:	940

Links from network (1–20)

1. downsyndrome.at.ua
2. downsyndrome.narod.ru
3. ds-health.com
4. miloserdie.ru
5. community.livejournal.com
6. sunchildren.narod.ru

Links to network: 8

Figure 6.1 Web Link Analysis for Downside Up. Source: Author's research and output of IssueCrawler (www.issuecrawler.net).

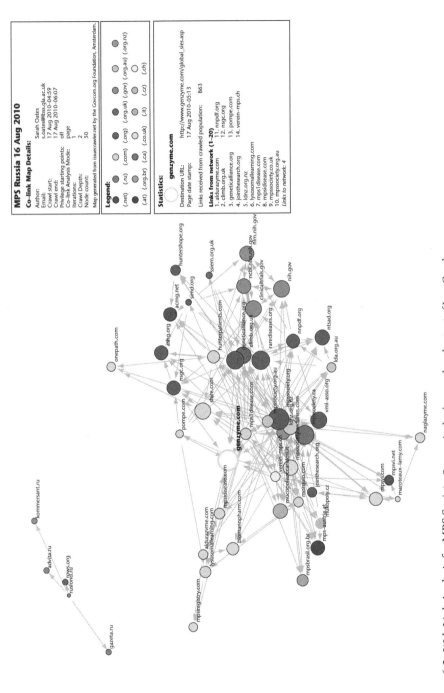

MPS Russia 16 Aug 2010

Co–link Map Details:

Author:	Sarah Oates
Email:	s.oates@lbss.gla.ac.uk
Crawl start:	17 Aug 2010–04:59
Crawl end:	17 Aug 2010–06:07
Privilege starting points:	off
Co–link Analysis Mode:	page
Iterations:	1
Crawl Depth:	2
Node count:	50

Map generated from issuecrawler.net by the Govcom.org Foundation, Amsterdam.

Legend:

(.net) (.ru) (.com) (.org) (.org.uk) (.gov) (.org.au) (.org.nz)

(.at) (.org.br) (.ca) (.co.uk) (.it) (.cz) (.ch)

Statistics:

genzyme.com

Destination URL:	http://www.genzyme.com/global_sites.asp
Page date stamp:	17 Aug 2010–05:13
Links received from crawled population:	863

Links from network (1–20)
1. alduraymne.com
2. climib.org.uk
3. geneticalliance.org
4. jointhesearch.org
5. ldnz.org.nz
6. lysosomallearning.com
7. mps1disease.com
8. mpsdisease.com
9. mpssociety.co.uk
10. mpssociety.org.au

11. nnpdf.org
12. nsgc.org
13. pompe.com
14. verein–mps.ch

Links to network: 4

Figure 6.2 Web Link Analysis for MPS Society. Source: Author's research and output of IssueCrawler (www.issuecrawler.net).

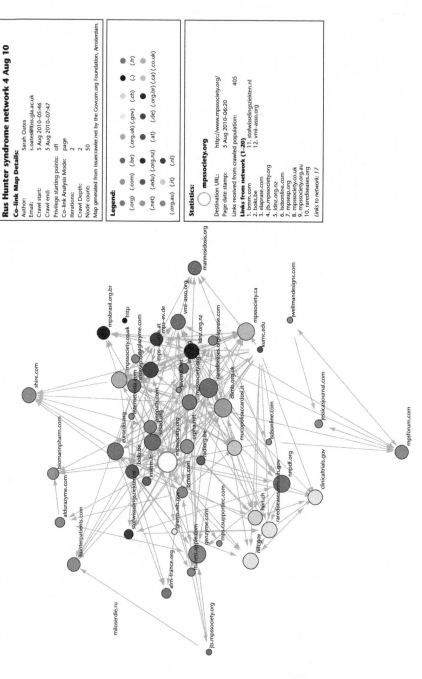

Rus Hunter syndrome network 4 Aug 10

Co–link Map Details:

Author:	Sarah Oates
Email:	s.oates@lbss.gla.ac.uk
Crawl start:	5 Aug 2010–05:46
Crawl end:	5 Aug 2010–07:47
Privilege starting points:	off
Co–link Analysis Mode:	page
Iterations:	2
Crawl Depth:	2
Node count:	50

Map generated from Issuecrawler.net by the Govcom.org Foundation, Amsterdam.

Legend:

(.org) (.com) (.be) (.org.uk) (.gov) (.ch) (.) (.fr)

(.net) (.edu) (.org.nz) (.at) (.de) (.org.br) (.ca) (.co.uk)

(.org.au) (.it) (.nl)

Statistics:

○ **mpssociety.org**

Destination URL:	http://www.mpssociety.org/
Page date stamp:	5 Aug 2010–06:20
Links received from crawled population:	405

Links from network (1–20)

1. bmm.com
2. boks.be
3. elaprase.com
4. jts.mpssociety.org
5. ldnz.org.nz
6. ladsonline.com
7. mpsesp.org
8. mpssociety.co.uk
9. mpssociety.org.au
10. rarediseases.org

11. stofwisselingsziekten.nl
12. vml–asso.org

Links to network: 17

Figure 6.3 Web Link Analysis for Hunter Syndrome Group. Source: Author's research and output of IssueCrawler (www.issuecrawler.net).

organizations in the instruction, training and integration into society of children with Down Syndrome, as well as positively influences the relation of society to people with disabilities."[9] Many of the central nodes in the web link map for Down syndrome in Russia are general blogging/web hosting or social-networking sites (such as narod.yandex.ru, livejournalinc.com, community.livejournal.com, and downsideup-blog.livejournal.com). There also were links to other Russian Down syndrome websites (such as sunchildren.narod.ru, downsyndrom-omsk.narod.ru, and downsyndrome.narod.ru),[10] Russian groups linked to charities or groups for other conditions (deafworld.ru, miloserdie.ru, detskie-domiki.ru), and some links to traditional mass media.

In contrast, the websites surrounding mpssociety.ru were linked much more heavily to non-Runet domains (although it should be noted that .ru is not an obligatory extension for a Russian organization). The links for MPS reflected interest in medical, rather than social or charitable, information. A central node defined by the link analysis was genzyme.org, a website for a biotechnology company that focuses on treatment for rare genetic disorders. Indeed, the web link map showed that traffic around the Russian MPS site was heavily defined by traffic to pharmaceutical and other informational sites (including www.mps.org that belongs to the National MPS Organization based in North Carolina). The web link analysis for Mitina's organization for Hunter syndrome showed a very interesting phenomenon—despite the fact that Mitina had established a separate, albeit similar domain (www.mps-russia.org), the web links also pulled users back to the U.S. MPS site (www.mpssociety.org). In fact, this site was the center of this particular information space and, unsurprisingly, the pattern of web linkages was similar to the MPS web link map with a large presence of international drug companies. There were a lack of links to generic online communication platforms (such as ones present on the web link map for Down syndrome), but a qualitative review did show a lively internal forum on both www.mps-russia.org and www.mpssociety.ru. It also revealed an impressive library of information on the original MPS (Russia) site, which could explain why it continued to rank so highly despite lacking new content for years. It would appear that the need for medical information for desperately ill children drives the MPS users to a range of international sites, while the Downside Up site was working within the Russian system to improve the social care and attitude toward individuals with Down syndrome.

The most striking aspect about the web link analysis map for MPS was the lack of Russian domain sites. Although activists report their blogging activity as important, it did not register on the map of linkages. Rather, it would appear that most of the links were scientific, educational, and non-Russian in origin. While there were an array of sites dedicated to knowledge and support relating to the syndrome, there was no presence of social-networking, blogging, or video-sharing platforms (with the exception of a relatively prominent node at itunes.apple.com). There was a small constellation of pharmaceutical sites, suggesting the presence of information or advertising for drugs that treat the condition. While in a sense all of this information would be useful to those interested in MPS, the web link map did not suggest much citizen/user-generated content. The controversy over the tabloid article suggesting "post-natal abortion" did not seem to leave permanent prominence or linkages to the blogs of the activists. A web link analysis of the kidney dialysis forum showed that this discussion essentially remained on LiveJournal, with little evidence that major media organizations, NGOs, or others were linking in or out of the central discussion thread (See Figure 6.4: Web Link Analysis of Dialysis Forum Relating to Closure Crisis in Rostov-on-Don).

Coding Analysis

What sort of information is offered to users of these websites? What elements of the information could be considered political in nature? What opportunities are there for many-to-many engagement on the central websites related to Down syndrome and MPS (the kidney dialysis group is not discussed in this section, as its activity was based mostly in a forum as opposed to spread over different websites)? By measuring the features of the websites for Down syndrome and MPS, it is clear that there was a fairly wide variation in information and resource provision among four different groups. (see Table 6.1: Quantitative Analysis of Health Condition Websites). While all of the websites offered article archives, medical research news, and detailed information on the condition, this was where significant overlap among the websites ended: downsideup.org was a complex and sophisticated website that was updated regularly during the analysis period (July and August 2010). It had detailed information about its activities, including extensive annual financial reports. The Downside Up website also offered information on the organization's structure, values, ideology, manifesto, policies, services, future strategy, and news coverage, as well as an archive of professional newsletters. This was unsurprising in that the annual report showed that Downside Up raised more than $1 million (USD) in 2009 and listed a relatively large staff. It launched from a distinctly modern, uncluttered front page that offered the reader three main alternatives—giving people a choice of "I want to support," "I want to say something," or "I want to find out more about Down syndrome." These three choices, in fact, defined the overall emphasis and function of the website, which was balanced among providing information to families of children with Down syndrome; advocating for better treatment and understanding of people with Down syndrome; and generating support for their organization.

Figure 6.4 Web Link Analysis of Dialysis Forum Relating to Closure Crisis in Rostov-on-Don.

Source: Author's research and output of IssueCrawler (www.issuecrawler.net).

Table 6.1 Quantitative Analysis of Health Condition Websites

Feature	Score (1 = present, 2 = absent)			
	Down Syndrome 1	*Down Syndrome 2*	*MPS*	*Hunter Syndrome*
URL	Downsideup.ru narod.ru	Sunchildren	Mpssociety.ru	Mps-russia.org
History/foundation	1	0	1 (not detailed)	0
Structure	1	0	0	0
Values/ideology/manifesto	1	1	0	1
Policies and service	1	0	0	0
Future strategy	1	0	0	0
News coverage	1	0	0	1
Newsletters	1	0	0	0
Media releases (i.e., speeches, statements, interview transcripts, conferences)	1	0	0	0
Staff/organizer	1	0	1	1
Some pages in English	1	0	0	0
Event calendar (prospective or retrospective) updated in last year	0[1]	0	0	1
Conference/annual meeting information	1	0	0	0

Table 6.1 (continued)

Feature	Score (1 = present, 2 = absent)			
	Down Syndrome 1	Down Syndrome 2	MPS	Hunter Syndrome
Frequently asked questions	1[2]	0	0	1
Article archive or library	1	1	1	1
Link to internal forum from home page	0	1	1	1
Link to internal forum from elsewhere	0	0	0	0
Link to external forum from home page	1	1	0	0
Link to internal forum from elsewhere	0	1	0	0
Funders	1	0	0	0
Annual financial report	1	0	0	0
Profiles/diaries of children with condition	0	1	1	1
Statement/diaries from parents of children (not on forum)	0	1	1	1
Sample document for use with health authorities	0	0	1	1
Presentation of medical research	1	1	1	1
Details on condition	1	1	1	1
Laws/legal material	0	1	1	1
SUBTOTAL	17	9	10	12

continued

Table 6.1 (continued)

Feature	Score (1 = present, 2 = absent)			
	Down Syndrome 1	Down Syndrome 2	MPS	Hunter Syndrome
	Resource generation			
Feature	Score			
	Down Syndrome 1	Down Syndrome 2	MPS	Hunter Syndrome
(i) Donation index 0–4	4	0	0	1
(ii) Merchandise index 0–4	0	0	0	0
(iv) Associate membership/volunteer solicitation 1 = present 0 = absent	1	0	0	0
SUBTOTAL	5	0	0	1
TOTAL	22	9	10	13

[1] Can be found in News section.
[2] But not linked from home page or easy to find.

Code: For each index (1) reference made and postal address listed; (2) download form and post; (3) online enquiry (specific email or online form); (4) online transaction (0) no references made.

Source: Author's research. The coding scheme is modified from Gibson and Ward (2003). This analysis also included a second Down syndrome website (sunchildren.narod.ru) because over the course of August 2010 it often outranked Downside Up in Yandex.

The profile of the organization was very clear from the information presented online, which told the story of its founding by a British man with a Down syndrome niece. He and his family were moved to found Downside Up in Russia, in which 85 percent of families turn over Down syndrome children to state care at birth (according to Downside Up). Finally, the more political nature of the organization was apparent in a quote provided on the website by Russian journalist Valerii Panyushkin reminding us that "children absolutely have the right to life."

The Sun Children website was more overtly political and challenging of the Russian custom of turning over newborn children with Down syndrome to state orphanages at birth. However, Sun Children was a difficult organization to assess because, as reflected by the scores on Table 6.1, there was no history, structure, or even contact name listed. Perhaps most tellingly, the site did not ask for donations to its organization, but rather directed site users to donate to other organizations (with Downside Up the first one listed). Hence, while the Sun Children site was providing an important voice and forum—it had a section of photos and letters written by Down syndrome individuals as well as glossy pictures of Down syndrome models from a Spanish campaign—it was impossible to tell if this was the work of an individual or a particular group. It should be noted, however, that there was some solid evidence of both online interest aggregation and the politicization of health issues on the Sun Children website. This included a copy of a letter to President Medvedev to complain about the *Speed-Info* article that was electronically signed by 1,577 people as of March 10, 2010.

The MPS website offered a more amateur, yet quite touching, face of disability. The organization, which appeared to be completely volunteer and spread across Russia (judging by the list of names and addresses that appeared on the site) focused on the personal side of treatment. In a section called "Ours" (*Nashi*), there were profiles of children with MPS, with details of their treatment (and sometimes notification of their death). In "Mamas and Papas," there were diaries and statements from parents about coping with MPS. There was a very detailed section on the syndrome itself, with many links to scholarly references and pharmaceutical companies, which reflected the difficulty for parents in getting treatment and information on this relatively rare condition. The website provided image files of letters to officials to help parents negotiate Russian bureaucracy in dealing with a rare and painful health condition for their children. Thus, while Downside Up reflected an organization focused on helping individual families cope with the challenges of raising a child with Down syndrome in a hostile environment, the MPS society was centered on supporting parents in attempting to deal with a typically fatal condition in a chaotic, overburdened health bureaucracy. While the issue of social acceptance of children with disabilities was clearly a part of the MPS group, it was secondary on the website to the pressing need to find effective treatment.

Beyond the differences shown in information and resource provision, the MPS website revealed another side to the nature of internet communication. Although the "news" section had not been updated since 2006 (despite being on the home page), the forum section was up to date and very active (discussion below). Of particular interest was that the main voice of the forum was that of Mitina, one of the mothers who brought the complaint about the *Speed-Info* article. Thus, while it would appear that the original founders/owners of the website no longer updated it, the website continued to function via its internal forum as an important source of contact for parents of those with MPS. Overall, the look and feel of the www.mpssociety.ru website was that of *samizdat*, with a cluttered layout and a small font. However, there also was the impression that the voices were quite genuine, sad, and sometimes desperate. The most practical part of the website at the time of analysis was the forum, in which information on how to contact officials and which institutions to visit for specific medical help (such as for prenatal genetic screening for families who already had one child with MPS) were offered in a timely manner. Forum comments sometimes redirected participants to Mitina's website on Hunter syndrome (www.mps-russia.org). While the focus and home page of www.mps-russia.org was very much on Hunter syndrome, it was clear from the lively website forum (with 2,389 postings on 231 themes from 245 users as of August 17, 2010, according to the site statistics) that many of the questions were about MPS in general. Mitina herself has reported that she managed to find more than 200 children with Hunter syndrome in Russia to convince officials to pay for extremely expensive medication[11] and it was clear from some posts that this was done online.[12]

From this analysis, it is clear that some Russian online networks related to health causes appear international in nature and some are more domestic in character. For example, Downside Up linked quite heavily to other websites in Runet and was clearly part of the broader charity community in Russia. On the other hand, neither MPS website was connected heavily into the wider Runet community. Rather, the links tended to cluster around medical and pharmaceutical websites as parents searched for basic care and treatment options for their severely ill children. At the same time, the link on the Hunter syndrome website showed that MPS received reasonable attention in the mainstream Russian media (including on television). Thus, it may be more important to consider the *nature of the cause* in the online sphere than the *national origin* of a specific group to predict whether particular websites will be embedded within domestic or international information spheres.

Catalyzing Events and Forum Content

What was the effect of a catalyzing event—the outcry over the tabloid article suggesting euthanasia for newborns with disabilities—on existing online support and advocacy networks for children with disabilities on Runet? What was the effect of the threatened exclusion from dialysis on a group of patients? In both cases, it would appear that the role of individual bloggers as types of online social entrepreneurs seemed to be particularly important. The voices of these individuals moved across media platforms, particularly in fostering traditional media attention by aggregating interests and attention online. A natural assumption might be that discussion would lead to aggregation and possible social action. However, online discussion does not necessarily lead to consensus and group action. Indeed, online interaction can spur arguments and controversy, alienating people from further online or even offline interaction.

This section turns to an analysis of forum content for MPS and kidney dialysis. The MPS forum content for analysis consists of 104 comments posted between January 21, 2010, and July 3, 2011, in a thread called "I await developments"[13] as well as 42 comments in a related thread on provision of care for MPS patients in neighboring Belarus from March 18, 2009, to December 17, 2010.[14] This content was selected as it reflected a period of reaction to the tabloid journalist's suggestion of euthanasia as well as discussion about how to campaign post-Soviet governments to provide expensive medication to children with a relatively rare genetic disorder. As reflected in the forum content, the struggle of parents in Russia—who also became involved online with parents of MPS children in Belarus—was very much ongoing in 2010. The forum content is compared with that of an established forum for dialysis patients at http://www.moscowdialysis.ucoz.ru/forum/27-2534-1. This case study looks at a specific "spike" in online activity (what Fossato et al., 2008, would call a "firestorm") related to the attempted exclusion of some patients from dialysis in Rostov-on-Don. While acceptance and the right to treatment are not general issues for Russian dialysis patients at the same level as for the parents of children with disabilities, the attempted removal of critical dialysis demonstrated that the internet could be a place for successful challenge to the state relating to health treatment decisions.

The sheer wealth of data provided by the online sphere has exacerbated ongoing debates about the relative merits of large N studies that rely on measures such as the occurrence of particular words (either by themselves or within a certain distance from others), the number of posts, the percentage of posts from an individual within a forum, or the number of followers/responses to a post by a user. Quantity is a key factor, particularly when combined with web link analysis to show relative prominence in the online information sphere. Unsurprisingly, attempting to mine online content has attracted a great deal of interest in the field of business and management, notably in terms of the potential to track the attitude toward a brand. In addition, if one can identify important online points of exchange and information, companies can promote their brands more effectively through social marketing. While sentiment analysis is used in social science, it is difficult to understand exactly how the volume or even pattern of words in the online sphere are linked to a *nuanced* understanding of citizen attitudes.

However, there are ways that quantity can be balanced with quality in the analysis of user-generated content (Hopkins and King, 2010). Much of the relevant literature dealing with the issue of online content analysis is focused on Twitter content (for an overview see Dann, 2010). There are several reasons for this high level of interest: (1) Tweets are limited to 140 characters, providing relatively homogeneous size and format across the unit of analysis, i.e., a tweet; (2) it is (relatively) simple to access the Twitter archive as opposed to content in Facebook or other platforms; (3) the use of "hash tags," i.e., words preceded by the # mark, make it relatively easy to identify subject areas for study; and (4) the format of Twitter with identified tweeters and followers listed publically make it easy to identify a range of user characteristics linked directly to tweets. The size of the data available for analysis is staggering. For example, Java et al. (2007) were able to analyze almost 1.4 million tweets from over 76,000 users over a two-month period in 2007. Java et al. mixed quantitative and qualitative methods, establishing a "style of use" metric using followers and following numbers as well as a "user intention" measurement via manually coded tweets (they coded a sample of the 76,177 tweets in the study). In the qualitative coding, Java et al. found four broad categories of content: daily chatter about the everyday life of the individual; conversations with other users; information sharing that included URLs; and "news" reporting that included commentary on news, sports, and the weather. This is a useful study in showing that quantitative observations about users (such as comparing those who have many followers with those in more reciprocal tweeting relationships that mutually exchange information) are helpful in terms of understanding *how* people use the internet. However, it is necessary to use human content analysis to understand *what* people are saying— and speculate as to *why* they may do this. Pear Analytics (2009) also developed on the theme of content classification, using 2,000 tweets to generate the following categories: "pointless babble" such as personal comments, observations, and chat (40.6 percent); conversational comments with questions, survey information, and replies (37.6 percent); information passed along, including re-tweets (8.7 percent); self-promotion (5.9 percent); spam (3.8 percent); and reference to news such as mainstream media content (3.6 percent). The Pear Analytics study parallels a frustration in content analysis for this project in that many of the comments in forums resisted meaningful categorizations in a coding scheme. There is an enormous amount of "pointless babble" online—the trick is finding the meaningful content amongst the babble, as it creates a very high noise-to-signal ratio for researchers.

Dann's meta-analysis of Twitter coding research is useful in terms of showing not only how quantitative and qualitative methods are best used in combination, but also in suggesting the broad range of approaches to online content analysis. The challenge is in moving on from Twitter to a broader range of platforms, types of content, and types of interaction that tend to be more complicated. This is particularly relevant in the Russian case, as Twitter was not widely used there during the period under review. Some of the concepts are useful, but the heterogeneity of forum comments in the area of Runet studied for this book make it more challenging. In addition, it is impossible to understand online activity without a comprehension of both the general political and media environment in Russia. It is difficult to grasp the meaning of the online discourse without details about the offline activity (organizations, protests, legal appeals, etc.).

The questions for content analysis are even more nuanced for these Russian user-generated comments. Sentiment analysis that measures the presence or absence of certain words—even in a particular spatial relationship to one another—would not be meaningful for unpacking rather complex ideas about rights and protest. For example, we know that many people commented on Mitina's blog about the "post-natal" abortion issue. But what did they say? If they were angered by the idea, how did they formulate their arguments? Did they merely abuse the journalist? If they were "negative," were they negative about the journalist or the children themselves? If they did disagree, or even agree, with the journalist, how did they express their views on children with disabilities? Who did people blame for the problems in gaining care for their children— national officials, local officials, their hospitals, or even fate itself? There are some quite useful and nuanced development of models of sentiment analysis (such as Hu and Liu, 2004) that could be adapted and deployed across a large corpus of user-generated content. However, as the discussion and findings below highlight, there is still work to be done in refining the parameters of online discussion relating to politics, particularly in countries in which the discourse is not readily linked to parties, elections, or other traditional democratic institutions.

As this book is interested in the political use of the internet, it was decided to analyze the forum comments through the lens of rights. Did the users construct arguments based on the idea that children with disabilities had rights as human beings? Or did they argue in a slightly different way as suggested by studies of post-Soviet citizens, not showing evidence of demands for rights on a broad scale, but demanding their state benefits? In addition, which (if any) political

institutions did they reference in their comments? How did they offer information or encouragement? Did they make calls to action in their posts?
Once the parameters were established,[15] a coding scheme was developed
(see Appendix).[16]

While these case studies are linked by the issue of government medical provision, concerns about dialysis provision and care for children with genetic disabilities are somewhat different. Both groups were able to use the online sphere
to gather information, aggregate interests, and possibly carry out actions linked
to addressing their specific needs. However, dialysis patients often were campaigning for services or rights on their own behalf, as opposed to the way in
which the voices of parents were most heard in the discussions of children with
genetic disabilities. In addition, dialysis treatment does not carry the same struggle of societal acceptance.

Coders, who were all native Russian speakers, noted the date, time, poster
name, and location. They attempted to define the user's behavior in the post,
ranging from challenging or disagreeing with the information offered; attacking
a poster; asking a question; answering a question; and/or urging people to take
part in actions such as protests, signing petitions, commenting on government
websites, and so on. In addition to user actions, the coders were asked to determine various aspects of the online discourse, in particular looking for mentions
of rights that included any mention of the state failing to provide services to any
discussion of what people should have (in terms of rights or privileges or benefits) in society as well as mention of state benefits. The project searched for mentions of the "moral economy" as advanced by writers such as Scott (1977) or the
notion of the "political economy." A moral economy argument is one that posits
that the state has an obligation to provide certain services to citizens as it serves
as a protector figure, a sort of parent to the people. This also has links to the
Soviet economy (or the Leninist ideal of "from each according to his abilities, to
each according to his needs"). Profit and individuals operating in a free market
are not part of the understanding of how society should work under the moral
economy. A "political economy" argument is one in which profit, individualism,
and the free market are understood to be how society should work. Final
categories in the content analysis looked at whether posters mentioned international or Russian issues and concerns (see Appendix for full details).

Coders also were instructed to list any mention of political institutions, including the president at the time (or Medvedev himself), the prime minister (or
Putin himself), the parliament, and political parties. Additionally, we asked
coders to note if posters justified their online participation. Coders also included
a brief qualitative overview of the post.

Perhaps the most successful—and surprising—category was that of "rights"
(see Table 6.2: Post Contents: MPS and Dialysis Forum compared). There was

a surprisingly large amount of commentary that touched on the issue of rights. In addition, the discussions often illuminated the ways in which post-Soviet citizens conceived of their rights and their relationship with the state. Unsurprisingly as rights and benefits are strongly interrelated in Russian civic culture, benefits were also mentioned quite frequently. However, it must be noted that the coders remained rather idiosyncratic in their definition of rights, benefits, and the differences between the two, which suggests that either the definition must be improved before further coding or one must accept that it is not possible to code for a broad discussion of rights with high inter-coder reliability. It was apparent that comments on the dialysis forum were more focused and relevant. This was certainly in part due to the catalyst of a threatened withdrawal of critical dialysis to a specific group of people. Most of the offline action was performed by people directly involved with the situation, and they also were very active in online discussion. Although clear leaders emerged in the discussion, it was far less asymmetric than the MPS discussion, which was heavily moderated and "led" by Mitina herself. This again illuminates the point that forums—and the way in which they can be coded, interpreted, and analyzed—cannot be separated from the broader political context.

Rights were mentioned in 34 percent of the comments on the dialysis forum and in 21 percent of the comments on the MPS forum (see Table 6.2). The dialysis forum also had a greater focus on benefits, with 27 percent of the comments discussing benefits, compared with 16 percent of the comments on the MPS forum. The MPS forum provided more specific responses to queries and concerns: More than half of the comments (55 percent) were coded as replies to questions. On the other hand, specific replies were almost nonexistent in the dialysis forum, with just

Table 6.2 **Post Contents: MPS and Dialysis Forum Compared**

	MPS		Dialysis	
	Number	*% of comments*	*Number*	*% of comments*
Rights	31	21.1	86	34.4
Benefits	23	15.6	68	27.2
International aspect of issue	24	16.3	2	0.8
Russian aspect of issue	15	10.2	13	5.2
Action	27	18.4	38	15.2
A question	21	14.3	45	18.0
Replies to questions	81	55.1	4	1.6
N (comments)	147		250	

Source: Author's research.

four (2 percent of the comments). It was not that the dialysis forum participants were callous or unconcerned about individuals; rather, the discussion was more about legal rights for groups and the fate of dialysis patients in regions, while the MPS forum often responded directly to the concerns of individual parents for diagnosis and treatment. As MPS is a relatively rare condition, the MPS forum often referenced information or action in other countries, including information relating to drug development or treatment. Action was suggested in slightly more of the MPS forum posts (18 percent compared with 15 percent for the dialysis group) but it should be noted that detailed study showed that the dialysis group was more focused on *group* action while the MPS forums often gave advice to *individuals* on how to lobby for drugs for their children.

Detailed Comment Analysis from MPS Forum: "Tell Them about the Situation and Cry for Help"

It is impossible to separate the MPS forum from the figure of Mitina, mother of a child with MPS and a longtime campaigner for treatment for MPS children in Russia. Refused expensive medication for her son based on the argument that few Russians needed the treatment, Mitina went online to find sufficient families to build her case for the government to pay for treatment. Along the way, she established herself as an online social entrepreneur. Mitina is intriguing in that she was not the only parent in this situation, yet she appears to be the one parent able to effectively inform, mobilize, and organize parents from across Russia. Mitina made 37 out of the 147 comments (25 percent) on the forum under analysis, the most dominant participant across both case studies for forum content. In particular, Mitina's participation in the forum is reflected in the high level of posting of responses to questions. Her replies are sometimes quite specific to an individual, with a recommendation of a name and an address through which to seek help. At other times, she gives the list more generic information, such as by posting links to news stories about the "post-natal abortion" controversy or the struggle for MPS treatment in general. Thus, the online conversation was both initiated and supported by Mitina, although it was not simply a one-to-many interaction. Comments were analyzed from the thread "Our affairs" under several popular sub-threads.[17]

The main point of the discussion was to provide links to the successful complaint filed by Mitina and another parent about the tabloid journalist with the Russian Union of Journalists, as well as links to news articles about the controversy. In addition, the constant struggle of parents to obtain proper diagnosis, treatment, and medication runs through all of the threads. Thus, while 45 participants in the discussion threads congratulate Mitina on her victory with the complaint against the journalist, the support for the concept of dignity for children with MPS is mingled with the ever-present struggle for the proper treatment of the children. In particular, it is clear that the rare nature of the disability makes it very difficult for parents to get help from an under-resourced public health system. However, at least some of the children were getting treatment and it was apparent from comments as well as suggestions in the forum that parents were using legal arguments (i.e., the right of citizens to necessary medical treatment) to try to obtain up-to-date treatment for their children. In contrast, a thread started by Liliana from Belarus[18] made it clear that the situation was even more difficult for MPS children in Belarus, as the comments indicated that the government had a widespread refusal to provide ongoing treatment with the expensive Elaprase drug. While the Russian MPS forum participants tried to provide moral support, it was clear that the ability to pressure the government—in particular by using the traditional mass media to make the denial of health treatment to children public—was not available to citizens of Belarus. This underlines the point made throughout this book that the informational and organizational capabilities of the online sphere are constrained by national political environments.

Overall, how did the MPS forum participants view their rights as they mentioned them in more than 20 percent of the comments (see Table 6.2)? Clearly, the notion of rights and benefits were linked, as participants mentioned benefits in just under half of the comments that also discussed rights (15 out of 31 comments that included rights). But what did rights mean in the post-Soviet context for the parents of children with MPS? Some of the information under "rights" related to practical information, such as how to file grievances with local officials (for the right to medical treatment) or addresses of people to write to "tell them about the situation and cry for help" (*rasskazyvaem o proiskhodyashchem i krichum o pomoshchi*) provided by Mitina on May 27, 2010.[19] The addresses were for the leader of the State Duma Committee on Family, Women and Children; the president of the Federation Council's Committee on Social Policy and Public Health; and the presidential representative for children's rights in the Russian Federation. This shows evidence of the "mixed" approach discussed by Turbine and others above, in that the internet was being used as a conduit for contact with formal government representatives rather than a political entity in its own right. Forum posts by Mitina on both May 25 and May 27 (2010) called for forum participants to support a demonstration for the treatment of children with MPS and other rare diseases outside health administration buildings in Yekaterinburg on June 1, 2010. A forum poster from Ireland (who is apparently originally from Russia) posted about the state medical care and support for children with disabilities in Ireland, where she lives with her child with MPS. She highlighted the difference between the broad provision of medical services and benefits to families of children with disabilities in Ireland and Russia, saying that families in Russia deserved this as well.

Overall, there was constant reinforcement that children with disabilities not only deserve to live (to counter the argument by the tabloid journalist), but deserve the best possible medical treatment. There was a strong identification with the idea of the moral economy as outlined above, with 25 percent (57 out of 227) of the forum comments being identified as mentioning some element of a moral economy. This compares with just three posts (1 percent) that linked to the idea of the political economy. None of this may sound particularly radical, but both attitudes are challenging to the poor state of government health care as well as the long-held prejudices against people with disabilities in Russia. One wonders, however, if the advice by the Russian forum participants to the Belarus forum participants was particularly helpful. For example, a participant named Masha wrote, in response to the situation in Belarus:

> All of this is just an OUTRAGE!!! We support you, Liliana. We are strong as flint. And we are able to appreciate the pleasant and beautiful things that life gives us. We appreciate it, love it, and admire it more than ordinary people. This is what nature has given to us. I hope and believe that we nonetheless do not live in a fascist society . . . All, to those in need. All, to those who have even the slightest chance. Don't give up![20]

Other forum participants chimed in about the importance of organizing, with one noting that a new NGO was the way to "become active, meet up, consolidate your association, find funding for medication—you can't just sit around and wait!" (Taisa from Belarus, August 29, 2009, http://mps-russia.org/forum/index.php?topic=380.30). This seemed somewhat optimistic—much more so than Liliana, the central figure in the online discussion from Belarus (with 14 posts), including the following one:

> We will fight . . . [But] what can we do? They are many and they are stronger. Even our great desire to live could not break through this wall. Of course, we will write, march, now and in the future. But sometimes your own time and strength are exhausted.[21]

THE DIALYSIS FORUM: DETAILED COMMENT ANALYSIS

The dialysis support forum was more focused than the MPS forum, in that the discussion thread under analysis was directly related to one catalytic event. The catalyzing event, which was outlined in the first post of the thread (http://www.moscowdialysis.ucoz.ru/forum/27-2534-15), was the exclusion of 11 dialysis patients from a facility in Rostov-on-Don. The hospital claimed to no longer be receiving funds for these patients and could not legally transfer any money from the rest of the hospital budget to cover the costs. This was essentially a death sentence for the patients, as there were no other suitable dialysis facilities available to them (this was apparent from comments to the forum as well as from coverage in the mass media).

As is clear from Table 6.2, the concept of rights played an even larger role in the dialysis discussion (more than a third of the comments addressed the issues of rights) than on the MPS forum. As with the comments on the MPS forum, the notion of benefits was strongly linked to rights—53 out of 86 comments (62 percent) of the posts referring to rights also carried a mention of benefits. In the dialysis forum, the issue of the rights of patients was not linked to an argument about the right to life as it was for children with disabilities. However, it was clear that the dialysis patients viewed themselves as a class of people who had to struggle for decent treatment. There was broad reference to the lack of dialysis availability, poor treatment, or delayed treatment that left people seriously ill or even had caused the premature death of loved ones. Thus, while the MPS forum participants felt that much of their poor treatment stemmed from a lack of care for children born with a rare and hard-to-treat disability, the dialysis patients on this forum felt the Russian medical system was failing in general. That being said, dialysis patients often expressed the frustration that their condition made them apparently disposable and powerless. Still, when they talked about rights, they were less likely to make emotive arguments. Instead, they were more apt to refer to the legal aspects of rights. There were very detailed posts on the implications of Article 124 of the Russian criminal code,[22] and about documentation needed to fulfill the terms of post-Soviet bureaucracy. Indeed, the 11 patients and their supporters engaged in a multilevel strategy, which included private meetings with hospital officials; meetings with local health officials; contacts with local and national media; and the rallying of supporters via the online sphere. Most of the discussion related to actions and information from dialysis patients across Russia. Hence, unlike the MPS forum, the discussion was not a question-and-answer between the main poster (Igor22) and the other forum participants. Rather, it was more of an online collaboration of tactics and information, with a much less prominent emotional element than on the MPS forum.

There were two central themes to the discussion on this dialysis forum thread: (1) the right of dialysis patients to have state-financed treatment; and (2) corrupt and inefficient practices in local and national health institutions, from the hospitals to the ministries. A less prominent theme about the ethical considerations in providing or taking away dialysis—and whose job it was to make these decisions—also was present in the forum. From the comments it was clear that many people were discussing the ideas of rights and benefits, as well as appealing to the concept of a "moral economy," i.e., that state services should be based on principles of goodness, fairness, and justice (in opposition to the affordability of the services). This was discussed both specifically for the provision of dialysis as well as for the more general concept of health care provided by the state to the people. Phrases such as "the state should," "the Ministry is obligated," "the hospital's duty is" are clear illustrations of this idea. The fact that rights were being discussed also was evidenced by the numerous calls to action to defend patient rights and suggestions of how this could be done. Among the suggestions were calls to contact officials with written petitions; raising awareness via getting coverage in the traditional mass media; going online to discuss the issue on government websites; posting on President Medvedev's blog; and calling for legal action against the hospital and the local/federal health agency. Unlike the MPS forum with its discussion of treatment advances in other countries and the superior provision of state health care in countries such as Ireland, the dialysis forum framed the discussion within the Russian context of health care (only two posts were international in nature).

Forum participants, many of whom were themselves dialysis patients from all over Russia, shared their stories (including problems with getting treatment) and fears. However, unlike in the MPS forum in which emotion and forlorn hope often dominated, the emotional component in the dialysis forum was enriched with a lot of information on how to rectify the problem in Rostov-on-Don and where to go to defend the rights of the patients for dialysis. Users cited Article 124, pointing out the illegal nature of stopping procedures, suggested talking to the media (based on their own previous experience with similar cases), and offered other ways of putting pressure on hospital/health authorities. Some offline action was planned, including media interviews, petitions, and appeals to government agencies, but most of it was carried out by local activists (typically one or two people), while other forum participants forwarded reports on action and advised on how to proceed. There were some calls to stage protests among the dialysis forum participants, but no major offline protests were reported in the forum.

It is worth noting that some participants stressed the role of the internet, blogosphere, and social media in raising awareness of the Rostov-on-Don issue. Indeed, the material in the forum illuminated the way in which media are manipulated by state officials through informal pressures and how the group managed to combat this. One cannot say that there is a complete dearth of media freedom in Russia (see Chapter 2), but the experience of the dialysis forum shows how media control works in Russia. Although group members were able to engage the attention of journalists, news organizations came under pressure not to report the story. For example, Ludmila reported on May 18, 2010, that the health ministry in Rostov-on-Don had called the commercial television network NTV and stated that the dialysis problem had been resolved. The patients had to then convince journalists that it had not been resolved. With an even more flagrant disregard for the truth, hospital officials would make promises to the media that the situation would be resolved, then later renege on treatment promises. This is outlined in the following post on the dialysis forum:

> Latest news: As soon as the noise died down, then [one of hospital staff] reneged on his promises, he became impudent with the health ministry, saying that patients remained on dialysis and that everything was in excellent order. I had to again connect with journalists and post on the President's blog. The effect was lightning-fast. Today in Hospital No. 1, a five-person commission from the health ministry arrived, spoke with the patients, promised again to buy new machines and begged them not to go to journalists or make any more complaints to [Igor] Stepanyukov [e.g., Igor22, the poster]. The repairs, which have been going on for three years, have been completed with two teams. Still another machine will be obtained via rent-purchase next week. I will continue to monitor these unscrupulous people who do not fulfill their promises.[23]

Igor22, May 28, 2010

It was clear that it was not the comments in a relatively small forum that were feared by the state officials. Rather, there were many references and links to television coverage of the issue—both local and national—as well as references to LiveJournal blogs, such as the one maintained by Stepanyukov/Igor22. In particular, Stepanyukov made use of Medvedev's blog by posting about the issue—and refusing to stop commenting when the president's blog falsely claimed the issue had been resolved. A poster named Userss articulated the nature of the campaign in a comment, linking back to the notion of the moral economy and emotion more common in the MPS forum:

> Don't stop communicating with the mass media. Our weapon is transparency [*glasnost'*] (and this is not trite). Their weapons are lies and silence. Forget the word "objectivity." If you're going to give an interview with the patients, go for maximum emotionality. Society must feel our condition. That is, they must "feel" it and not just "be informed." It's only then, when promises are realized, that you can relax.

Userss, May 18, 2010

Many LiveJournal users would have learned about the issue from key bloggers who reposted the initial appeal letter, and the text was widely reposted on Live-Journal and on other stand-alone blogs, such as exler.ru (http://exler.ru/blog/item/8000/). The excluded dialysis patients also went on Dmitry Medvedev's LiveJournal blog to post about the issue, and got reaction from the blog modera-tors.[24] It is clear the posts did not go unnoticed, but it is difficult to say whether this had any real effect on the situation, since there were no visible connections found in this analysis between Medvedev's blog reaction and the changes that subsequently took place in dialysis provision in Rostov-on-Don.

There was little evidence of a political discussion among participants about political parties, the Duma, or national political leaders such as Putin or Medve-dev (although Medvedev's official blog did figure in the discussion at one point). Rather, forum participants articulated much of their discontent with what they found to be disorganized, corrupt, and uncaring officials (with no political affili-ation mentioned) on all levels—local, regional, and federal, as well as with the general chaotic nature of health-care provision. It was in this respect that the state was somewhat challenged, although there were a few comments that re-flected the sentiment that things were better abroad or even that things were better in Moscow than in the regions. There was no evidence of users giving up or convincing others the fight was not worth it. The general reaction was of shock and horror at the initial decision to deny the 11 patients their dialysis procedures, yet at the same time the forum remained upbeat and optimistic, al-though at times frustrated by the Russian bureaucratic machinery and its dis-tance from the citizens and their concerns.

The two key online social entrepreneurs in this case were Stepanyukov (user Igor22) and Lyudmila Kondrashova (user Ludmila). They are both representa-tives of Nephro-Liga, a national NGO of patients with kidney disorders in Russia (http://nephroliga.ru/). At the time of the analysis, Kondrashova was the head of the NGO, while Stepanyukov was head of the local branch of Nephro-Liga. They were quite active on the forum thread, which was evidenced by both of them being the users with the most posts in the thread: Igor22 had 37 posts (out of a total of 250 posts or 15 percent of total posts), while Ludmila made 32 posts (13 percent). The rest of the 44 active users in this thread had significantly fewer posts on average. However, while the online social entrepre-neurs were the most common voices, they did not overwhelmingly dominate the discussion. Qualitative analysis of the forum postings supports this claim: Most of the posts by Igor22 and Ludmila were reports on action taken or infor-mation about the issue, as well as reactions to other forum posts. Thus, the two central posters were taking part in a discussion rather than "leading from above" all the time. In addition, both Stepanyukov and Kondrashova were fre-quently mentioned in news stories on the subject posted in online media and referenced on the forum, as well as in television news items mentioned by users on the forum.

The Rostov-on-Don dialysis provision case is interesting for several reasons. Most significantly, the forum can claim an important role in reversing the hospital's action to cut off treatment to the patients. While the evidence suggests this was through both online campaigning as well as offline actions, there is compelling evidence that the forum informed and inspired people with a stake in the situation or the broader issue of dialysis provision to take action. In addition, although the discussion and comments on the key forum were very specific and centered around the local hospital and the 11 patients, the discussion eventually branched out to encompass broader issues, such as the state of dialysis care in the Rostov region and in other regions of Russia; provision of dialysis care for children; and even state obligations to patients with chronic conditions in general. While researching ways to campaign in defense of the 11 patients in Rostov-on-Don, the online social entrepreneurs and forum users discovered problems in other hospitals providing dialysis procedures, such as outdated or broken equipment; inadequate patient treatment; and poor food and conditions for patients tethered to dialysis machines for hours each week. The issue gained wide coverage in local media (online and offline), as well as some national coverage in Russia. This evidently helped bring about changes in the form of funding for dialysis procedures; new equipment; and promises of a new dialysis center in Rostov-on-Don. In June 2011, a new dialysis center was opened in there with 10 new dialysis machines available to the city patients.[25] In addition, a children's dialysis center in Rostov-on-Don received new equipment in September 2010 as part of a United Russia charity program.[26] This also was a point of discussion at the forum, with the general feeling being that United Russia was taking credit for work brought about by the activists, but there was not a sense of rejection of the party involvement (even after the goal had been achieved).

Conclusions

It was clear by mid-2011 that the internet was a key informational resource for Russian citizens and could challenge the Russian state, although this study shows relatively limited health issues and small victories. For the children with disabilities, there was evidence of tangible change brought about by online aggregation. It is unlikely that the Russian government could have been persuaded to provide highly expensive drugs for a relatively rare condition without the ability of the MPS website to identify and collect details on patients across Russia. In particular, Mitina was effective at leveraging her blog via Radio Liberty/Radio Free Europe and gaining international attention. This was helped by a particularly insensitive tabloid article about euthanasia for infants with disabilities. While the article was the catalyst, it was clear that Mitina had gained important experience and credibility through her online activities. In the case of Downside Up, the rise in the number of families registered with the organization grew from 519 in 2004 to 1,458 in 2009. There is also evidence that Downside Up is reaching across the country, with two-thirds of its registered children living outside of the Moscow region. This would have been very difficult to organize in a pre-internet era in Russia. Both through the provision of information and resources online and victory in causes brought about by specific catalysts such as fighting prejudice or funding medication, children with genetic disabilities and their families in Russia have received concrete benefits from the online sphere. A group of dialysis patients in Rostov-on-Don managed to keep their life-sustaining dialysis services and saw significant improvements to their facility after a national campaign that was linked via online activism.

The arguments in the MPS forum tended to be more emotive and less focused, which was connected to problems of fighting for care for children with genetic disabilities in Russia. These forum participants were waging a battle on two major fronts—for acceptance of their children into society as well as for the rights for their children to gain treatment even if their condition is rare. The arguments often blended together and overlapped. At the same time, the forum was a venue for parents to share and try to alleviate their worry and grief over the often painful, short lives of their beloved children. The dialysis crisis forum was more focused and dynamic. Although there were elements of emotionalism in the posts, generally there was a more strategic and forceful shape to the conversation. While the instigator of the thread and the first post (Igor22) was a dominant voice, there were other important voices. On the MPS forum, the tone was more maternal, with Mitina as the central figure who responded to most posts personally. The coding scheme, despite its flaws, allowed us to highlight the central issues and differences between the two forums.

The MPS forum was concerned with rights and benefits, but replies to queries and discussions of actions were the most common factor in user comments. However, it is important to note that qualitative analysis is key here, as the actions discussed tended to be about personal appeals for care for individual children. There was also a broader discussion about the rights of children with MPS and other rare conditions for treatment, but personal concerns were mingled quite closely with the political point about health rights. On the other hand, the analysis of user-generated comments showed that the question of rights (and benefits) played a greater role for the dialysis patients. The qualitative analysis highlighted a more politicized group that was fighting for a specific right (access to critical health treatment), but also a group arguing for this on the grounds of both what is legal under Russian law *as well as* what is right and just.

This parallels the MPS argument, but is more overt and less emotional. It plays less on the notion of "maternal" politics, such as found in the arguments made by groups such as Soldiers' Mothers Union, that children and parents are deserving of a particular compassion and aid from the state. Rather, the dialysis patients argued as a politicized group for their rights.

In addition to the specific findings about these groups, this chapter represents the challenge of applying systematic content analysis schemes to user-generated content. There were several lessons learned—as well as findings uncovered—in this process. Coders differed in their interpretation of rights, although greater inter-coder reliability was found in terms of identifying suggested actions. The breadth of language, the different rhetorical styles of those who posted, and even the variations in language use that ranged from English-based slang to very formal Russian, all made it challenging to codify each comment. In addition, some comments were a word or a phrase, while others were small essays with complex and nuanced content. However, while it was not particularly straightforward to translate the words into valid and reliable numerical scores, the investigation of user-generated content did provide rich data on the actions, attitudes, and exchanges among the participants in political protest in Russia. Indeed, this offered a new and interesting way to understand Russian attitudes toward the notion of rights and their ability to challenge state policy. While the forums were generally closed groups of like-minded individuals, they revealed much about how Russians think about rights. In particular, the forum comments show that Russians tend to link together the notion of rights and state privileges. They overwhelmingly rejected the more modern idea of a "political" economy, basing their arguments on the state's obligation to provide care under a "moral" framework.

The comparative analysis of the two forums shows us that one cannot consider the role of online political communication without mapping how the internet interacts with the traditional mass media. Throughout both forums, it was clear that the attention from the traditional mass media was critical to the success of the campaigns. In particular, the relationship among dialysis patients, local bureaucrats, mass media reports, and the threat of ongoing publicity was central to understanding how the dialysis ward was not only kept open, but eventually improved. In many ways, the dialysis patients had the "perfect storm" of a media event for the post-Soviet political environment. Despite attempts to fob them off with inferior dialysis, the patients were able to argue convincingly that a reduction in the quantity or quality of their treatment would shorten their lives, if not kill them quite quickly. They were an articulate, organized group who garnered nationwide support, especially via LiveJournal. They leveraged their existing social capital.

Where does this leave us vis-à-vis the quantitative versus qualitative divide in the study of user-generated content in the online sphere? The sheer volume of online content makes it possible to identify key trends, in usage and content. However, the very nature of content resists easy quantification. For example, one might find a sudden rise in user-generated content in the mention of Putin near elections. Although there are claims that sentiment analysis could code whether these are "negative" or "positive," exposure to user-generated content on Runet through this project suggests that automated coding is very vulnerable to problems of a lack of validity and reliability. In particular, the variation in how people post, the rise of slang-like language replete with transliterated English words and text abbreviations, as well as the heavy use of irony and humor in Runet all make meanings complex and slippery. However, quantitative methods such as search results and web link analysis can point us to "islands" of interesting content online, places that are prominent and relatively important in terms of understanding the link between online content and political action. With content found through quantitative triangulation, qualitative content analysis can be deployed via coding or through qualitative framing analysis. Thus, mixed methods still yield the best results, although there is room for improvement and greater synergy between automated and human analysis of user-generated content.

While there is little evidence that web pages, blogs, and forums *alone* will spur offline action, there is the indication that networks "come alive" at moments of crisis, such as when a Russian journalist wrote in December 2009 that parents should be allowed to kill children with disabilities at birth or when local officials made the inhumane decision to deny dialysis to 11 patients. It is also worthy of note that both in the context of Russian politics and the character of internet charisma in general, online social entrepreneurs play a key role in information sharing and political action. In the tradition of the Union of Soldiers' Mothers, it is unsurprising that these social entrepreneurs present their primary persona as mothers, in this case of children with chromosomal differences. This study reinforces the idea that we need to look for "political" action online in places that might be considered more personal or even social in nature. Political discussion is not confined to any particular website or forum; rather, political issues spread across the internet in a variety of locations and forms.

7

The Winter of Discontent

Elections, Protests, and the Internet in Russia, 2011–12

In the autumn of 2011, it appeared that the internet in Russia was indeed "stalled" in terms of political impact. Despite the dramatic evidence of online political movements in the Arab Spring, Russian politics seemed to remain firmly offline, with little evidence of the potential for the internet to foster widespread political change. However, over the course of a few weeks at the end of 2011, it became clear the internet had changed the political landscape in Russia, as the largest street protests since 1993 were triggered by reports of election falsification. The evidence suggests that there were three critical elements to this transformation. First, the internet has limited the Kremlin's ability to shape critical information flow to citizens. At the same time, the internet has empowered citizens in specific ways that the Kremlin apparently finds hard to understand, much less to co-opt or control through its traditional way of dealing with Russian citizens. Finally, compelling evidence of falsification in the December 2011 Duma elections, spread in different ways through the online sphere, triggered a particularly visceral response from Russian citizens.

This chapter examines what the winter protests in 2011–12 in Russia demonstrate about the role of internet in Russian society and beyond. What were the protests about and how were they linked to the online sphere, both in terms of information provision and mobilization? How did the Russian government's reaction to the rising power of the internet alleviate or exacerbate political tensions? What evidence was there that the internet had become embedded in the political life of Russian citizens, signaling the "end of the virtual" (Rogers, 2009; Greene, January 2012) and the beginning of the understanding of a new era in political communication for the Russian state? What does this suggest for the future of Russian citizens, Russian leaders, and Russian democracy? This chapter analyzes a combination of factors that all contributed to the Russian "winter of discontent": (1) the failure of state "soft" controls that relied on traditions of self-censorship;

(2) an online sphere that was freer than traditional mass media; (3) an explosion in internet use that erodes the dominance of state-run television; (4) a lack of understanding about citizen attitudes and the online sphere on the part of the Kremlin; (5) crowd-sourcing; (6) online political networks; and (7) the role of online social entrepreneurs. In conjunction with these factors, studies of Russian attitudes and elections suggest that reports of widespread electoral falsification would serve as a particularly emotive and powerful protest trigger for Russian citizens. In the identification and analysis of these factors, we can recognize a pattern of online political evolution in general. As discussed throughout this book, the role of the internet in political protest in Russia did not take the form of a single group or event. Rather, the way in which the internet challenged "politics as usual" for the Kremlin took many forms. Although there are a range of protests linked to the online sphere, as identified earlier in this book, this chapter looks specifically at events from late November 2011 through early March 2012, with a particular focus on large demonstrations in December. These protests took place throughout Russia, but the largest demonstrations were in Moscow.

Protests Linked to the Russian Internet in 2011–12

While the mass protests were linked to reports of electoral violations, the first significant sign of unrest reflected in the online sphere in Russia was linked to a video of then-Prime Minister Vladimir Putin at a martial arts match in the Olympic Stadium in Moscow on November 20, 2011. After the fight between Russian Fedor Emelianenko and American Jeff Monson, Putin stepped into the ring to congratulate the victorious Emelianenko, calling him a "real Russian he-man [*muzhik*]." As Putin spoke, booing broke out in the crowd. In a review of the tape, which is widely available on YouTube, it is difficult to tell exactly how the crowd is reacting. Certainly, the booing appears to be louder when Putin is speaking, but it is hard to say whether this was a political reaction to the prime minister, sports fans who were annoyed with any politician in the ring, or a reflection on the match itself. It was highly unusual to see any public disapproval of Putin, who had announced his rebid for the presidency in September, and it was highlighted when the tape was shown on Russian television with the booing edited out. This only served to underline the difference between the official, sanitized discourse and Russian reality—a gap that has existed and widened since the first days of the new Russian state in the early 1990s—but one that is generally tolerated by many Russian television viewers (Oates, 2006). However, the decision to clean up the tape was evidence that Russian PR managers seemed not only unaware that the tape already had become part of the public sphere via video sharing online, but that attempts to doctor it for television would only serve to highlight the incident still further. The incident was covered widely in the Western media, particularly as Putin prepared to run for his third term as president in March 2012.

Although the booing at the martial arts fight made international news, it was only a shadow of the challenges the internet provided for the state in the coming weeks, with protests over the parliamentary elections occurring on December 4, 2011. While elections in Russia have passed with little public controversy since President Boris Yeltsin was forced into a runoff with Communist contender Gennady Zyuganov in 1996 (Oates, 2006; White, 2011), elections have been a central area of contention and tension in Russia. This is to be expected, in that competitive elections are designed to highlight struggles among different power bases, parties, candidates, and constituencies within societies. The key difference between elections in Russia and elections in established democracies is the way in which the incumbents have worked so effectively at rigging the system in Russia. Some of this could be considered within the normal electoral "rules of the game," such as government increases in state benefits and cuts in taxes just prior to election day. However, tactics surrounding Russian elections have far exceeded democratic electoral politics. In particular, the government has changed electoral rules to favor large, state-sponsored parties and fostered a media environment in which opposition parties or candidates are belittled, ignored, or become subjects of smear campaigns (particularly on state-run television). There were reports of voter manipulation, rigged ballots, and even outright fraud in many Russian elections prior to 2011. Yet both presidential and parliamentary elections had passed with little protest or comment within Russia, despite reports of problems from international organizations, until the end of 2011.

What changed in the 2011–12 election cycle? Critical clues to this are found in a review of Russian attitudes toward democracy and elections compiled by Hale, Henry E. (2011), who argues that Russians will support authoritative leaders if they are elected through a relatively free process. Rejecting claims that Russians prefer authoritarianism or do not seek a democratic society, Hale uses public opinion data to show that Russians do value democracy, although their definition of democracy can be somewhat unfamiliar to Western researchers. Within a framework of "delegative democracy," Russians are willing to cede a large amount of power and authority to a strong leader such as a president or prime minister (Hale). In other words, they are supportive of strong leaders, but there are trade-offs for this leader. He must be willing to stand for election in a relatively free and fair contest. In addition, this strong leader must show respect for and understanding of the electorate. This particular social contract was violated in the 2011–12 cycle, in that there were signs of falsification that were disseminated to a growing audience by a vastly more integrated and organized online sphere than ever before in Russia. In addition, as discussed below, the respect for the electorate was sadly lacking in the Kremlin's response to the protestors.

Elections to the State Duma attracted widespread complaints of falsification from Russians in late 2011.[1] Seats in the Russian parliament are won through a national party-list contest, which grants seats in proportion to vote won only to those parties that gain 7 percent or more of the national vote. United Russia, the central state party, actually lost seats in the 2011 Duma elections, but retained a comfortable lead with 49.3 percent of the vote and 238 seats, down from 315 seats in the previous Duma (see Table 7.1: Predicted and Actual Vote in 2011 Russian Duma Elections). The other parties who won seats in the 2011 elections were the Communist Party of the Russian Federation (92 seats), A Just Russia (64), and the Liberal Democrats (56). This means that United Russia still maintained a majority in the 450-seat parliament (despite winning just under 50 percent of the popular vote due to the seat distribution system), while the Communists and A Just Russia together formed a Left bloc of 156 seats. The Liberal

Table 7.1 **Predicted and Actual Vote in 2011 Russian Duma Elections**

Party	Political orientation	Predicted vote, Levada Center	Predicted vote as "expert prognosis," VCIOM	Actual vote result	Number of seats in 2011 (out of 450)	Change in seats from 2007
United Russia	Pro-state	53%	53.7%	49.3%	238	– 77
Communist Party	Left	20%	16.7%	19.2%	92	+ 35
A Just Russia	Left/socialist-democrat	12%	11.6%	13.2%	64	+ 26
Liberal Democrats	Nationalist but pro-state	9%	10%	11.7%	56	+ 16

Source: Political orientation was determined by the author's research, which can be found in more detail in Chapter 5. The vote predictions from the Levada Center can be found at http://www.levada.ru/25-11-2011/noyabrskie-reitingi-odobreniya-i-doveriya-reitingi-partii, last accessed March 30, 2012. This is based on a national survey of 1,591 adults carried out from November 18–21, 2011. For the prognosis from the All-Russian Center for the Study of Public Opinion (VCIOM), see their report (in PowerPoint format) at http://www.old.wciom.ru/fileadmin/news/2011/prognoz_23-11-2011.pptx, last accessed March 30, 2012. The research firm used 10 experts to predict the vote between November 18 and November 23, 2011. The number of seats is from reporting by the Russian Central Election Commission, see http://www.vybory.izbirkom.ru/region/region/izbirkom?action=show&root=1&tvd=100100028713304&vrn=100100028713299&region=0&global=1&sub_region=0&prver=0&pronetvd=null&vibid=100100028713304&type=233 (last accessed August 29, 2012).

Democrats, led by nationalist Vladimir Zhirinovsky (see Chapter 5 for more details), have historically voted with the ruling party. While the Duma can shift the agenda and influence politics in Russia (Remington, 2001), it lacks the constitutional strength and popular mandate of a dominant president or prime minister such as Putin. Thus, the loss in seats for United Russia promises relatively little policy change in Russia. Despite the concerns about falsification, there was little expectation that Putin would not secure quick victory with at least 50 percent of the vote the following March. He won easily, with 63.6 percent of the vote.[2]

What were the size and scope of the Russian protests linked to the December 2011 Duma elections and the March 2012 presidential election? Spontaneous protests broke out in Moscow on the Monday and Tuesday after the Duma elections on Sunday, December 4. Defying a ban against unapproved rallies, anti-Putin demonstrators appeared in central Moscow to face off against pro-Putin demonstrators. On Monday, a protest against electoral violations drew several thousand people and resulted in at least 300 arrests (participation in non-sanctioned rallies is a crime in Russia). On Tuesday, police arrested at least 250 protestors, according to the BBC, which estimated the crowd at "hundreds, possibly thousands."[3] The BBC report also noted that footage from protests, which were not covered in any substance in the mainstream media, was followed by at least 30,000 viewers online on the Ridus news website in the hours after the rally. In addition, around 200 protestors were arrested in St. Petersburg and 25 in Rostov-on-Don. Blogger Alexey Navalny and the leader of the opposition Solidarity party were both arrested and jailed for 15 days for their part in the protests.[4]

A review of the Russian media by the BBC foreign media monitoring service found the main Russian television stations made "no mention of the opposition protests."[5] On Tuesday, December 6th, the main nightly news on the three major national television channels (First Channel, state-owned Rossiya-1, and commercial NTV) had "low-key" reports focused on the pro-Putin rallies held in Moscow.[6] On Wednesday, they "largely ignored even those stories."[7] Instead of covering the grassroots protest, Rossiya-1 showed a video report of the rally by one of United Russia's youth wings, Molodaya Gvardiya (Youth Guard). There was coverage elsewhere in the traditional mass media, however. A smaller commercial station, REN-TV, reported on the opposition protests. In addition, major Russian newspapers such as the daily *Kommersant* covered the protests, including by reporting violence by security forces against the protestors. The *Kommersant* editor was fired over his coverage of Putin a few days later.[8] By December 8th, the protestors were more organized, with thousands attending a planned rally calling for fair elections on Bolotnaya Square in Moscow. The BBC estimated the crowd at 50,000 (the organizers claimed 100,000, while Russian officials put the estimate at 25,000). With a focus on the fraud in the Duma elections, the protest attracted a wide range of different groups, including communists, nationalists, and liberal groups, marking the first significant manifestation of a coalition in Russian opposition politics.[9] In addition, there were protests reported in St. Petersburg, Vladivostok, Kurgan, Novosibirsk, and Yekaterinburg. The protests peaked on December 24, with a massive demonstration on Sakharov Avenue in Moscow, with an estimated 80,000 people.[10] Navalny, who had served his jail sentence for participating in the earlier protest, was a central speaker. Again, the state organized pro-regime demonstrations on the same days and state television news coverage focused on these rallies. Significant protests continued in February and March, although the numbers were smaller.[11]

Evidence of Electoral Falsification

The decline in support for United Russia had been predicted both by opinion polls and the United Russia party itself. The Levada polling organization, known for its relative independence from the Kremlin, predicted 53 percent for United Russia, 20 percent for the Communists, 12 percent for the Liberal Democrats, and 9 percent for A Just Russia. As noted on Table 7.1, the final results were not too far from public opinion results within weeks of the election. What attracted attention, both in Russia and around the world, was a large number of eyewitness accounts of falsification, bolstered by some statistical oddities in the results. Although Russian television coverage emphasized the orderly and democratic nature of the elections—as well as the approval of international observers that was reported in a selective way[12]—online sources claimed widespread falsification. Among the concerns were "carousels" of voting in which people travelled together to vote at numerous polling stations, falsification of ballots, and fabrication of results. These concerns were supported by evidence uploaded to the internet. Some of this was in the form of videos, but one of the primary sites for reporting purported election violations was through an "electoral violations" map run by the Golos[13] NGO in Russia at http://www.kartanarusheniy.org/. The government's response was to either ignore the reports—they were not covered in any serious way in the mainstream media—or to engage occasionally in mudslinging in an attempt to undermine either the credibility or the motivations of those reporting the violations. There also was evidence of "dirty tricks," particularly in that the Golos website was the subject of distributed denial-of-service attacks.[14] In addition, reports were made that Golos was in the pay of the United States, including in an NTV documentary called *Anatomy of a Protest* that was aired in March and claimed that the anti-government protestors were mostly paid to demonstrate. The head of Golos, Liliya Shibanova, was detained at a Moscow airport for several hours on December 3, 2012, and only released when she surrendered her laptop computer to authorities.[15] The Central Election Commission of the Russian Federation launched an investigation into the electoral manipulation, but dismissed widespread fraud.[16] Indeed, one of their key findings was a claim that many of the videos of alleged falsification had themselves been falsified.

Regular observers of elections in Russia and similar post-Soviet countries have long noted a range of violations in fair electoral process (OSCE/ODIHR, June, 2004; OSCE/ODIHR, January, 2004; European Institute for the Media, February 1996, September 1996, March 2000, August 2000).[17] Indeed, the OSCE report on the 2011–12 election cycles noted problems with both the Duma and presidential elections.[18] The difficulty comes in separating isolated issues from systematic falsification. The falsification in the 2011 Russian Duma elections, despite the relative closeness of the actual results to the predicted results, seemed unusually compelling due to the way in which the internet was able to identify an apparent pattern of orchestrated manipulation. This was bolstered by a study of the actual results, which were easier to find in detail due to the internet as well. By categorizing electoral violations, mapping them, and collecting them via a range of citizen reports, the Golos map showed how widespread and pervasive electoral manipulation appeared to be across the country. This type of monitoring of electoral violations has always been a huge challenge for both domestic and international election observers, who struggle to provide enough informed coverage on the ground. It is particularly easy for international observers to be misled or to simply lack the capacity to observe enough of the process—from voter coercion to misleading polling procedures to outright stuffing of ballot boxes—to make authoritative reports about the overall fairness of elections. That being said, international and national election observers have noted worrying issues in a range of Russian elections, most notably biased media and a lack of transparency in vote counts in some areas. There also have been concerns over curious results in some districts, such as very high pro-Kremlin votes from Chechnya.

The 2011 Duma elections were no exception to concerns about election result anomalies, which were highlighted in an investigative report led by *The Wall Street Journal*. The *Journal* worked with political scientists to analyze the detailed precinct results from the 2011 elections and found compelling evidence of ballot stuffing. To obtain the data for individual precincts, the newspaper downloaded 2,957 web pages posted on Russia's Central Election Commission website.[19] Analysis by political scientists for the project estimated that as many as 14 million of the 65.7 million votes cast (21 percent) were part of vote rigging. Suspicions were raised as United Russia fared unusually well in precincts in which turnout was well above the national average, which "suggests ballot stuffing" according to the *Journal*, and tallies with reports from individuals who said that they witnessed electoral fraud (such as those who reported it to the Golos election monitoring website). As no other parties benefited in this way from high turnout, the figures suggest that ballots or even just vote totals for United Russia were added to the actual results in many precincts. Although Russian officials were dismissive of the analytical reports suggesting ballot stuffing for United Russia, Putin did decide to install video cameras to stream live video in all of the precincts in Russia for the presidential elections on March 4, 2012.

For its report, the *Journal* designed a computer program to analyze the official voting totals from 95,228 electoral precincts in Russia and a "subsequent statistical analysis revealed phenomena that scholars who study vote data say are suggestive of vote-rigging." Scholars, including Alberto Simpser and Walter Mebane, found pervasive evidence of fraud in the analysis. Anomalies included a large number of precincts that reported an exact round number (e.g., 50 percent or 60 percent) for turnout. More than a handful of round numbers would be statistically highly unlikely, so this suggests that electoral officials falsified returns to fulfill targets. According to the *Journal* analysis, several groups of precincts also reported similar, high round figures as the vote return for United Russia. The *Journal* provided a caveat: "Scholars point out the statistical studies can't prove vote fraud, and the statistical analysis doesn't show how the possible falsification could have occurred. United Russia's strong performance in high-turnout regions could reflect concentrated pockets of enthusiastic support among disciplined voters." However, given eyewitnesses who reported other fraud, including vote totals that were rewritten by election workers after the initial count was completed, it is hard to believe the vote for United Russia was not significantly enhanced.[20]

The Failure of the State Media Frame

Three of the seven factors listed at the beginning of this chapter that contributed to mass protest in Russia in the winter of 2011–12 were linked to the traditional media: the failure of state "soft" controls on the media; an online sphere that was freer than traditional mass media; and the growth in internet audience at the expense of the attention to state-run television. The Kremlin has enjoyed dominance of the main media frame, primarily through its effective control of the state-run First Channel television. Unlike during the Soviet era of censorship and control, much of the effective control of media framing and agenda setting is via the inculcation of self-censorship of media outlets as well as a relatively minor and essentially powerless opposition media such as small newspapers and radio stations. This system of control relies on widespread attention and allegiance to state television, with citizens relatively tolerant of information distortion in the greater interest of the state (Oates, 2006). However, as the analysis of the Russian media audience in Chapter 3 suggests, both the attention and the allegiance are slipping at the same time. While statistics show that more and more people (especially the younger generation) are now prioritizing the internet over television, people who use the internet heavily are more likely to question state authority and support freedom of speech. Thus, while the state perceived the internet as a "talking shop" or "safety valve" that did not threaten the dominant information sphere of television, the pace of growth in internet use, the rise in information sources online, and the increasing trust in information online have all combined to undermine the government's information dominance via television. Nor was there much evidence that attempts to control and intimidate journalists in the online sphere were particularly effective, as the role of information provision steadily widened from a Moscow-centric elite to a far broader group of bloggers and citizens with little allegiance to the power structures in the Kremlin.

Used to a highly attentive audience that accepted coverage that was uncritical of the president and ruling party on all but trivial matters, the Kremlin did not appear to understand how the information space had been transformed by mutually reinforcing factors: as state television lost audience share, more and more important information was becoming available online. This gap became a chasm during the first major protest on December 5, as television failed to cover the demonstrations in any meaningful way. At the same time, there was a wealth of commentary and—even more importantly—documentary evidence about the protests from videos and news via online sources. For example, the online television channel Rain (*Dozhd'*) gained steadily in online usage during this time period, with peaks of use around the Duma elections, the presidential elections, and the protests.[21] This gap between traditional media coverage and online coverage reached critical levels, until finally the traditional media began using Twitter as a source to report on the demonstrations on December 24.

The December protests were the first time that the state's agenda-setting power was seriously challenged and, arguably, undermined by the online sphere. The credibility gap between the public knowledge of the large protests—NTV just dared to mention a large police presence in the evening news on December 5—and the dearth of coverage was simply too great. While this is in part due to the rising importance of the internet in quantity of audience, quality of material, and presence of online networks, it also has to be acknowledged that the winter demonstrations were the largest protests in decades in Russia. Thus, it was not the internet alone that challenged the traditional media—it took a very powerful issue of the election falsification and catalyst of street protests to do so. As the analysis by Hale suggests, election falsification would touch a particular nerve with Russians, who would view this as a fundamental violation of their understanding of the political contract between themselves and the state.

A Stalled Government Reaction

The reaction of the Kremlin to the election protests could be characterized as one of disbelief—and disdain. Aside from failing to take into account information, including video clips, being spread online about the demonstrations, the Kremlin chose to denigrate the movement and belittle those involved. In part, this took the form of constantly understating the attendance at the rallies, which led to wildly divergent crowd estimates at various protests as well as a lack of serious or professional coverage of the events on state-run television. Putin mocked the protestors for wearing white ribbons as symbols of outrage at electoral manipulation, saying in a live television call-in show broadcast on December 15th that the ribbons looked like condoms.[22] Runet immediately reacted with its characteristic enthusiasm for Photoshop caricature, creating pictures of Putin's face wrapped with condoms. People appeared at rallies with huge balloons on their heads to symbolize condoms. The most memorable reaction from Russian President Dmitri Medvedev was the re-tweeting of an obscene tweet about Russian blogger Alexey Navalny. Konstantin Rykov, a United Russia Duma deputy and online PR specialist, tweeted that: "Today it became clear that a person who writes in their blog the words 'party of crooks and thieves' is a stupid, c*cksucking sheep." This was linked both to Navalny's popularization of this nickname for United Russia (discussed in Chapter 5) to a viral online video clip of the blogger shouting "c*cksucking sheep" at the December 5 protest meeting before he was arrested. The Kremlin moved quickly to claim "an incorrect retweet of an entry appeared on Dmitry Medvedev's Twitter account . . . A check revealed that during a routine password change, an employee in charge of technical support for the account made an inadmissible interference in @MedvedevRussia's feed. The guilty will be punished."[23] Whether it was due to an overenthusiastic anti-Navalny PR tweeting for the president, the president himself (which would be unlikely), or merely a mischievous prank using the president's account, none of it speaks well for professionalism, oversight, or security of Medvedev's online PR team.

Arrests at rallies are relatively frequent in Russia, but the number of people detained increased as the scale of the protests grew during the 2011–12 winter rallies. Hundreds including Navalny, other movement leaders, and opposition politicians, were arrested. The government claimed those arrested were a threat to public security, while activists—particularly those in the Strategy-31 movement to protest abuse of Article 31 of the Russian Constitution that guarantees free assembly—have asserted that arrests at protests in Russia are made chiefly to harass and intimidate peaceful protestors. Certainly, the detention of Navalny made headlines around the world and was held up as an example of government repression. Indeed, the arrest helped to transform

Navalny from a well-known blogger to an international leader for the Russian opposition. Overall, it was clear that the Kremlin strategy was to ignore or denigrate the opposition, following the same pattern that had been established for years for political opponents. However, this denigration now embraced a sizable number of citizens instead of a handful of critics. Formerly, the Kremlin had been careful to separate denigration of particular politicians from criticism of ordinary citizens or the people. While much of the criticism was leveled at specific political opponents—Navalny, liberal politician Grigory Yavlinsky, longtime government critic and former party leader Boris Nemtsov—much of the rhetoric reflected, albeit in less crude terms, the "sheep tweet." At best, people were being fooled; at worst, they were engaging in antisocial and dangerous behavior. This represented a noteworthy and ominous shift in the Kremlin's attempts to establish a news frame for the situation. Previously, this frame had kept a respectful tone toward the masses while denigrating specific political enemies or groups. This signaled an end to at least the façade of respect for the citizens.

Motivations of the Protestors

What was the motivation to turn out on some very cold winter days in Russia to attend protest marches and demonstrations? Cyber-optimistic champions of online democracy would describe this as a crossover from virtual politics to street politics, a physical manifestation of the networking and empowerment that takes place in the online sphere. The Kremlin labeled it as opportunists seeking entertainment or attention at the expense of civil society. Research into who was protesting and why—carried out both online and offline—gives important insights into the motivations of the protestors. What emerges is further evidence for two central ideas of this book. First, it is not useful to attempt to separate "online" engagement from "offline" engagement, as protestors who were interviewed by a public opinion firm during the demonstrations did not attribute their participation solely to online mobilization. That being said, it was a meaningful factor amongst a range of elements in motivating people to demonstrate. In addition, as discussed in Chapter 3, there is evidence that more committed online users in Russia are politically distinctive and more anti-state than those who use the internet less regularly or not at all. The second point is that evidence from a study of tweets relating to the protests underlines the concept of one nation and two media audiences, as there was distinctive pro-government Twitter use fueled by aggressive marketing/spamming and a more genuine, albeit quieter, "public sphere" for the opposition reflected in Twitter networks at the same time. While the evidence discussed below often appears to point in different directions, it aids research in two key ways. First, it gives a broad range of data and insights into the individuals, their motivations, and the way in which these are expressed via the online sphere. Second, it shows the impossibility of separating "virtual" from "actual" politics.

In a survey of 791 protestors at the December 24 demonstration on Sakharov Avenue in Moscow, the Levada Center found that just over half of the people interviewed had participated in another protest (mostly on December 10).[24] More than half of the participants (56 percent) had heard about the protest via "internet publications," a third (33 percent) cited "other internet sources," and another third had heard about them via friends, relatives, or neighbors.[25] Although much of the traditional mass media—especially state-run television—was slow to cover the protests, it was still a significant way in which people had heard about them. Eighteen percent had heard about the protests on television and 10 percent from newspapers. It is clear through these figures that television played a relatively minor role in informing citizens. Indeed, even in terms of traditional media, radio played a far more important role, as 27 percent of those surveyed during the demonstration had heard about the protests on radio. This is unsurprising in that radio can be allowed more latitude in discussing politics than television in Russia.

Despite concerns that the internet is more a place for play than for politics, the Moscow demonstrators were clearly using the online sphere as a venue to discuss and deliberate about traditional politics. More than two-thirds of those surveyed at the December 24 demonstrations said they had discussed the Duma elections on social-networking sites in the past three months (37 percent of them regularly and 31 percent of them periodically). Yet almost a third (32 percent) of the protestors surveyed had not discussed Duma politics at all on social-networking sites. Interestingly, engagement in the online sphere did not seem to drive more regular attendance at the demonstrations. When divided into groups of those who regularly discussed politics online, those who discussed it periodically, and those who did not discuss it online at all, those who talked about politics the most online were only slightly more likely to have attended previous protests (Greene, May 2012). This suggests there was not a core of internet activists who were joined by a small group at protests; rather, it would indicate that protest was not strongly linked to online political discussion. Nor did their reasons for protests vary much. Overall, those surveyed had two overwhelmingly strong reasons for protesting: 73 percent said both that they wanted to express their "outrage" over falsification as well as express anger over their "accumulated dissatisfaction" over the political situation regarding the country/ political leaders (protestors could report more than one reason for their participation). Other reasons included dissatisfaction with undemocratic policymaking (52 percent), disappointment with Medvedev and/or modernization (42 percent), solidarity with parties participating in the protest (15 percent), affinity with protest organizers (13 percent), accompanying friends (10 percent), and finding protesting interesting and "trendy" (6 percent).

Where the protestors were very distinctive was in their party preference. There was an overwhelming preference overall for Yabloko (24 percent), the relatively liberal party led by Yavlinsky that has failed to cross the party-seat threshold for the Duma since 2003. However, Yabloko traditionally has enjoyed substantially more support in the urban centers such as Moscow and most of those surveyed at the protest were indeed from Moscow (only 4 percent of those surveyed said they were from outside Moscow or the Moscow region). Those who have analyzed and observed Russian party politics over the past two decades would also note that Yabloko, as the most long-term, liberal option in Russia, has been a sustained target of media bias (Oates, 2006). This would suggest that party could experience a resurgence of support or interest by gaining a "voice" online. Interestingly, the habit of discussing politics online made a meaningful difference in support for political parties. Those who regularly discussed politics online had a preference for a (then nonexistent) "party founded by Navalny" (28 percent), with about 20 percent favoring Yabloko and about 7 percent choosing the Communist Party (Greene). This was in quite distinct contrast to those who only periodically discussed politics online, 30 percent of whom favored Yabloko and less than 15 percent who would favor a party founded by Navalny. Those who did not discuss politics online also picked Yabloko as their favorite, but 17 percent chose the Communist Party. This is likely an artifact of age and online use: Communist supporters tend to be older and hence are much less likely to be engaged in social networking or online in general. Indeed, the offline group had less interest in a party founded by Navalny (10 percent), but a relatively strong interest in the People's Freedom Party (15 percent, far more than any other group measured by online political discussion; this analysis is from Greene). This would suggest that there are distinct constituencies fostered by online political discussion. The idea of a party around a popular blogger found credence with a significant percentage of those who talk about politics online, while traditional parties such as Yabloko and the Communist Party held sway for those who were not engaged in online political discussions. Indeed, it would appear that the more one discusses politics online, the more likely one is to be attracted to a party founded by a blogger—a logical conclusion, but still one that suggests the latent power of the internet to weld together "online" and "offline" politics. It is also interesting to note that this interest in bloggers-as-politicians would appear to erode support for parties that might conceivably use the online sphere to rally support, particularly parties such as Yabloko that have a younger appeal than the Communists and could be seen as the type of party to be able to adapt to new media technologies.

While there were interesting differences among the protestors based on their internet use, the larger issue was how distinctive the protestors were from the general population in Russia. In particular, their presidential vote choices differed wildly from the electorate at large. Even in December 2011, Putin still had strong support from the voters, while he had virtually no support from the street demonstrators on December 24 in the Levada Center survey. The protestors surveyed were interested in a range of presidential candidates who shared the characteristic of not being Putin, with vote preferences reported as 29 percent for Yavlinsky, 18 percent for billionaire entrepreneur Mikhail Prokhorov, 11 percent for Communist leader Gennady Zyuganov, 5 percent for Liberal Democrat leader Vladimir Zhirinovsky, and 5 percent for former Just Russia leader Sergei Mironov. Putin came last, at 1 percent. On the one hand, this is not particularly surprising, as those who supported Putin would be far less likely to protest. However, one would expect at least some support for the former president and current prime minister. Part of this divergence can be explained by the exercise itself, in that people were picking a "fantasy" president rather than considering who to favor from a list of realistic possibilities for victory.

Online Mobilization

One of the most pervasive interests of states and citizens alike has been the ability of online communication tools to organize protest demonstrations. Indeed, state officials often label internet service providers such as Facebook (in Egypt) or Twitter (in Iran) as not just effective in the *communication* of unrest, but key players in the *creation* of the unrest. In other words, without the particular internet platform, many believe there would not be social unrest on the scale seen in Egypt in 2011 or Iran in 2009. The same concerns were voiced about the role of social media—namely Twitter and BlackBerry messaging—in the August 2011 riots in London and other English cities. While the central media frame in Britain was that ICTs were accelerants to the violence, in particular by giving voice to antisocial groups and gathering mobs for looting, a study by a group of scholars at the University of Manchester and the London School of Economics suggested otherwise.[26] This Reading the Riots study found that the most dominant (re-tweeted) texts on Twitter referred to mass media reports. Indeed, the mass media at the time extensively covered the riots, even providing detailed maps of their location.[27] The problem with analyzing the role of online communication in crisis situations is disentangling the issues relating to the broader socioeconomic factors and political environment from the specific mobilization tools offered by ICTs. It is easier for states to "blame" Twitter or Facebook for unrest rather than explore the causes of the discontent.

Two studies of Twitter in Russia provide an insight into its use for recent protest mobilization in Russia. As part of a three-year study of the Russian internet, The Berkman Center for Internet & Society mapped patterns in more than 50 million Russian-language tweets collected between March 2010 and March 2011 (Kelly et al., March 2012). The project examined both content and connections among Russian-language users (most of them in Russia itself) in the period prior to the 2011–12 protests. Using human content analysis to establish categories, the researchers divided the Twitter users into five main groups: political, instrumental, CIS regional, technology, and music. They also noted the presence of clusters around Russian regions outside of Moscow and St. Petersburg. However, not all of the tweets were linked to citizen activity. The analysis found that a large volume of activity on Twitter was generated by "marketing campaigns and search engine optimization (SEO) initiatives, including both automated and coordinated human actors" (p. 3).

Once these marketing groups were filtered out, the researchers found a democratic movement cluster linked to former chess champion and opposition politician Garry Kasparov and the Solidarity movement. However, the analysis of the tweets also showed some gaps: for example, although the Berkman Center found Russian nationalists very active in the Runet blogosphere (Etling et al., 2010), they lacked a meaningful presence on Russian Twitter as of March 2011. Although the analysis showed that pro-Putin youth groups were active on Twitter, their presence—along with other pro-government presence—was eliminated when the results from human and search-engine optimization manipulation were filtered out. While it is noteworthy that there was what appeared to be grassroots politics on Twitter, it seemed to be overwhelmed by the more professional marketing by pro-government groups. Although more sophisticated users could themselves filter or select their content to avoid mass marketing, it would suggest that pro-government forces had colonized Twitter, making it less effective for grassroots politics in Russia. This is particularly noteworthy as there has been recent growth in the use of Twitter in Russia, although there were only 3.8 million users by April 2012.[28]

An analysis of the meeting participants on VKontakte and Facebook showed few links between the protestors or any sense of community among those who appeared at the protests in Moscow on December 10 or 24 (Suvorov, January 2012). In a project for Basilisk Labs, Suvorov mined 19,664 user profiles on VKontakte and 2,600 user profiles on Facebook by analyzing social-networking groups relating to the protests. In addition, he was able to mine data about the participants through their stated preferences as well as via their online "friend" links. Overall, the research found those who claimed to have attended the protests to be overwhelmingly male (80 percent, compared with 52 percent male usage of VKontakte overall), typically between 21 and 26 years old, relatively well educated, and fairly well off financially. As with the Levada Center survey data cited above, the social-network analysis found this group of protestors politically distinctive from general internet users. By comparing the profiles of the participants to a sample of 15,000 profiles of non-protestors on VKontakte, Suvorov found that protest participants were much more likely to label themselves as "liberals" (more than 30 percent for the protestors, compared with just over 10 percent for the general social-network users) and were somewhat more likely to label themselves "socialists" (just under 10 percent compared with about 6 percent). On the other hand, the protestors were far less likely to pick "moderate" as their ideology: Only about 14 percent of the protestors chose this label, compared with over 50 percent of the general social-network users.[29] However, Suvorov notes that 60 percent of the social-network participants declined to pick any ideological label at all from the menu provided by the social-networking site.

In addition to establishing a profile of the December Moscow protest participants through social-networking sites, Suvorov used the data to assess the resilience of the protests if those leading the protests were removed or repressed. In addition, the study looked at whether there was a sense of a robust network or community of the protestors that was reflected in the online sphere. In both cases, the analysis by Suvorov of the online data suggested that the protests lacked depth and resilience. A network analysis of those who identified themselves with the two protests showed no pattern of networks among the protestors, despite a study of 17,000 meeting participants and a total of 1.6 million linkages in the online sphere. What emerged was a pattern of isolated groups of individuals, with no single network through which they could connect. In addition, while the study found a network surrounding popular bloggers and online social entrepreneurs during the protests, there was no network connecting them to the people who showed up to protest (i.e. to a wider audience in general). There remained what Suvorov termed "islands" of protest, without the type of networks identified by the Berkman study. Most likely this is linked to the fact that the Berkman analysis used a broader sweep of terms to define issues as political. Suvorov notes that this lack of a protest movement with identifiable, connecting ideology meant that the Moscow protests did not "turn into a Maidan," a reference to the central protest area for the Orange Revolution in Ukraine. Instead, Suvorov concluded that the meetings on December 10 and 24 in Moscow were more "political flash mobs" rather than gatherings or demonstrations in the traditional political sense. As a result, he did not perceive the Moscow demonstrations as vehicles for political change due to a lack of connection and a lack of shared political goals among the protestors. At the same time, he noted that this lack of a centralized movement highlights the independent motivation of a large number of people to choose to protest. This could then be interpreted to mean that levels of political interest and dissent are relatively robust, albeit without a particular unified direction by late 2011—although this is not a conclusion that Suvorov draws from the data. While Suvorov predicted no further protests— and the protests for the presidential elections were smaller—it is interesting to speculate that his research shows a rising political activism that could possibly be harnessed by an effective opposition movement.

Another study examining the use of Twitter during the protests suggests that the communicative features of Twitter as portable, immediate, and working via networks, may resist attempts to tame it as a democratizing tool. The Center for the Study of New Media & Society at the New Economic School in Moscow analyzed more than 11,000 tweets sent by over 8,500 users during a period of peak political protest around the March 4 presidential elections (Greene, May 2012).[30] The analysis examined both anti-government and pro-government activity on Twitter. The data collection began from the identification of Twitter hashtags that "were clearly and uniquely associated" either with the March 4 presidential election or with the ensuing pro- and anti-government demonstrations. The researchers then used snowballing to identify other hashtags and keywords, eventually identifying nine hashtags and five keywords that were central to communication relating to election protests.

Unlike Suvorov's conclusions that protestors were relatively atomized in the online sphere, the center's research found that Twitter performed "multiple functions simultaneously and at differing stages of mobilization (Greene, p. 1)". These functions included serving as an aggregator of information, ideas, and memes for mobilization; a medium to spread information, ideas, and memes to a broader audience; and as an "echo chamber" that could reinforce group solidarity. In addition, the research found that the pro-government and anti-government "camps" displayed significantly different social structures in that the opposition networks were more diverse and dispersed, as well as being linked with media outlets that had a meaningful Twitter presence. This linkage meant that the protestors were able to dominate the Twitter landscape during a period of peak protest around the presidential elections. Meanwhile, the pro-government networks (or "camps") were relatively more concentrated, had communication along established channels, and placed more emphasis on formal role-players rather than informal participants. Finally, the research on Twitter activity found that a "key role" during the protest period was played by professional journalists and media outlets, full-time bloggers, established civic groups, NGOs, and political organizations. The impact of "informal" tweeters or "accidental" tweets appeared minimal, which parallels the findings of the Reading the Riots project in the United Kingdom.

Twitter can simultaneously fulfill various functions such as informing, mobilizing, networking, and even providing surveillance of society at the same time. Greene (pp. 12–13) notes that the Twitter analysis for the electoral protests found that the communication tool

> took on a much more dispersed and interactive character during the election phase, when the emphasis was on collecting and aggregating information on what was happening during the voting process, including evidence of fraud. Moreover, the transition, particularly within opposition networks, from more dispersed to more concentrated communication over time suggests a process by which information is collected, aggregated, processed and then re-broadcast for mobilizational purposes. It is also noteworthy that the emphasis within the pro-government networks is more heavily on broadcast.

This study suggests that Twitter—or any online communication tool—cannot be understood to have a single role within a society or even a particular protest. Rather, online communication tools both reflect and refract existing power and informational networks within a country. To make matters even more complicated, different online tools may play different roles for different groups even at the same time. Thus, Suvorov's research found little evidence of a social-networking community arising among those who went to two major protest rallies in December, although the research did underline that those who identified themselves as protestors on social-networking sites were more likely to be male, more educated, wealthier, and to consider themselves liberal than the general online population. However, the study of Twitter by Greene suggests that there is a "strength of weak ties" among activists, finding an identifiable community of interest during the peak protest period after the Russian presidential elections in March 2012. Street surveys on December 24 found that the protestors supported a distinctly different group of politicians than those on the ballot. Yet both the street survey and the examination of social-networking sites did not suggest that this was a group of people who were lured into a sort of internet cult—an argument put forward in an anti-protest "documentary" on NTV in March—but that these were people who had a range of different information sources and ideas. This is positive for Russian democracy in the sense that it shows people have often independently come to the protests, not driven by one ideology or one leader. Suvorov said his research on social-networking sites suggested that this is little more than a "political flash mob" and cannot last. Yet the Twitter research, as well as the analysis of both Twitter and blogs by Berkman, shows more resilient networks of interest in the Russian online sphere. Overall, there is compelling evidence of disquiet and discontent with the falsification of Russian elections, a rising sense of anger and opposition in Russia. So far, it would appear to be sentiment without a central organization. However, with a large number of engaged—and often enraged—citizens, it would seem that a cogent opposition movement could engage the public.

Conclusions

How does the evidence from the role of the online sphere in protests contribute to the seven factors discussed in the introduction to this chapter? There is compelling support for the idea that there has been a fundamental shift in the way in which information can be created, consumed, and disseminated in Russia. Although it would be misleading and unhelpful to call this a revolution based on Russian blogging or social networking, it is clear from the study of both online content and the protest participants themselves that a shift in orientation toward political communication has occurred. Television is still immensely important in Russia, as noted in Chapter 3, but it can no longer control the shape and flow of information in the same way. This does not mean revolution per se, but it does mean when citizens have a particular focus of discontent—in this case the falsification of the elections and associated rallies—the online sphere provides an effective, authoritative, and rapid means of disseminating both ideas and organizational tactics. Some of this is linked to crowd-sourcing, as evidenced by the Golos voting violation maps. Most of it, however, would appear to be connected to the way in which information and central online social entrepreneurs (such as Navalny) become important nodes in information networks. The evidence from the study of blogs and Twitter is mixed: while the Berkman Institute and the Center for New Media & Society found evidence of relatively robust networks, Suvorov argues that the protests were little more than "political flash mobs." Yet we know from the study by the Levada Center that there were compelling differences among the protestors, with some characteristics linked to heavier use of the online sphere to discuss politics. In hindsight, Russia was vulnerable to "political flash mobs" due to the growing credibility gap between the traditional media, exploding internet use, and the information that could be found online relating to the emotive issue of vote falsification. The question remains as to whether this was indeed a political "flash" or whether the protests are evidence of a rising political consciousness on the part of Russian citizens. Whatever the depth or endurance of the political moment surrounding this winter of discontent, it has shown the ability of the internet to change the rules of the political game in a very short period once preexisting conditions such as significant online content, community, and weak controls are in place. The political consequences were not as profound as those in the Orange Revolution in Ukraine, in which protests led to new elections. Here, the victories for democracy were more subtle and could probably be identified as more concern about transparency (not necessarily fairness) in the 2012 presidential elections as well as changes in the Duma electoral laws announced by Medvedev in Spring 2012 that make party formation less cumbersome.

As much as it would be inaccurate—and misleading—to claim that the 2011–12 winter protests in Russia changed the political system, it did shift some of the power to control political communication away from one set of elites. Arguably, bloggers are another set of elites and, as the study by Suvorov suggests, it is difficult to tell how much information is linked among the grassroots in Russia. In thinking about the way in which the internet inculcates political change, we can consider change on different levels. In terms of society itself, Russia remains essentially an oligarchy or a "delegative democracy" in which citizens have limited opportunities to effect political change. In terms of groups, the experience of the winter of discontent has shown the opportunities and risks of either forming opposition online or using the online sphere to bolster an offline group. Arrests of organizers were frequent and the open nature of the online sphere makes these groups quite vulnerable to co-optation and control. The most intriguing and significant change may have taken place on the part of the Russian citizen, who learned that it is possible to participate in politics in a range of new ways, from acquiring more independent information, to contributing their views and information via crowd-sourcing, to discussing new ideas, to taking part in or even helping to organize a protest march. It is this change for the individual, who is below the radar of state retaliation and attention, that could hold the most promise for a long-term shift toward a more open, inclusive, and fair society in Russia.

8

Conclusions

This study of the Russian internet had two primary goals. The first was to explore, in detail, the effect of the internet on political communication in Russia. The second, broader endeavor of this project was to use the Russian experience to develop a comparative framework for understanding how the internet interacts with existing political communication norms and institutions within a nation. In other words, how do domestic factors shape and constrain the democratizing potential of the online sphere? How do states—and citizens—use the internet in surprising or enlightening ways? The book began with a research framework of the "5C" categories: content, community, catalyst, control, and co-optation. While the research does not always neatly fit into one of these categories, approaching the study through five different pathways has been useful. It has value in terms of understanding the Russian case, but more significantly it has aided in building theory about the interplay between international norms and domestic factors in understanding how the internet fits into a national political landscape.

Over the course of writing this book, both international and domestic factors shifted significantly in relation to the online sphere. The role of the internet in the Arab Spring changed global perspectives about the potential of the internet to foster revolution. Until the events in Egypt, political analysts had remained relatively unconvinced that online politics could transform entrenched institutions in the offline world. Although there was excitement over the way in which the internet enlivened President Obama's election campaign in 2008, it was questionable whether the online sphere was ultimately the reason for his victory. While Twitter was prominent in foreign reporting about unrest in Iran surrounding the presidential elections in 2009, the shocking image of a young woman shot during protests did not lead to a shift in elite power there. It was not until the street protests linked to Facebook and other online networks became visible in Egypt in early 2011, that leaders and the public alike started to realize the broad potential of the internet in political change. Over the same period, a combination of forces was bringing about a fundamental shift in internet use in the Russian Federation. When research for this book began in 2008, Russia still lagged behind other European and Western countries in terms of internet use. By 2011, growth in the Russian online population had exploded, making Russians second only to Germans as the largest group of Europeans online. In the space of a few years, Russia had moved from a narrow internet society to one in which the internet was reaching into a wide and engaged group of citizens. It would seem that both the international and domestic potential of the internet to inform, engage, and transform the society was at hand.

This book argues that the collision of online factors (growth, content, networking, online social entrepreneurship) with the political catalyst of election falsification marked a significant new era in political communication in Russia. It has shifted the role of the internet—in the eyes of the public and the leaders— from a marginal arena for malcontents into an important source of political information and aggregation. The evidence is not only through the tens of thousands of people who attended rallies in Russian cities in the winter of 2011–12, demonstrations that would have been impossible without the informative and organizational role of the internet. The proof is also in the rising evidence of critical political content and community in the online sphere.

Two key questions emerge from this study that parallel the twin aims of this book. First, does the rise of online communication and community signal a fundamental political change in Russia? In addition, is the experience in Russia generalizable? In other words, can we both understand the Russian case through evidence from the Arab Spring and other movements linked to online campaigns elsewhere, as well as use the Russian "winter of discontent" to further our understanding of how the internet can function as a "game-changer" in political communication in non-free states?

Even before the 2011–12 election protests, there was no doubt that the internet had enriched and enlivened the nature of political and social debate in Russia. In particular, Russians had developed domestic platforms such as Live-Journal (which combines features of blogging and social networking) and the search engine Yandex. A major study of the Russian blogosphere (Etling et al., 2010) found that by 2010 Russians were engaging in a wide political debate online, linking to and from a range of political viewpoints. Unlike the more insular political bloggers in the United States who tend to stay within ideological boundaries (Davis, 2009), the Berkman report found that Russian bloggers were straying across a range of political camps. However, this is also reflective of the fact that there was not really contested political space between government and opposition in Russia; rather, there was little effective opposition to the Kremlin and the pro-Kremlin parties in the Russian parliament. Thus, it was not surprising that Chapter 5 found little evidence that Russian political parties used the online sphere to increase their political presence and power. Rather, the online sphere tended to parallel, rather than transform, the role of political parties in Russia. The only evidence of a novel contribution from Russian political parties online came from the publicity for some alternative voices and protests that lacked a presence in the traditional mass media.

The greatest promise for fundamental political change in Russia was not present via traditional political institutions, such as parties, online. Rather, more significant challenges to the state appeared "under the radar" of traditional politics in the way that Russian patients and families sought rights and benefits by using Runet (Chapter 6). This rise of online communities, energized by specific concerns about the status and treatment of people with health issues or disabilities, stood in direct contrast to "politics as usual" in Russia. A review of website information provision, web links, and user-generated content shows that Russians can and do organize campaigns and seek redress from the state. However, as bitter comments from family members of kidney patients on the dialysis forum suggest, other people who were less empowered and more isolated were not as successful, dying due to a lack of proper treatment.

All of this raises the general question about the Russian internet: How representative of the Russian political and social sphere is the activity on Runet? What do either wide-ranging studies of online data with the aid of automated coding or the more detailed analysis of internet content by human coders tell us about political communication in Russia? Are power relationships merely replicated—or even augmented—by the online sphere? Or is it possible for Russian citizens to become more enlightened and empowered through the range of information and communication tools via the internet? For the cyber-optimists, there is some very persuasive evidence that the internet could fundamentally change the relationship between the elites and the masses in Russia. Perhaps one of the strongest arguments for fundamental change is simply quantitative: As penetration rates approach 50 percent of the population, internet usage among those under 40 has reached the rate of the United States and Western Europe. In the Russian government's own estimates, based on a large number of independent sources, internet penetration will grow until it reaches almost all of the population under 40 by 2014 (Russian Federal Agency on the Press and Mass Communication, 2011). This will make Russia one of the most wired nations in the world. At the same time, there is compelling evidence, such as in the 2010 survey cited in Chapter 3 and the survey of December 2011 protestors in Chapter 7, that online citizens are more liberal and engaged than average Russian citizens. Although it is impossible to tell the direction of the effect—whether those who are going online were more liberal to begin with or to what extent the internet may have "transformed" them—the correlation is significant. It would lead one to speculate that the more citizens get online, the more likely they are to gain exposure to a wider range of views than those offered by the limited Russian traditional mass media, to become acquainted with global points of view, to aggregate interests, and to become more politically empowered in general.

While there is evidence of the transformative nature of the online sphere in Russia, cyber-pessimists also have a compelling case to make. As Chapter 2 outlines, it is not inevitable that the globalizing potential of the internet is realized within national boundaries. In particular, the Russian mass media is controlled through a neo-Soviet media model (Oates, 2007) that inculcates self-censorship, the obedience to political sponsors, and avoidance of topics that directly challenge the government. Russia remains an unusually violent place for journalists to do their jobs, with many being murdered or attacked each year. As the internet rises in prominence in the Russian political communication sphere, so will efforts to harness it as another outlet for state-centric messages. This is evidenced already by a share of the violence against reporters being directed at online writers. There are also signs that the Kremlin and the dominant United Russia party use the internet, including some bloggers, to spread "white" propaganda about their cause and attack opponents with "black" propaganda. In addition, there is indication from the Berkman Institute that pro-state forces have attempted to "colonize" Twitter (Kelly et al., 2012). Indeed, state regulations and the legal system—which offer relatively poor protection for journalists in general—are designed more to protect the government's right to use the internet as a tool for monitoring and controlling citizens in Russia than to provide an open exchange of ideas (see Chapter 4). A range of laws, from regulations that require Russian internet service providers to give data to the state security system to measures to protect the president against slander, actively work against freedom of speech in the online sphere. More worryingly, Deibert et al. (2010) detect a trend in states such as Russia to incorporate the internet into its broader policy of state repression and control of citizens.

Where does this leave us, both in terms of Russia online and the broader question of understanding the political role of the internet in comparative perspective? The following key points emerge that parallel the "5C" model of content, community, catalyst, control, and co-optation.

Content

The study of content remains both the most elusive and most promising aspect in analyzing the Russian internet as well as the online sphere in general. The internet makes public a vast treasure-trove of data, so much information that it is enormously difficult to isolate what might be its critical elements, although many projects are starting to make this attempt in Russia (Etling et al., 2010;

Kelly et al., March 2012; Suvorov, 2012; Greene, May 2012). The audience is open to all, at least for now, but what can we make of it? We can make a great deal of it through quantitative analysis, by tracking what people search, which websites they visit, and even how those websites are linked to one another. Thus, we can see the informational architecture of an online society, although parts of this map tend to be overwhelmed with particularly popular sites that draw the bulk of the traffic. Thus, we know where Russians tend to go online and we know generally what they do. This does not differ markedly from other societies, which makes it necessary to think about what content they may consume and—even more interestingly—produce in their online lives.

Some studies, notably Internews (August 2011), have suggested that the brave and interesting reporting on blogs and via other online outlets fundamentally challenge the information hegemony of the Kremlin. There is some evidence to suggest this might be the case, particularly given the relatively high penetration and rapid expansion of internet use. Other evidence is a range of case studies of individual bloggers such as Alexey Navalny who have attracted a large following (and the unwelcome attention of the government) by publishing allegations of bribery and corruption online. Indeed, Navalny served as a central rallying figure—both online and in person—for the 2011–12 winter protests. There is no question that the range of discussion is broader in the online sphere in Russia than in the relatively controlled traditional media, especially on central television channels.

However, has online reporting in Russia *fundamentally* changed the agenda of the mainstream media? It would appear that the Russian government still holds an asymmetrically large amount of power over bloggers, able to deploy controls ranging from informal pressure (Fossato at al., 2008), to lawsuits, to even arrest and imprisonment in order to control bloggers who violate the accepted norms of coverage in Russia. It is clear that the mainstream media use online sources and that groups are able to utilize the internet (as did the dialysis patients and the parents of disabled children) to seek benefits or even gain what some would perceive as rights. The internet was a key element in the winter of discontent, ranging from the way in which information was gathered, to how it was distributed, to how people were mobilized, and even to the organization of the events themselves. The question remains, in this symbiotic relationship between the traditional mass media in Russia and the grassroots internet, whether the traditional mass media still are more powerful. At the same time, there is nothing to stop the traditional mass media, particularly the powerful and influential First Channel, from pursuing a more aggressive and successful online presence. So far, the online sphere has been left to information entrepreneurs such as Navalny and Marina Litvinovich highlighted in the Internews report, but there is no reason that this could not change in the future. While some cyber-optimists would argue that the online audience would not accept the intrusion of slick PR or blogs written as marketing tools, many would assert that the bulk of the internet audience lacks deep political conviction and essentially seeks to be entertained rather than politically transformed.

Another central question is whether there are quantitative or qualitative measures for online content that can reliably predict political action in a society. It is clear that we can learn a significant amount about how people gather, disseminate, and even feel about particular issues from online content. In particular, user-generated content gives us insight into audiences and citizens on an unprecedented level. Yet, it is the lack of precedents that remains a problem for scholars, analysts, policy-makers, and citizen activists alike. What are the significant "trigger" points for online content to make a difference? Is it the scale of online content, i.e., the amount of information provision and user-generated comments? Is it the location of the information within the informational architecture as illuminated via web link analysis or other mapping tools that can visualize the spread of information along online pathways? Is there a particular quantity or pattern of usage that can be generalized, allowing states and citizens to predict when online content may have reached a critical mass to generate social change? For example, the development of Google Trends has shown that search patterns for flu symptoms can predict the level and spread of influenza within a population, given that individuals will search for relief from symptoms as they start to arise. Thus, one can see a type of electronic "flocking" in the online world that can help societies prepare for peaks in the flu season through the provision of medical supplies. Can search behavior data be harnessed the same way in the political world? For example, does the rise in the search terms for an opposition party—such as the Communist Party in Russia—suggest a greater interest in opposition politics and possible support in upcoming elections? The notion that online search and other user data can provide new ways of understanding and predicting human behavior is one of the most popular and growing fields, but exactly how to harness this phenomenon remains far more elusive in the sphere of politics, as opposed to the relatively straightforward field of marketing.

This has led to a growing use of sentiment analysis for online content (as discussed in Chapter 6). Indeed, a $40 million USD hedge fund, based on a trading strategy linked to sentiment analysis in Twitter messages, was launched in the United Kingdom in 2011. The fund used a sentiment-analysis system that added a language algorithm based on the content analysis of about 10 million tweets sent daily with other trading algorithms to predict the confidence level of investors.[1] Could the same sort of sentiment analysis be used to track political mood, allowing politicians in both government and opposition to tailor their policies to attract the most votes at critical elections? Will the evolution of automated content analysis reveal the thoughts, attitudes, and even feelings of citizens to a degree that politicians can predict or even manipulate public moods as well as public actions?

While sentiment analysis and other forms of automated content analysis seem to be effective at predicting and even explaining some behaviors, this study found that content analysis of both information provision by political institutions and users was very problematic to reduce to an automated system. A significant element of the problem is sampling. In standard public opinion work, one can factor national attitudes from a sample that is defined through tested statistical procedures. But what is a significant sample in the online sphere? Is it comments or a subset of comments on the most popular blogs? Is it the information provided on the website of the country's most influential television channel? Is it through the comments underneath the controversial stories on the television website? What weight does the presidential blog carry? While it might not be the most popular blog in the country, it may be read by the most influential people in the nation, who can glean important changes in policy and direction through the president's words (or the words of those hired to write for him). Once we identify important content, how do we analyze it for complex political concepts? As noted in Chapter 6, researchers found it difficult to code even within a relatively well-defined coding frame that used political concepts such as arguing for rights and benefits. How can this type of research be deployed on a scale that is of significant scope, yet also valid and reliable, to mine online content to understand political attitudes? In particular, how can we set up valid and reliable ways to measure signals of change or contestations within states? The evidence in this book would suggest that content can only be usefully employed in political analysis against a backdrop of other factors, which are discussed in the following four categories of the 5C model.

Community

What is an online "community"? In online methodological terms, a community is often represented by a web link analysis that allows one to see the map of connections among websites or users. Further advances in internet methodology make it possible to measure communities on a range of platforms, including the relationship between those who tweet and networks that are reflected on social-networking sites such as Facebook or VKontakte. As LiveJournal straddles the divide between social networking and blogging, it offers a particularly interesting way to analyze how ideas, bloggers, followers, and those who post comments come together in a particular way online. The idea employed about online "communities" is somewhat deeper in this book, in that the case studies relating to political parties, families of disabled children, patients, and the 2011–12 winter protestors have looked at communities that are defined by offline characteristics. Thus, the idea of community in the online sphere reflects—and often intensifies—the community in the offline world. Social scientists are left with trying to measure how the online community maps onto the offline community and vice-versa. Evidence in this book suggests that the online sphere can offer specific enhancement to offline communities in non-free states such as Russia. It provides a way to exchange information on topics that are too narrow (health-care provision for children with mucopolysaccharidosis) or too controversial (state corruption) for the mainstream Russian media. Through this exchange, the narrow strata of particular issues or interest groups that stretch across Russia are brought together and intensified. Rather worry-ingly, this type of resilient community did not seem to arise out of the 2011–12 winter protests (Suvorov), although other studies suggest that there are some relatively robust relationships online between those who engage politically in Russia (Kelly et al., Greene, May 2012).

Although political parties do not seem to be fundamentally changed or enhanced by the online sphere in Russia, there is compelling evidence from the studies in this book that the internet fundamentally changes the ability of some groups to mobilize. For example, the campaigns for the rights of children with disabilities or access to critical health services most likely would have failed without the help of the communicative tools and features of the internet. Thus, there is evidence of issue "community" enhancement, if not an essential redistribution of power from elites to citizens in Russia. Case by case, we can see that citizens manage to access privileges and even rights through online campaigns. This book only looked at some examples. As noted by the 2011 Internews report, there were also compelling examples of citizen mobilization with the protests over the development of the Khimki forest and the crowd-sourced response to massive wildfires in Russia in 2010 when government assistance faltered.

The question is whether these will remain isolated examples or whether, once some campaigns are successful, these tactics will become widespread enough to fundamentally redress the power imbalances between rulers and citizens in Russia. For this to happen, the type of challenge launched in the online sphere would have to develop from the relatively small causes (although they often reflect broad principles) to fundamental concerns in Russian society—the right to fair elections, the right to effective political parties, the right to free speech, the right to fair trial, the right to rule of law—in general, the right for a transpar-ent and democratic system in which citizens ultimately control who is in charge of the government. This begs the question of whether the smaller movements supported by the online sphere were linked to the larger protests in the winter of

2011–12 supported by Runet. It would certainly suggest that both citizens and groups had acquired significant new skills in gathering information, building networks, and organizing responses to challenge a state that had failed to deliver on what they perceived to be key issues. Whether this will lead to a fundamental redistribution of power remains to be seen and, as argued by scholars such as Rogers and Greene, depends more on a broad range of political factors than on just what happens in the online sphere.

Catalyst

One element of internet scholarship has focused on how intense events affect the online sphere. The syndrome of a sudden and penetrating spread of content and activity in the online sphere surrounding large protests, coups, natural disasters, or other extraordinary events has been called "firestorms" by Fossato et al. in a study of three prominent Russian protest movements. Jungherr and Jürgens (2011) introduced the idea of "peakiness" in online content in their study of tweets relating to a protest against urban development in Stuttgart, Germany. Whether content flames or peaks, the conceptualization is very evocative in terms of understanding that online dynamics may shift quickly and fundamentally during extraordinary events. Thus, there may be a relatively stable community of activists, but their behavior (both online and offline) may shift radically due to police actions, riots, counter-protests, arrests of the participants, and so on. The volume and nature of both the information provided by the groups as well as that fed back via user-generated content may bear little resemblance to the usual online traffic and activity. Yet, if we cannot establish patterns of online behavior during crisis, it is very difficult to establish comparable patterns and theories to explain the role of the internet in crisis. Do users stay within their usual communicative "maps" as expressed by web link analysis? Do they employ different ways of communicating in an emergency? Are the usual norms of communication and online behavior changed, or even broken, during a crisis? Does the noise-to-signal ratio grow, i.e., do a large number of new or angry users overwhelm the fundamental discussion or direction of the online community during a crisis event? These are all issues that are still relatively poorly understood.

This book examined the nature of online catalyst in a relatively modest way in an attempt to understand how extraordinary events challenged, changed, or consolidated online content and community for patients and families of children with disabilities. In Chapter 7, the book looked at these issues through studies of online content by Greene and Suvorov. The issue of catalyst becomes much more persuasive in understanding the internet's role in the 2011–12 winter demonstrations. In the case of the families of children with Down syndrome or MPS, the catalyst was the heartless article suggesting that children with disabilities could be killed at birth. For the dialysis patients, the issue was the removal of treatment that would essentially condemn them to a rapid death. These "catalysts" were apparent through media coverage of the cases. The study of catalysts with these case studies highlighted two key points. First, the attitudes of the users making comments became much more focused and easier to code for attitudes toward important markers such as human rights and liberal values. A review of forums on health issues in Russia generally showed little content that generated meaningful information about user attitudes, as much of the discussion was everyday conversation, general greetings, queries, or personal issues. During a crisis event, however, forum content became much more focused and revealing about broader issues. This suggests that finding relevant and revealing content online is more likely to take place during a "firestorm" or "peaky" periods of comment related to a crisis for the group.[2]

The second key point about catalysts is that it would appear that the involvement of the traditional mass media is necessary for a successful "catalyzing" campaign. For this study, this is a self-fulfilling prophesy as it was the fact that the health case studies were covered by the mass media that made them visible to the researchers. However, through the comments in the forums as well as the fact that these online communities are essentially quite small, the involvement of at least regional mass media was necessary in order to pressure officials into action. In all of the cases, it was the attention of the media that helped the group to meet their goals—of trying to change attitudes about children with disabilities, to punish the tabloid journalist who was so grossly insensitive, to get the Russian government to fund expensive treatment for children with MPS, and to gain life-sustaining dialysis treatment unfairly denied by injudicious hospital bureaucrats. The interplay between traditional and "new" media became much more important during the 2011–12 winter protests. While the internet fostered a range of compelling information sources—ranging from the Golos electoral violation map to online Rain TV—traditional media such as state-run television clung to its post-Soviet model of selective news coverage within a distorted frame of high social consensus. This might work when internet penetration is low, but as the Egyptian authorities discovered to their peril, the lack of a dynamic state media strategy that takes into account the powerful information and networking capabilities of the internet is a dangerous proposition. Arguably, the Russian state lost a significant amount of credibility and the ability to control the information arena during the 2011–12 winter demonstrations. Although Russian citizens showed themselves amenable to "delegative democracy" (Hale, 2011) and a fair amount of media distortion in the service of the state (Oates, 2006), this stretched the credibility gap to the breaking point. Many Russian citizens probably did support the president and had relatively little sympathy for the protestors, but very few would appreciate television propaganda that showed blatant disrespect for the intelligence of the Russian viewers.

Control and Co-optation

For many years, Russia has pursued a relatively laissez-faire attitude toward internet control. In contrast to China, Russia seemed content to allow a far wider range of internet content and activity than many non-democratic regimes. However, as Chapter 4 delineates, Russia actually has a wide range of controls for the online sphere, ranging from strong anti-libel laws to the obligation of internet service providers to forward information to the state security services. Thus, while Russia does not have a system akin to the "Great Chinese Firewall" and probably does not fit the concept of "networked authoritarianism" advanced by MacKinnon (2011), taken together the barriers to free speech online in Russia are fairly formidable. This dovetails with the general problem of free speech in Russia, in that there are many protections for the state and few for the citizen, journalist, or media outlet. Given that there is little confidence in the Russian courts and general legal system to protect citizens, this presents a significant barrier to their ability to feel free to comment and post information online. Perhaps most chilling is the way in which prominent bloggers are pursued by the state, such as the charges filed against Navalny. This lack of tolerance for the Fourth Estate (online and offline) became apparent as bloggers and journalists were particular targets for arrest during the 2011–12 protests, although at no time did the Russian state attempt to shut down the internet.[3]

In terms of the type of control that the Russian state may pursue for the online sphere, it is most likely to parallel what Deibert and Rohozinksi (2010) define as third-generation internet control, a "highly sophisticated, multidimensional approach to enhancing state control over national cyberspace and building capabilities for competing in informational space with potential adversaries and competitors" (p. 7). In the third generation of internet control, at which Deibert and Rohozinski argue that Russia could be a world leader, the state proactively uses the internet for counter-information campaigns to "overwhelm, discredit, or demoralize opponents" (p. 7). At the same time, the government is able to mine the internet for rich data about users and content for better surveillance and control of the population. While the Russian online population may perceive the online sphere as a place for the creative expression of political views, it may actually function more effectively as a resource for the government to identify what it would perceive as dangerous individuals, communities, and thoughts as expressed in blogs, comments, websites, and a range of other forums online. Yet there remains the tension of a sort of cat-and-mouse game that pits the creativity and ingenuity of the users against the controlling strategy of the state.

The Russian government has put pressure on individual bloggers who have been perceived as particularly influential or challenging to the regime. The case of Navalny (discussed in Chapter 4) shows that Russian law can be deployed against individuals who chose to use the internet to challenge the lack of coverage on bribery and corruption in Russia, although in many ways this has only authenticated Navalny's opposition role. In addition, a study of three prominent protest movements in 2008 found that the Russian government was effective in co-opting an outspoken blogger who was aggregating complaints and information about how officials were evading responsibility for deadly car accidents (Fossato et al., 2008). Co-optation is a difficult and slippery subject to study in the online sphere. As with traditional journalists, it is sometimes difficult to ascertain the difference between adherence to the norms of self-censorship and censorship that is overtly imposed by a media outlet owner, local authorities, commercial sponsors, or even national authorities. However, given the Russian government's ability to co-opt a range of opposition politicians as well as media owners, it is likely that the same strategy is deployed in the online sphere to a much wider degree than has been uncovered by some entrepreneurial individuals.

If we were to add an additional C to the 5C model, would it be change or continuity? The research in this book suggests that there is an enormous amount that can be illuminated about a country through a study of the internet, particularly in the way in which audiences reveal so much about behavior and attitudes in their daily interactions online. It is still somewhat unclear how social scientists can effectively tame this information tide to create valid and reliable markers about political opinions harvested from the online sphere. However, we already can gain important insights by linking the information in the online sphere to existing political institutions—i.e., to understand the role of this political communication within the relevant political context. Thus, the online sphere never brings a set of uniform and global opportunities to the citizens within a particular country. Rather, it is a far more dynamic process. The evidence in this book suggests that while the uniform and global communicative tools of the internet will be shaped by existing political attitudes and institutions within Russia, these tools also can enhance the opportunity for citizens to seek redress. This has the potential to evolve, from the Russian ground up, into a more general movement for citizens' rights and a more democratic society. At this time, it is not clear how much citizens will choose to embrace this potential, which is tempered by the control and co-optation effectively deployed by the Russian government. There may be compromise and concession from the Russian state, as seen in a small way with the liberalization of laws on party formation in the spring of 2012. This leaves us, for now, with a revolution that is indeed stalled. At the same time, it is stalled rather than stopped, with evidence in this book suggesting that the steady empowerment of an ever-broader range of Russian citizens due to information and networking via the online sphere could yet present a serious challenge to the Russian status quo.

User-Generated Coding Frame

Date posted: day/month/year, i.e., if February 24, 2011, it's 24/02/11

Time posted: 24-hour clock, i.e., 23:22, will assume it is Moscow time unless noted

SPAMMER/suspected spam: if spam, stop coding this item and move to next user-generated text—no need to copy and paste text. If you suspect spam, code it as spam—better to leave it out if unsure

Name of Poster

If available, otherwise leave blank. We use screen name or whatever name they have listed there. We can cross reference this against any open registration information later, but intend to hide any real-life identifiers in the reporting of the research to protect online participants from any perceived unwanted attention.

Location of Poster

I.e. Moscow, St. Petersburg, just say "Russia" if clear from Russia and exact location not clear, unknown if you can't tell

Well-defined User Behavior (If Clear)

For many users, it is impossible to define their behavior from a single comment. However, in some cases users have very explicit behavior. If it is explicit, use the following categories:

UCHAL: Disagreeing/Challenging information presented—this is disagreement or challenge in general—doesn't have to disagree with the most recent poster, etc.

UATTAK: Attacking another poster personally and/or with offensive language

UASK1: Asking questions related to individual concerns, including appeals for legal or medical advice and/or asking questions related to broader societal issues

UANSW: Posting information/answering questions, including reporting on action elsewhere or action related to the particular central concern of the forum, etc. This also includes pointing people to information online.

UACT: Asking people to take part in actions, including signing petition (online or offline); contacting officials online or posting messages on government online spaces (i.e., e-mail officials or post messages in a forum); contact officials offline (either in person or by post, etc); seeking legal redress; contacting other online locations, i.e., spread word online by posting, linking, etc.; contacting traditional media (i.e., TV, radio, print media); calling for illegal action/civil disobedience; requesting donations.

Discourse: What Does What They Are Saying Mean?

Note: Some of these are relatively hard to code. If in doubt, put in a 99 to indicate a possible hit. You can have all of these categories in one comment (although that might be rare).

RIGHT: Mention of "rights"—interpret very broadly, any mention of the state failing to provide services to any discussion of what people should have (in terms of rights or privileges or benefits) in society. This would include complaints about health-care services or treatment of a disabled child.

DBEN: Mention of state benefit.

DINTL: International issues/concerns mentioned.

DRUS: Issues/concerns for Russia are mentioned—this includes all levels from national to local.

Mention of Political Institutions

(Put 1 for all mentioned; note that you can do a word search to code.)

PPRES: president
PPARL: parliament
PPARTY: political party (any)
PPUTIN: Putin by name
PMEDV: Medvedev by name
POTHER: Other, such as a regional Duma

Text: Cut and paste text of post here.

Links: Are there links in the comment?

Comments (Free text area): for further details/comments, as noted above. Note that the codes will point the qualitative coders to particular comments for further study.

WHEN YOU HAVE FINISHED the quantitative coding, make a report on the following:

What are the central themes of the discussion? Are people really talking about benefits or rights? Are they reacting to a particular catalyst? Is there evidence that people are either (a) learning from each other about their rights and benefits; (b) having a political discussion; (c) planning offline "political" activities ranging from contacting the mass media, to forming an action group, to staging a protest; (d) challenging the state itself; (e) giving up, trying to convince others that the fight isn't worth it.

Notes

Chapter 1

1. See http://www.whitehouse.gov/contact/.
2. The World Telecommunication/ICT Indicators Database is compiled by the International Telecommunications Union and uses figures reported by countries themselves. See http://data.un.org/Data.aspx?d=ITU&f=ind1Code%3aI99H (last accessed February 27, 2012).
3. Available at www.issuecrawler.net.
4. One of the most prominent Russian opposition journalist, *Novaya Gazeta* reporter Anna Politkovskaya, was assassinated in October 2006 in her apartment building. No one had been convicted of her murder by August 2011. The Committee to Protect Journalists has estimated that 29 journalists were killed in a decade in post-Soviet Russia. Many have died covering the wars in Chechnya, but the organization estimated that at least 11 (not including Politkovskaya) were murdered in contract-style killings in the four years after Putin came to power in 2000.
5. BBC, February 21, 2007. As part of its remit, the BBC monitors media outlets from around the world. This report is available online at http://news.bbc.co.uk/1/hi/world/europe/4315129.stm.

Chapter 2

1. Article 19 of the United Nations' Universal Declaration of Human Rights reads: "Everyone has the right to freedom of opinion and expression; this right includes freedom to hold opinions without interference and to seek, receive and impart information and ideas through any media and regardless of frontiers." See http://www.un.org/en/documents/udhr/index.shtml#a19.
2. I owe the link to this theory to my former PhD student, Gordon Ramsay.
3. Internet World Stats, http://www.internetworldstats.com/stats.htm.
4. There was widespread evidence that the British *News of the World*, a tabloid newspaper owned by News Corporation, used illegal tactics such as phone hacking and bribery of officials to obtain information for stories. The newspaper was shut down by News Corporation in the wake of the scandal in 2011.
5. See http://data.un.org/Data.aspx?d=ITU&f=ind1Code%3aI99H (last accessed April 16, 2012).
6. According to the Association for Education in Mass Communication and Journalism, see http://www.reportr.net/2010/08/05/aejmc-trends-newspaper-industry/ (last accessed April 16, 2012).
7. The author would like to thank David Brake at the University of Bedford (UK) for compiling a very useful list of academic literature relating to the Arab Spring. The list, which was

circulated via the Association of Internet Researchers e-mail list, is available at https://docs.google.com/document/d/1DU8AOlkTV6F0ZyoGcbk_060iBZG5tWKwj_n97EJPe9M/edit (last accessed August 27, 2012).

8. From http://www.alexa.com/topsites/countries/US and http://www.alexa.com/topsites/countries/GB (both accessed July 15, 2011).

9. One of the most intriguing cases is that of the website of the British liberal newspaper, the *Guardian*. In mid-2012, the *Guardian* website was receiving 21 percent of its traffic from the United States (and only about 30 percent from the United Kingdom), see Alexa statistics via http://www.alexa.com/siteinfo/guardian.co.uk#, (last accessed April 16, 2012).

10. See www.digitalicons.org for information and free downloads.

11. Author's translation, the Russian transliterated text is: *ZhZh ispol'zyut ne tol'ko kak privatnyi ili publichnyi dnevnik, no i kak sprestvo sotsialiizatsii sposov polucheniya informatsii i novostei, sposov priobreteniya novykh druzei, mesto diskussii i sozdaniya sovmestnykh proektov.*

12. In the 2010 Corruption Perceptions Index by Transparency International, Russia placed 154th, close to the worst of the 178 countries in the study. Medvedev made anti-corruption a central theme of public messages and 4,500 corruption cases were brought to court in the first half of 2009. However, out of those cases, only 1,232 people who work in the public sector and law enforcement were convicted. Indeed, Transparency International actually found that Russia's problems with corruption were getting worse, with the country's ranking dropping slightly from 2009 to 2010.

13. In Russian (translation by author, website accessed February 19, 2012): *Zachem vce eto nuzhno? Zatem, shto pensionery, vrachi, uchitelya nakhodyatsya na grani vyzhivaniya v to vremya kak zhuliki u vlasti pokupayut ocherednuyu villu, yakhtu ili eshche chert znaet shto. Eto nashi den'gi. Eto normal'noe meditsinskoie obsluzhivanie. Eto kachestvennoe obrazovanie. Eto dorogi, po kotorym mozhno ezdit'. Eto chistye ulitsy. Eto vozmozhnost' vsem zhit' luchshe.*

14. http://lenta.ru/news/2012/02/04/montage/ (accessed February 19, 2012): *SKR ob'yavil roliki s narusheniyami na vyborakh cmontirovannymi* (State Investigatory Committee announces that videos of election violations were falsified).

15. As noted by Aleksei Venediktov, editor-in-chief of the Ekho Moskvy radio station, reported by the *Washington Post*, see http://articles.washingtonpost.com/2011-12-06/world/35286895_1_alexei-navalny-russian-alexei-venediktov, last accessed December 4, 2012.

16. Jamie Coomarasamy, "Russia: Protests and opposition to Vladimir Putin," February 3, 2012, BBC News Online, available at http://www.bbc.co.uk/news/world-europe-16487469 (last accessed on February 19, 2012).

Chapter 3

1. In 2011, Russian ranked in online linguistic popularity after French and before Korean, and was much less common than the use of English or Chinese, see http://www.internetworldstats.com/stats7.htm.

2. It should be noted that Russia has significantly lower life expectancy than the rest of Europe, according to the World Fact Book published by the Central Intelligence Agency (see https://www.cia.gov/library/publications/the-world-factbook/geos/rs.html), making the consideration of who is a pensioner or considered elderly start earlier in life. According to the CIA Factbook, Russian life expectancy at birth in 2011 was 59.8 years for males and 73.15 years for females. This compares with a life expectancy of 75.7 years for men and 82.13 years for women across the European Union, according to the same source (https://www.cia.gov/library/publications/the-world-factbook/geos/ee.html).

3. From a survey of 2,000 Russian adults carried out by Russian Research Ltd. from December 2003 to January 2004. The author gratefully acknowledges support for this research from the United Kingdom Economic and Social Research Council.

4. For newspapers, 31 percent routinely read local newspapers and 22 percent routinely read national papers.

5. From a survey 2,000 Russian adults conducted by Russian Research Ltd. in 2001.

6. The main state-run television channel that is found on Channel 1 has gone through several name changes in the past two decades. Its current name is *Pervyi Kanal* (First Channel) in Russian; for convenience it will be referred to simply as Channel 1 in its past incarnations.

7. It is unclear in the report whether "Europe" included Ukraine, but given the relative popularity of Russian media in Ukraine, it is logical to assume that it was included in these figures.

8. BBC Online is the fifth most popular website in the United Kingdom, according to the web tracking company Alexa, see http://www.alexa.com/topsites/countries/GB (accessed July 18, 2011).

9. As measured by whether the respondent lived in a city of 200,000 or more.

10. Although this enthusiasm for universal internet access and use may wane if the Russian government finds further evidence, such as that from the 2010 survey cited above or the winter 2011–12 protests, that regular internet use leads to a challenge to the state. It is clear from the tone of this report that the Russian government was confident that the internet will serve as a tool for state support, not state challenge, in addition to being a key element of economic modernization for the country. The government's control of the online sphere will be discussed in Chapter 4.

11. See the organization's mission statement at http://www.freedomhouse.org/template.cfm?page=2.

12. See http://www.levada.ru/26-12-2011/opros-na-prospekte-sakharova-24-dekabrya (last accessed February 27, 2012).

Chapter 4

1. Taylor Nelson Sofres (TNS), *Auditoriya mobil'novo internet priblizilas' k 10 mln* [The Mobile Internet Audience Has Reached 10 Million], RuMetrika, November 22, 2010, http://rumetrika.rambler.ru/review/0/4578, cited in Freedom House 2011, p. 269.

2. Transparency International ranked the Russian Federation as 154th in the world in its 2010 corruption perception index that ranked 178 countries. See http://www.transparency.org/policy_research/surveys_indices/cpi/2010/results.

3. It should be noted that there is an unusually large amount of cyber crime in Russia and in many parts of the former Soviet Union. The combination of relatively high levels of technical education combined with low levels of compliance to international legal norms has fostered this situation. The problem of cyber crime is highlighted by the 2011 report from the Russian Federal Agency on the Press and Mass Communication and in a range of other reports about Russia. However, criminal issues will not be used in this discussion of Russian internet policy, which is not focused on criminal behavior such as piracy or fraud.

4. The resolution states that the "rights and freedoms of a person and citizen may be limited only by a federal statute to the extent necessary to protect the foundations of the constitutional system, morals, health, rights and legal interests of other persons, and to defend the country and the security of the state" (as cited in Richter, p. 9).

5. For example, see the limits set on speech that constitutes "clear and present danger" by the U.S. Supreme Court in Schenck v. United States (1919), later modified by Brandenburg v. Ohio (1969).

6. The author would like to acknowledge excellent research assistance by Anna Kvit in preparation of this chapter.

7. As Richter (p. 11) notes, online content is still subject to other regulation. The resolution notes that those who "violate the law when disseminating information through Internet websites not registered as mass media outlets shall be subject to penal, administrative, civil, and other liability under the legislation."

8. An abbreviation for the Russian Federal Service for Supervision in the Sphere of Telecom, Information Technologies, and Mass Communications.

9. The Federal Security Service of the Russian Federation (*Federal'naya sluzhba bezopasnosti Rossiiskoi Federatsii*) is the successor security agency to the Soviet KGB.

10. *Sistema operativno-rozysknykh meropriyatii.* (System hardware to ensure the operational-search measures).

11. *Prikaz Goskomsvyazi RF No. 47 "Ob utberzhdenii Obshchikh tekhnicheskikh trebovanii k sisteme tekhnicheskikh sdredstv po obesnepcheniyu funktsii operativno-rozysknykh meropriyatii na setyakh (sluzhbakh) dokumental'noi svyazi"* [Order of the State Committee of the Russian Federation No. 47 "On the approval of the general technical requirements for the system hardware to ensure the operational-search measures of the networks (services), documentary communication], paragraph 1.3.

12. *Prikaz Ministerstva Svyazi RF ot 25.07.2000 N 130 "O poryadke vnedreniya sistemy tekhnicheskikh sredstv po obesnecheniyu operativno-rozysknykh meropriyatii na setyakh telefonnoi prodvizhnoi i besprovodnoi svyazi i personal'novo radiobyzova obshchevo pol'zovaniya."* [Order of the Ministry of Communication of the Russian Federation on July 25, 2000, Number 130 "On the order of the introduction of technical means to ensure the operational-search measures on the networks of telephone, mobile and wireless communications, and paging public"].

13. *Prikaz Ministerstva informatsionnykh tekhnologii svyazi Rossiiskoi Federatsii ot 16.01.2008 No. 6 "Ob utverzhdenii trebovannii k setyam elektrosvyazi dlya provedeniya operativno-razysknykh meropriyatii Chast' 1. Obshchie trebovaniya"* [Order of the Ministry of Information, Technologies, and Communication of the Russian Federation on January 16, 2008, Number 6, "On the approval of requirements for telecommunication networks for conducting operational search activities. Part I. General Requirements"].

14. Order of the Ministry of Information, Technologies, and Communication of the Russian Federation on January 16, 2008, Number 6.

15. As of mid-2011, foreign internet service providers were not required to comply with SORM information collection and redirection rules. However, it is unlikely that a foreign company could long resist the demands of the Russian government for information, particularly as foreign companies must comply with extensive regulations to do business in the country.

16. *Federal'nii zakon "ob operativno-rozysknoi deyatel'nosti"* [Federal Law "On operative-search activity"].

17. V. Novyii. *FSB podklyuchilas' k Skype i ISQ* [FSB joined with Skype and ICQ]. Available online at: http://www.infox.ru/business/net/2009/09/02/FSB_kopayet_pod_inos.phtml (last accessed July 9, 2011).

18. *Deputati Gosudarstvennoi Dumu Rossii predlagayut skanirovat' pasporta pri prokupke SIM karty.* [Deputies of the Russian State Duma required the scanning of passports for purchase of SIM cards], see http://news.org.ua/view2.php?id=43468 (last accessed May 7, 2011).

19. See http://www.politzeky.ru/politzeki/drugie-dela/22470.html (last accessed August 31, 2012).

20. See Matthew Schaff, "Criticism = extremism," in the *New Statesman* (London), July 11, 2008. Available online at http://www.newstatesman.com/international-politics/2008/07/russia-extremism-rights.

21. Voronov K. (2009) *Silovikov zashchishchayut ot "Oborony"* [Those in Power Protect Themselves from "Oboronists"]; Lenta.Ru (2011) User of VKontakte came up for trial for the slogan *"Bei mentov"* [Beat the cops], see http://www.kommersant.ru/doc/1146974/print (last accessed August 21, 2012). The Agora Human Rights Association group notes that this is a play on words for an infamous Russian anti-Semitic slogan from the pre-Soviet era "Beat up the Yids and Save Russia."

22. Human Rights in Russia (2008).

23. See http://www.rightsinrussia.info/internet/report.

24. See article by Pavel Goroshko on Kompromat.ru (2006) Real term for virtual murder [*Real'nyi srok za virtual'noe ubistvo*] http://compromat.ru/page_18231.htm (last accessed August 21, 2012).

25. New Region [*Novyi region*] 2 (2007) Is the Internet threatened by censorship? LiveJournal users could not dissuade State Duma Deputy Alksnis from dismissing a case on insult via the Internet [*Rozit li Internetu tsenzura? ZhZhisty ne smogli otrovorit' deputata GD Alksnisa prekratit' delo ob oskorblenii v Internete*]. For a discussion in English, see http://eng.cnews.ru/news/top/indexEn.shtml?2007/03/06/238881.

26. New Region 2 (2007).

27. Korolev I. (2008) A Virtual Insult to Putin draws a real punishment [*Za virtual'noe oskorblenie Putina dali real'nyi srok*], available online at http://www.cnews.ru/news/top/index.shtml?2008/11/01/325760 (last accessed August 21, 2012).

28. Motorin V. (2006) Journalist responds to "fallacy" [*Zhurnalist otvetit za "fallos"*]. This article is no longer available online. Internet discussions about the case suggest that the article itself did not have radical political context, but rather offensive comparisons and sarcastic comments on Putin's speech about the need to increase the birth rate in the Russian Federation. A discussion about the issue is available (in Russian) in an article entitled "Putin as a phallic symbol" [*Putin kak fallicheskii symbol*] posted on May 23, 2006, on the Israland website, see http://www.isra.com/news/67472 (last accessed September 18, 2011).

29. See http://korrespondent.net/russia/201844-v-rossii-izymaetsya-zhurnal-s-putinym-v-obraze-mishki.

30. See Schreck, Carl. May 2, 2006. "Web Sites Under Scrutiny in Wake of Extremist Acts," Issue #1166 (32), Tuesday, May 2, 2006. *The St. Petersburg Times* (Russia), No. 1166 (32). Available online at http://www.sptimes.ru/index.php?action_id=2&story_id=17489.

31. See http://www.rg.ru/2008/09/04/a257796.html (last accessed June 5, 2011).

32. Reported on the newsmsk.ru website, see http://www.newsmsk.com/article/22Jun2009/ter_posobie.html (last accessed September 18, 2011).

33. The discussion (in Russian) of this case can be found on the Radio Liberty website: http://www.svobodanews.ru/content/transcript/451849.html. It is also discussed in Agora Human Rights Association.

34. Lenta. Ru (2011) Bashkir opposition bloggers were sued for extremism [*Bashkirskikh oppozitsionnykh blogerov osudili za estremizm*], see http://lenta.ru/news/2011/04/19/extremeways/ (last accessed August 21, 2012).

35. This is despite the fact that Russian law does not specifically allow government officials to block web pages or to compel internet providers to block web pages.

36. Details of this case come from an article posted by Denis Legezo on August 27, 2010, on the cnews technology website, see http://www.cnews.ru/news/top/index.shtml?2010/07/27/402821 (last accessed August 31, 2012).

37. The opening to *Anna Karenina*, first published in full in 1878.

Chapter 5

1. See "Nice website, shame no-one visits it: Politics still a turn-off, even in cyberspace," press release from the Economic and Social Research Council, February 23, 2005, available at http://www.eurekalert.org/pub_releases/2005-02/esr-nws022305.php (last accessed September 1, 2012).

2. While it was originally intended that party politics would play a role in the election to both houses of the Russian parliament, members of the Federation Council have essentially been appointed (rather than directly elected in a nationwide vote) after the initial election of representatives to the upper chamber in 1993.

3. This was modified by Medvedev in 2012, which will be discussed in Chapter 7.

4. These rules were changed to make it somewhat easier to found political parties after the winter protests of 2011–12 in Russia.

5. The data were generously shared by Professor Stephen White (Glasgow), from research funded by the Economic and Social Research Council in collaboration with the Australian Research Council (RES-000-22-2532 *Crafting Authoritarian Politics*).

6. According to the Central Election Commission of the Russian Federation, see http://cikrf.ru/eng/.

7. Russian national elections are generally held every four years, although the president does have the ability to dissolve the parliament and call for early elections.

8. http://er.ru/persons/supreme_council/.

9. It should be noted that in mid-2011 United Russia also maintained a separate, less popular website for its Duma fraction (http://www.er-duma.ru/).

10. http://er.ru/party/programme/.

11. http://er.ru/core/news/theme/15.html.

12. This book does not explore the use of the web for attacking opponents with rumors or what Russians called "kompromat," which is the amalgam of the Russian words for "compromising" and "materials." This indicates "news" of dubious validity, but a relatively high salacious interest. For a discussion of this, see March, 2004.

13. In the interest of remaining an observer at this point, the author did not register in order to gain access.

14. https://www.facebook.com/home.php?sk=group_101763483249659&ap=1, (last accessed August 22, 2012).

15. This is, of course, a quite cursory judgment. An in-depth content analysis of the website would need a much larger sample and would require comparison to other party social-networking pages. It should also be noted that an analysis of the use of videos via YouTube is beyond the remit of this study. The "curs and thieves" spam had been removed by the following day (August 18, 2011).

16. The constituency formation of Russian political parties is discussed in more depth in Oates, 2006 and White, 2011. There is not space here for a discussion of the socioeconomic demographics of Russian party support, but it is relevant to note that the Communists tend to have older, less urban, and poorer supporters. All of these factors contribute to a relative lack of online access in Russia, according to Russian Federal Agency on the Press and Mass Communication (2011).

17. These would all be good questions to ask the party, which is planned in the next phase of the research.

18. http://kprf.ru/party/howto/.

19. In its party program section, see http://ldpr.ru/#party/Programme_LDPR/Questions_attention.

20. A study of news framing in the 1993, 1995, and 1999 Duma elections showed that Zhirinovsky, while both successful at garnering coverage and avoiding the worst attacks by the government on state-run media, was not framed as a particularly intellectual or rational politician. However, his outrageous sound bites and antics seem to resonate well with his supporters.

21. http://srduma.ru/.

22. http://www.spravedlivo.ru/information/partners/.

23. http://www.obrzdrav.ru/.

24. As of August 18, 2011.

25. For a discussion of the old website and web statistics in March 2010, see Oates, 2010.

26. According to Alexa, http://www.alexa.com/siteinfo/er.ru on August 9, 2011.

27. Further investigation into Alexa rankings of the LDPR and A Just Russia websites yielded little information because the traffic was so low.

28. See p. 27 of the paper for the web link analysis; the paper is available for free download at http://www.media-politics.com/publications.htm.

29. This iteration of the web link analysis did not include LDPR, as it was not originally part of the research.

Chapter 6

1. National Association for Down Syndrome, see www.nads.org.
2. The full text of the original article, the complaint, and the response by the Union of Journalists are reprinted in a UNESCO report on bioethics and journalism in Russia, see http://unesdoc.unesco.org/images/0019/001918/191823e.pdf (last accessed September 1, 2012).
3. http://www.svobodanews.ru/content/feature/1944765.html.
4. See the report on the Russian Radio Liberty website, http://www.rferl.org/content/In_ Russia_Call_For_Postnatal_Abortion_Sparks_Furor_Among_Parents_Of_Disabled/ 1952215.html (last accessed September 1, 2012).
5. http://www.svobodanews.ru/content/feature/1944765.html.
6. The thread on the Rostov-on-Don issue is http://www.moscowdialysis.ucoz.ru/forum/27-2534-1.
7. It should be noted that significantly different results were returned when the search was made in English, even on Yandex.ru, so it is important to search in the native language of the online audience.
8. A group called Sun Children (www.sunchildren.narod.ru) sometimes came slightly higher in the Yandex rankings than Downside Up. However, it would appear that Sun Children is an online-only organization.
9. http://www.downsideup.org/down.php?PHPSESSID=cea670a76e48cb6657d1fe6451cf b4d3.
10. There is an argument that these should have been selected for analysis as they have more Russian origins—Downside Up was founded by a British citizen who was working in Russia. However, the point was to start with the most popular site from a Russian search and this returned Downside Up on August 5, 2010.
11. Indeed, the drug used to treat the condition (idursulfase, marketed as Elaprase©) costs about $375,000 USD per year per patient and was listed as one of the most expensive drugs in the world by *Fortune* magazine in February 2010, see http://www.forbes.com/2010/02/19/ expensive-drugs-cost-business-healthcare-rare-diseases.html (last accessed September 1, 2012).
12. http://www.svobodanews.ru/content/feature/1944765.html.
13. http://mps-russia.org/forum/index.php?topic=550.0.
14. http://mps-russia.org/forum/index.php?topic=380.0.
15. An initial coding scheme was too ambitious, particularly because of the uneven length of the posts.
16. The coding scheme was developed as part of the work for a British Academy grant as well as a grant from the U.K. Economic and Social Research Council. Vikki Turbine (Glasgow) and Tetyana Lokot (National University of Kyiv-Mohyla Academy) codesigned the coding scheme with the author.
17. http://mps-russia.org/forum/index.php?topic=551.0;   http://mps-russia.org/forum/ index.php?topic=551.0; http://mps-russia.org/forum/index.php?topic=553.0; http:// mps-russia.org/forum/index.php?topic=1008.0;   http://mps-russia.org/forum/index. php?topic=2111.0;   http://www.guestbook.ru/?user=mpssociety&page=4&language= russian; http://mps-russia.org/forum/index.php?topic=380.0.
18. "The Status of MPS in Belarus," http://mps-russia.org/forum/index.php?topic=380.0.
19. http://mps-russia.org/forum/index.php?topic=1008.0.
20. July 27, 2009, http://mps-russia.org/forum/index.php?topic=380.0.
21. August 8, 2009, http://mps-russia.org/forum/index.php?topic=380.0.
22. This article deals with punishment for people who refuse to provide necessary medical help to patients with serious health issues.
23. Translations of posts by author.
24. http://community.livejournal.com/blog_medvedev/48625.html?thread=28547057# t28547057.

25. http://www.dontr.ru/Environ/WebObjects/dontr.woa/wa/Main?textid=46266.
26. http://www.moscowdialysis.ucoz.ru/forum/27-2534-118961-16-1285609394.

Chapter 7

1. A useful and well-sourced discussion of this can be found on Wikipedia under "Russian legislative elections, 2011" at http://en.wikipedia.org/wiki/Russian_legislative_election,_2011, (last accessed March 30, 2012).
2. See the official Russian Central Election Commission results at http://www.vybory.izbirkom.ru/region/region/izbirkom?action=show&root=1&tvd=100100031793509&vrn=100100031793505&region=0&global=1&sub_region=0&prver=0&pronetvd=null&vibid=100100031793509&type=227, (last accessed April 10, 2012).
3. "Russia election: Protesters defy rally ban in Moscow," BBC Online, December 6, 2011, available at http://www.bbc.co.uk/news/world-europe-16052329, (last accessed April 19, 2012).
4. "Russia election: Protesters defy rally ban in Moscow," BBC Online, December 6, 2011, available at http://www.bbc.co.uk/news/world-europe-16052329, (last accessed April 19, 2012).
5. "Russian election: Biggest protests since fall of USSR," BBC Online, December 10, 2011, available at http://www.bbc.co.uk/news/world-europe-16122524, (last accessed April 19, 2012).
6. "Protestors barely seen on Russian TV," BBC Online, December 7, 2011, available at http://www.bbc.co.uk/news/world-europe-16067899, (last accessed April 19, 2012).
7. "Protestors barely seen on Russian TV," BBC Online, December 7, 2011, available at http://www.bbc.co.uk/news/world-europe-16067899, (last accessed April 19, 2012).
8. Kremlin-Connected Oligarch Fires Publishing Execs Over Vote Coverage, Radio Free Europe/Radio Liberty, December 13, 2011, available at http://www.rferl.org/content/russia_kommersant_publisher_fires_executives_over_putin_text/24420401.html, (last accessed April 19, 2012).
9. "Russian election: Biggest protests since fall of USSR," BBC Online, December 10, 2011, available at http://www.bbc.co.uk/news/world-europe-16122524, (last accessed April 19, 2012).
10. "'First we take Sakharov Avenue': The capital sees its biggest demonstration yet against the Kremlin," *The Economist*, December 31, 2011, online at http://www.economist.com/node/21542205, (last accessed April 19, 2012).
11. "Moscow: Thousands join pro- and anti-Putin protests," BBC Online, February 4, 2012, available at http://www.bbc.co.uk/news/world-europe-16885446, (last accessed April 19, 2012).
12. Author's observation.
13. *Golos* means both "voice" and "vote" in Russian.
14. See " 'Hacking attacks' hit Russian political sites", December 5, 2011, on the BBC website, available at http://www.bbc.co.uk/news/technology-16032402, (last accessed April 6, 2012). A distributed denial of service attack (DDoS) occurs when multiple systems flood the bandwidth or resources of a targeted system, making it incapable of carrying out its planned function. These systems are compromised by attackers using a variety of methods. The article also notes that other sites, including the Echo of Moscow radio station, opposition newspaper *New Times*, the political site Slon.ru, and a daily business paper suffered DDoS attacks at the same time.
15. See "Russian election monitor chief held for several hours," December 3, 2011, on the BBC website, available at http://www.bbc.co.uk/news/world-europe-16016733, (last accessed April 6, 2012). The incident also was reported on the Golos website at http://www.golos.org/news/4500, (last accessed April 6, 2012).
16. Their report (in Russian) can be found here: http://www.cikrf.ru/news/relevant/2012/02/03/kniga.doc, (last accessed April 10, 2012).

17. The author has served as an elections observer for the former European Institute for the Media (Düsseldorf) in Russia and Kazakhstan.
18. The report on the Duma elections is here: http://www.osce.org/odihr/elections/82441, (last accessed April 10, 2012). The report on the 2012 Russian presidential election is here: http://www.osce.org/odihr/elections/Russia/87410, (last accessed April 10, 2012).
19. Gregory L. White and Bob Barry, "Russia's Dubious Vote: Analysis of Parliamentary Results Points to Widespread Fraud," December 28, 2011. Retrieved online March 30, 2012, from http://online.wsj.com/article/SB1000142405297020339110457712454054482220.html?mod=googlenews_wsj#mjDropdown.
20. The *Wall Street Journal* highlighted the case of Chechnya, in which turnout was reported at 99 percent, with all but 6,200 of the 614,109 registered voters voting for United Russia.
21. Analysis by Alexa (www.alexa.com) shows that the website traffic for the channel's website grew five-fold during the Duma elections and almost tripled during the presidential elections, see the analysis for tvrain.ru at http://www.alexa.com/siteinfo/tvrain.ru, (last accessed April 6, 2012).
22. http://www.guardian.co.uk/world/2011/dec/15/vladimir-putin-mocks-moscow-protesters, (last accessed April 10, 2012).
23. From coverage by the British *Guardian* newspaper, see http://www.guardian.co.uk/world/2011/dec/07/medvedev-tweet-russian-blogosphere-frenzy (last accessed November 11, 2012).
24. Full results are provided here by the Levada Center (which carried out the research at the request of the protest organizers): http://www.levada.ru/26-12-2011/opros-na-prospekte-sakharova-24-dekabrya, (last accessed April 10, 2012).
25. The respondents could choose more than one answer.
26. http://www.guardian.co.uk/uk/interactive/2011/dec/14/reading-the-riots-investigating-england-s-summer-of-disorder-full-report.
27. Author's observation.
28. http://blogs.yandex.ru/, (last accessed April 10, 2012).
29. No exact figures are given—the results are presented in a bar graph, see http://basilisklab.com/boloto-analis-2.html, (last accessed April 6, 2012).
30. The center collected a database of 11,113 tweets from a total of 8,565 unique accounts, 99.8 percent of which were sent during between March 4–6, 2012, see Greene for more details.

Chapter 8

1. The initial Twitter fund has now been expanded into an application for trading based on sentiment analysis by Derwent Capital Markets; see http://www.derwentcapitalmarkets.com/dcm_dealer/ (last accessed September 1, 2012).
2. In fact, the coders for this project complained that forums were "boring" when divorced from catalyzing events. In addition, inter-coder reliability increased significantly when concrete events and problems were being discussed, as opposed to general chat. This would suggest that a more ambitious coding scheme, including those that could use automated algorithms, would more usefully be deployed during crisis events. It also highlights that different approaches should be used during crisis and non-crisis periods relating to specific online communities.
3. However, groups such as Golos reported being taken offline with dedicated denial-of-service (DDoS) attacks.

References

Abbott, Jason P. 2001. Democracy@internet.asia? The Challenges to the Emancipatory Potential of the Net: Lessons from China and Malaysia. *Third World Quarterly* 22(1): 99–114.

Adkeniz, Yaman. 2000. Policing the Internet: Concerns for Cyber-Rights. In Rachel Gibson and Steven Ward (eds) *Reinvigorating Democracy?: British Politics and the Internet*. Aldershot: Ashgate.

Agora Human Rights Association. 2011. *Threats to Internet freedom in Russia, 2008–2011: An independent survey*. Russia: Agora Human Rights Association. Available online in English at http://www.openinform.ru/fs/j_photos/openinform_314.pdf and in Russian at http://www.openinform.ru/fs/j_photos/openinform_313.pdf.

Alexander, Marcus. 2003. The Internet in Putin's Russia: Reinventing a Technology of Authoritarianism. Department of Politics and International Relations, University of Oxford. Online at http://www.psa.ac.uk/journals/pdf/5/2003/Marcus%20Alexander.pdf, last accessed March 15, 2011.

Altheide, David L. 1997. The News Media, the Problem Frame, and the Production of Fear. *Sociological Quarterly* 38(4): 647–68.

Altheide, David L. and R. Sam Michalowski. 1999. Fear in the News: A Discourse of Control. *Sociological Quarterly* 4(3): 476–503.

Anstead, Nick and Andrew Chadwick. 2008. The 2008 Digital Campaign in the United States: the real lessons for British parties. *Renewal: a Journal of Labour Politics* 16 (3/4): 86–98.

Anstead, Nick and Andrew Chadwick. 2009. Parties, election campaigning, and the Internet: toward a comparative institutional approach. In Andrew Chadwick and Philip Howard (eds) *Handbook of Internet Politics*. London: Routledge: 56–71.

Anstead, Nick and Will Straw (eds). 2009. *The change we need: What Britain can learn from Obama's victory*. London: The Fabian Society.

Becker, Jonathan. 2004. Lessons from Russia: A Neo-Authoritarian Media System. *European Journal of Communication* 9(2): 139–63.

Berelson, Bernard R., Paul F. Lazarsfeld and William N. McPhee. 1954. *Voting: A Study of Opinion Formation in a Presidential Campaign*. Chicago: University of Chicago Press.

Blumler, Jay and Michael Gurevitch. 1977. Linkages Between the Mass Media and Politics. In James Curran, Michael Gurevitch, and Janet Woollacott (eds) *Mass Communication and Society*. London: Edward Arnold: 270–90.

Brandenburg, Heinz. 2006. Pathologies of the Virtual Public Sphere. In Sarah Oates, Diana Owen and Rachel K. Gibson (eds) *The Internet and Politics: Citizens, voters and activists*. London: Routledge, 207–22.

Bruns, Axel. 2007. Methodologies for Mapping the Political Blogosphere: An Exploration Using the IssueCrawler Research Tool. First Monday 12(5). No pages (online at http://firstmonday.org/htbin/cgiwrap/bin/ojs/index.php/fm/article/view/1834/1718).

Calvert, Martin. 2010. Identity, Strategic Essentialism and Informal Networks among Social Activist LiveJournal Bloggers in Nizhny Novgorod: Implications for Information Transfer and the Individual. Paper presented at The New Media in New Europe-Asia Conference, University College London, May 2010.

Campbell, Angus, Philip Converse and Warren Miller. 1960. *The American Voter*. Chicago: University of Chicago Press.

Carlson, Tom and Göran Djupsund. 2001. Old Wine in New Bottles? The 1999 Finnish Election Campaign on the Internet. *Harvard International Journal of Press Politics*, 6(1): 68–87.

Chadwick, Andrew. 2006. *Internet Politics: States, Citizens, and New Communication Technologies*. Oxford: Oxford University Press.

Chandler, Andrea. 2008. The Social Promise: Rights, Privileges and Responsibilities in Russian Welfare State Reform since Gorbachev. In Thomas Lahusen and Peter H. Solomon, Jr. (eds) *What is Soviet Now: Identities, legacies, memories*. London: LitVerlag: 192–214.

Chomsky, Noam. January 18, 2006. War on Terror. Amnesty International Annual Lecture Presented at Trinity College (Dublin). Available online at http://www.chomsky.info/talks/20060118.pdf.

Christensen, Christian. 2011. Discourses of Technology and Liberation: State Aid to Net Activists in an Era of "Twitter Revolutions." *The Communication Review* 14(3): 233–53.

Colton, Timothy J. 2000. *Transitional Citizens: Votes and What Influences Them in the New Russia*. Cambridge, MA: Harvard University Press.

Cooper, Julian. 2008. The Internet in Russia—Development, Trends and Research Possibilities. Presentation at the CEELBAS Post-Soviet Media Research Methodology Workshop, March 2008, University of Birmingham.

Dahl, Robert A. 2000. *On Democracy*. New Haven, CT: Yale University Press.

Dann, Stephen, 2010. Twitter content classification. *First Monday* [online] 15(12): (November 24 edition). Online, free access at http://firstmonday.org/htbin/cgiwrap/bin/ojs/index.php/fm/article/view/2745/2681.

Davis, Richard. 2009. *Typing Politics: The Role of Blogs in American Politics*. New York: Cambridge University Press.

Deibert, Ronald, John Palfrey, Rafal Rohozinski and Jonathan L. Zittrain. 2010. *Access Controlled: The Shaping of Power, Rights, and Rule in Cyberspace*. Cambridge, MA: The MIT Press.

Deibert, Ronald, John G. Palfrey, Rafal Rohozinski and Jonathan Zittrain (Open Net Initiative). 2009. *Access Denied: The Practice and Policy of Global Internet Filtering*. Cambridge, MA: The MIT Press.

Deibert, Ron and Rafal Rohozinski. 2010. Beyond Denial: Introducing Next-Generation Information Access Controls. In R.J. Deibert et al. *Access Controlled: The Shaping of Power, Rights, and Rule in Cyberspace*. Cambridge, MA: MIT Press. Available online at http://mitpress.mit.edu/catalog/item/default.asp?ttype=2&tid=12187&mode=toc.

Dyson, Esther. 1998. *Release 2.1: A Design for Living in the Digital Age*. London: Penguin.

Elmer, Greg. 1997. Spaces of Surveillance: Indexicality and Solicitation on the Internet. *Critical Studies in Mass Communication* 14(2): 182–91.

Entman, Robert M. 2003. Cascading Activation: Contesting the White House's Frame after 9/11. *Political Communication* 20: 415–32.

Etling, Bruce, Karina Alexanyan, John Kelly, Robert Faris, John Palfrey, and Urs Gasser. 2010. *Public Discourse in the Russian Blogosphere: Mapping RuNet Politics and Mobilization*. Cambridge, MA: The Berkman Center for Internet and Society at Harvard University.

Etzioni, Amitai and Oren Etzioni. 1999. Face-to-Face and Computer-Mediated Communities: A Comparative Analysis. Paper presented at the Virtual Communities Eighth Annual Conference on Computers, Freedom and Privacy, University of Texas, Austin.

European Institute for the Media. August 2000. *Monitoring the Media Coverage of the March 2000 Presidential Elections in Russia*. Düsseldorf: European Institute for the Media. Available online at http://www.media-politics.com/eimreports.htm.

European Institute for the Media. March 2000. *Monitoring the Media Coverage of the December 1999 Parliamentary Elections in Russia: Final Report*. Düsseldorf: European Institute for the Media. Available online at http://www.media-politics.com/eimreports.htm.

European Institute for the Media. September 1996. *Monitoring the Media Coverage of the 1996 Russian Presidential Elections*, Düsseldorf, Germany, The European Institute for the Media, available online at http://www.media-politics.com/eimreports.htm.

European Institute for the Media. February 1996. *Monitoring the Media Coverage of the 1995 Russian Parliamentary Elections*, Düsseldorf, Germany, The European Institute for the Media, available online at http://www.media-politics.com/eimreports.htm.

European Institute for the Media. 1994. *The Russian Parliamentary Elections: Monitoring of the Election Coverage of the Russian Mass Media*, Düsseldorf, European Institute for the Media, available online at http://www.media-politics.com/eimreports.htm.

Foot, Kirsten A., Michael Xenos, Steven M. Schneider, Randolph Kulver and Nicholas W. Jankowski. 2010. Electoral web production practices in cross-national perspective: The relative influence of national development, political culture, and web genre. In Andrew Chadwick and Philip N. Howard (eds) *Routledge Handbook of Internet Politics*. London: Routledge: 40–55.

Fossato, Floriana. 2009. Discussion: Is Runet the Last Adaptation Tool? *Russian Cyberspace* 1(1): no page numbers. Online at http://www.digitalicons.org/issue01/pdf/issue1/Web-as-an-Adaptation-Tool_N-Fossato.pdf, last accessed August 9, 2010.

Fossato, Floriana and John Lloyd with Alexander Verkhovsky. 2008. The Web That Failed: How Opposition Politics and Independent Initiatives Are Failing on the Internet in Russia. Oxford: Reuters Institute for the Study of Journalism. Available for free download at http://reutersinstitute.politics.ox.ac.uk/fileadmin/documents/Publications/The_Web_that_Failed.pdf.

Freedom House. 2011a. *Freedom in the World 2011 The Authoritarian Challenge to Democracy: Selected data from Freedom House's annual survey of political rights and civil liberties*. New York: Freedom House. Available online at http://www.freedomhouse.org/report/freedom-world/freedom-world-2011 (last accessed December 4, 2012).

Freedom House. 2011b. *Freedom on the Net 2011: Global Scores*. New York: Freedom House. Available online at http://www.freedomhouse.org/report/freedom-net/freedom-net-2011 (last accessed August 20, 2012).

Galston, William A. 2003. The Impact of the Internet on Civil Life: An Early Assessment. In Elaine Ciulla Kamarck and Joseph S. Nye Jr. (eds) *Governance.com: Democracy in the Information Age*. Washington, D.C.: Brookings Institution Press.

Gel'man, Vladimir. 2008. Party Politics in Russia: From Competition to Hierarchy. *Europe-Asia Studies* 60(6): 913–30.

Giacomello, Giampiero. 2008. *National Governments and Control of the Internet: A Digital Challenge*. London: Routledge.

Gibson, Rachel K. 2010. "Open Source Campaigning?": UK Party Organisations and the Use of the New Media in the 2010 General Election. Paper prepared for presentation at the Annual meeting of the American Political Science Association, Washington, D.C.

Gibson, Rachel K., Michael Margolis, David Resnick and Stephen J. Ward. 2003. Election Campaigning on the WWW in the USA and UK: A Comparative Analysis. *Party Politics* 9(1): 47–75.

Gibson, Rachel K. and Ian McAllister. 2008. Do Online Election Campaigns Win Votes? The 2007 Australian *YouTube* Election. Paper presented at the Annual Meeting of the American Political Science Association, Boston, MA.

Gibson, Rachael K., and Stephen J. Ward. 2000. A Proposed Methodology for Studying the Function and Effectiveness of Party and Candidate Web Sites. *Social Science Computer Review* 18: 301–19.

Glassner, B. 2000. *The Culture of Fear: Why Americans are Afraid of the Wrong Things*. New York: Basic Books.

Goggin, Gerard and Mark McLelland (eds). 2008. *Internationalizing Internet Studies: Beyond Anglophone Paradigms*. London: Routledge.

Golynko-Volfson, Dmitry. 2009. Sotsial'nyie seti v nesetovom sotsiume [Social Networks in an Un-Networked Society]. *Digital Icons: Studies in Russian, Eurasian and Central European New Media* (formerly *Russian Cyberspace*) 1(2): 101–113. Online at http://www.digitalicons.org/issue02/dmitry-golynko/, last accessed August 9, 2010.

Goroshko, Olena I. and Elena Zhigalina. 2009. *Quo Vadis? Politicheskie kommunikatsii v blogosfere Runeta* [Political Interactions in Russian Blogosphere]. *Russian Cyberspace* 1(1): 81–100. Online at http://www.digitalicons.org/issue01/pdf/issue1/Political-Interactions-in-the-Russian-Blogosphere_O-Goroshko-and-E-Zhigalina.pdf, last accessed August 9, 2010.

Graber, Doris. 2009. *Mass Media and American Politics* (8th edition). Washington, D.C.: CQ Press.

Greene, Samuel A. January 18, 2012. The End of Virtuality? Moscow: The Center for New Media and Society. Available at http://www.newmediacenter.ru/2012/01/18/the-end-of-virtuality/, last accessed February 27, 2012.

Greene, Samuel A. May 2012. Twitter and the Russian Street: Memes, Networks & Mobilization. Moscow: The Center for New Media and Society. Available at http://www.newmediacenter.ru/2012/05/22/twitter-and-the-russian-street-memes-networks-mobilization/, last accessed November 1, 2012.

Greengard, Samuel. 2009. The First Internet President. *Communications of the ACM* 52(2): 16–18.

Habermas, Jürgen. 1989 (trans.). *The Structural Transformation of the Public Sphere: An Inquiry into a Category of Bourgeois Society*. Oxford: Polity.

Hale, Henry E. 2011. The Myth of Mass Russian Support for Autocracy: The Public Opinion Foundations of a Hybrid Regime. *Europe-Asia Studies* 63(8): 1357–75.

Hallin, David and Paulo Mancini. 2004. *Comparing Media Systems. Three Models of Media and Politics*. New York: Cambridge University Press.

Hamdy, Naila and Ehab H. Gomaa. 2012. Framing the Egyptian Uprising in Arabic Language Newspapers and Social Media. *Journal of Communication* 62: 195–211.

Harfoush, Rahaf. 2009. *Yes We Did: An Inside Look at How Social Media Built the Obama Brand*. Berkeley, CA: New Riders.

Hargittai, Eszter and Gina Walejko. 2008. The Participation Divide: Content Creation and Sharing in the Digital Age. *Information, Communication & Society* 11(2): 239–56.

Hartford, Kathleen. 2000. Cyberspace with Chinese Characteristics. *Current History* 99(638): 255–75.

Harwit, Eric and Duncan Clark. 2001. Shaping the Internet in China: Evolution of Political Control over Network Infrastructure and Content. *Asian Survey* 41(3): 377–408.

Haynes, Audrey A. and Brian Pitts. 2009. Making an Impression: New Media in the 2008 Presidential Nomination Campaigns. *PS: Political Science & Politics* 42 (1): 53–58.

Heydemann, Steven and Reinoud Leenders. 2011. Authoritarian Learning and Authoritarian Resilience: Regime Responses to the 'Arab Awakening.' *Globalizations* 8(5): 647–653.

Heilemann, John. 1996. Old Politics RIP. *Wired* 4(11). Online at www.wired.com/wired/archive?4.11/netizen.html.

Herman, Edward S. and Noam Chomsky. 2002. *Manufacturing Consent: The Political Economy of the Mass Media*. New York: Pantheon Books.

Hindman, Matthew. 2009. *The Myth of Digital Democracy*. Princeton, NJ: Princeton University Press.

Hirst, Paul. 1994. *Associative Democracy: New Forms of Economic and Social Governance*, Cambridge: Polity.

Homero Gil de Zuñiga, Eulàlia Puig-I-Abril and Hernando Rojas. 2009. Weblogs, traditional sources online and political participation: an assessment of how the Internet is changing the political environment. *New Media and Society* 11(4): 553–74.

Hopkins, Daniel J. and King, Gary. 2010. A Method of Automated Nonparametric Content Analysis for Social Science. *American Journal of Political Science* 54(1): 229–47.

Howard, Philip N. and Malcolm R. Parks. 2012. Social Media and Political Change: Capacity, Constraint, and Consequence. *Journal of Communication* 62: 359–362.

Hu, Minqing and Bing Liu. 2004. Mining and summarizing customer reviews. *KDD '04: Proceedings of the Tenth ACM SIGKDD International Conference on Knowledge Discovery and Data Mining*, pp. 168–77, and at http://www.cs.uic.edu/~liub/publications/kdd04-revSummary.pdf, accessed September 29, 2011.

Hutcheson, Derek. 2003. *Political Parties in the Russian Regions*. London: Routledge.

International Telecommunications Union. January 31, 2011. *World Telecommunications/ICT Indicators Database*. New York: United Nations Statistical Division. Available online at http://data.un.org/Data.aspx?d=ITU&f=ind1Code%3aI99H#ITU.

Iyengar, Shanto. 1991. *Is Anyone Responsible?: How Television Frames Political Issues*. Chicago: The University of Chicago Press.

Jankowski, Nicholas W., Kirsten Foot, Randy Kluver and Steve Schneider. 2005. The Web at the 2004 EP election: Comparing political actor web sites in 11 EU Member States. *Information Polity* 10(3/4): 165–76.

Java, Akshay, Xiaodan Song, Tim Finin and Belle Tseng. 2007. Why we twitter: understanding microblogging use and communities. Proceedings of the 9th WebKDD and 1st SNA-KDD 2007 workshop on Web mining and social network analysis: 56–65.

Jungherr, Andreas and Pascal Jürgens. 2011. One tweet at a Time: Mapping Political Campaigns through Social Media Data. Draft Version 1.0. Paper presented at the 6th ECPR General Conference: European Consortium for Political Research, Reykjavik, Iceland.

Kachkaeva, Anna., I. Kiriya and George Libergal. March 2006. *Television in the Russian Federation: Organisational Structure, Programme Production and Audience*, a report prepared by Internews Russia for the European Audiovisual Observatory. Moscow: Educated Media.

Khamis, Sahar and Katherine Vaughn. 2012. We Are All Khaled Said: The potentials and limitations of cyberactivism in triggering public mobilization and promoting political change. *Journal of Arab & Muslim Media Research*, 4(2-3): 145–163.

Kelly, John, Vladimir Barash, Karina Alexanyan, Bruce Etling, Robert Faris, Urs Gasser and John Palfrey. March 2012. Mapping Russian Twitter. Cambridge, MA: The Berkman Center for Internet & Society. Available for free download at http://cyber.law.harvard.edu/publications

Koltsova, Olessia. 2006. *News Media and Power in Russia*. London: Routledge.

Krasnoboka, Natalya and Holli A. Semetko. 2006. Murder, journalism and the web: How the Gongadze case launched the Internet news era in Ukraine. In Sarah Oates, Diana Owen and Rachel K. Gibson (eds) *The Internet and Politics: Citizens, voters and activists*. London, Routledge: 183–206.

Kurchakova, Natalya. 2006. Formy samoprezentatsii v bloge [Forms of self-presentation in blogs]. In V.L. Volokhonskii, Y.E. Zautseva, and M.M. Sokolov (eds) *Lichnost i mezhlichnostnoe vzaumodeistvie v Seti Internet Blogi, Novaya real'nost'*. [Personality and inter-personal interaction in Internet Blogs, the new reality]. Saint Petersburg: SPGGU: 132–63.

Langer, Ana Inéz. 2012. *The Personalisation of Politics in the UK: Mediated Leadership from Attlee to Cameron*. Manchester (U.K.): Manchester University Press.

Lawrence, Regina G. and Melody Rose. 2010. *Hillary Clinton's Race for the White House: Gender Politics & the Media on the Campaign Trail*. Boulder, CO: Lynne Rienner, 2010.

Lewiński, Marcin and Dima Mohammed. 2012. Deliberate Design or Unintended Consequences: The Argumentative Uses of Facebook During the Arab Spring. *Journal of Public Deliberation*, 8 (1): 1–11 (Article No. 11).

Li, Dan and Gina Walejko. 2008. Splogs and Abandoned Blogs: The perils of sampling bloggers and their blogs. *Information, Communication & Society* 11(2): 279–96.

Linaa Jensen, Jakob. 2006. The Minnesota E-Democracy Project: Mobilising the Mobilised? In Sarah Oates, Diana Owen and Rachel K. Gibson (eds) *The Internet and Politics: Citizens, voters and activists*. London, Routledge: 39–58.

Lipman, Maria. 2005. Constrained or Irrelevant: The Media in Putin's Russia. *Current History* 104: 684.

Lipman, Maria and Michael McFaul. 2010. The Media and Political Developments. In Stephen K. Wegren and Dale R. Herspring (eds) *After Putin's Russia: Past Imperfect, Future Uncertain*. Lanham: Rowman and Littlefield Publishers.

Lipow, Arthur and Patrick Seyd. 1996. The Politics of Anti-Partyism. *Parliamentary Affairs* 49(2): 273–84.

Lonkila, Markku. 2008. The Internet and Anti-Military Activism in Russia. *Europe-Asia Studies* 60(7): 1125–49.

Lonkila, Markku. 1997. Informal Exchange Relations in Post-Soviet Russia: A Comparative Perspective. *Sociological Research Online* 2(2), http://www.socresonline.org.uk/2/2/9.html (last accessed September 1, 2012).

Lusoli, Ward and Stephen Ward. 2006. Hunting Protestors: Mobilisation, Participation and Protest Online in the Countryside Alliance. In Sarah Oates, Diana Owen and Rachel K. Gibson (eds) *The Internet and Politics: Citizens, voters and activists*. London, Routledge: 59–79.

Lusoli, Wainer and Stephen Ward. 2005. Logging On or Switching Off? The Public and the Internet at the 2005 General Election. In Stephen Coleman and Stephen Ward (eds) *Spinning the Web: Online Campaigning during the 2005 General Election*. London: Hansard Society: 13–21.

MacKinnon, Rebecca. 2011. China's "Networked Authoritarianism". *Journal of Democracy* 22 (2): 32–46.

March, Luke. 2006. Virtual Parties in a Virtual World: The Use of the Internet by Russian Political Parties. In Sarah Oates, Diana Owen and Rachel K. Gibson (eds) *The Internet and Politics: Citizens, voters and activists*. London: Routledge.

March, Luke. 2004. Russian parties and the political internet. *Europe-Asia Studies* 56(3): 369–400.

Margolis, Michael. 2010. Review of *Typing Politics: The Role of Blogs in American Politics*, by Richard Davis. *Political Communication* 27(2): 218–21.

McNair, Brian. 1991. *Glasnost, Perestroika and the Soviet Media*. London: Routledge.

Mickiewicz, Ellen. 2008. *Television, Power, and the Public in Russia*. New York: Cambridge University Press.

Mickiewicz, Ellen. 1997. *Changing Channels: Television and the Struggle for Power in Russia*. New York: Oxford University Press.

Mickiewicz, Ellen. 1988. *Split Signals: Television and Politics in the Soviet Union*. New York: Oxford University Press.

Mickiewicz, Ellen Propper. 1980. *Media and the Russian Public*. New York: Praeger.

Morozov, Evgeny. 2011. *Net Delusion: The Dark Side of Internet Freedom*. New York: PublicAffairs.

Morris, Dick. 2000. *Vote.com*. Los Angeles, CA: Renaissance.

Mulgan, Geoff and Andrew Adonis. 1994. Back to Greece: The Scope for Direct Democracy. *Demos Quarterly* 3: 2–9.

Negroponte, Nicholas. 1995. *Being Digital*. London: Coronet.

Newhagen, John E. 1997. On hitting the agenda reset button for Net research, and getting it right this time. Paper presented at the Association for Education in Journalism and Mass Communication.

Nisbet, Erik C., Elizabeth Stoycheff and Katy E. Pearce. 2012. Internet Use and Democratic Demands: A Multinational, Multilevel Model of Internet Use and Citizen Attitudes About Democracy. *Journal of Communication* 62: 249–265.

Norris, Pippa. 2003. Preaching to the Converted?: Pluralism, Participation and Party Websites. *Party Politics* 9(1): 21–45.

Norris, Pippa. 2001. *The Digital Divide: Civic Engagement, Information Poverty and the Internet Worldwide*. Cambridge: Cambridge University Press.

Norris, Pippa. 2000. *A Virtuous Circle: Political Communication in Postindustrial Societies*. Cambridge: Cambridge University Press.

Nye, Joseph S. Jr. 2004. *Soft Power: The Means to Success in World Politics*. New York: PublicAffairs.

Oates, Sarah. 2011. Going Native: The Value in Reconceptualizing International Internet Service Providers as Domestic Media Outlets. *Philosophy & Technology* 24 (4): 391–409.

Oates, Sarah. 2008. *Introduction to Media and Politics*. London: SAGE.

Oates, Sarah. 2007. The Neo-Soviet Model of the Media. *Europe-Asia Studies* 59(8): 1279–97.

Oates, Sarah. 2006. *Television, Democracy and Elections in Russia*. London: Routledge.

Oates, Sarah. 2003. Television, Voters, and the Development of the 'Broadcast Party.' In Vikki. L. Hesli and William M. Reisinger (eds) *The 1999-2000 Elections in Russia: Their Impact and Legacy*. New York: Cambridge University Press.

Oates, Sarah. 1998. Voting Behavior and Party Development in New Democracies: The Russian Duma Elections of 1993 and 1995. PhD Thesis. Atlanta, GA: Emory University.

Oates, Sarah, Lynda Lee Kaid, and Mike Berry. 2009. *Terrorism, Elections, and Democracy: Political Campaigns in the United States, Great Britain, and Russia*. New York: Palgrave Macmillan.

Oates, Sarah and Gillian McCormack. 2010. The Media and Political Communication. In Stephen White, Richard Sakwa and Henry E. Hale (eds) *Developments in Russian Politics 7*. London: Palgrave Macmillan: 118–34.

Open Net Initiative. April 14, 2005. *Internet Filtering in China in 2004-2005: A Country Study*. Available online at http://opennet.net/studies/china

Organization for Security and Co-operation in Europe/Office for Democratic Institutions and Human Rights (OSCE/ODIHR). June 2, 2004. *Russian Federation Presidential Election 14 March 2004 OSCE/ODIHR Election Observation Mission Report*, Warsaw, Office for Democratic Institutions and Human Rights.

Organization for Security and Co-operation in Europe/Office for Democratic Institutions and Human Rights (OSCE/ODIHR). January 27, 2004. *Russian Federation Elections to the State Duma 7 December 2003 OSCE/ODIHR Election Observation Mission Report*, Warsaw, Office for Democratic Institutions and Human Rights.

Owen, Diana. 2006. The Internet and Youth Civic Engagement in the United States. In Oates, Sarah, Diana Owen and Rachel K. Gibson (eds) *The Internet and Politics: Citizens, voters and activists*. London: Routledge: 20–38.

Pasti, Svetlana. 2005. Two Generations of Contemporary Russian Journalists. *European Journal of Communication* 20(1): 89–115.

Patico, J. 2002. Chocolate and Cognac: Gifts and Recognition of Social Worlds in Post-Soviet Russia. *Ethnos* 67(3): 345–68.

Philo, Greg (ed) 1995. *Glasgow Media Group Reader Volume 2: Industry, economy, war and politics*. London: Routledge.

Pickup, Francine and Anne White. 2003. Livelihoods in post-communist Russia: Urban/Rural Comparisons. *Work, Employment & Society* 17(3): 419–34.

Polat, Rabia K. 2005. The Internet and Political Participation: Exploring the Explanatory Links. *European Journal of Communication* 20(4): 435–59.

Polumbaum, Judy. 2001. China's Media: Between Politics and the Market. *Current History* 100: 269–77.

Poster, Mark. 1997. Cyberdemocracy: The Internet and the Public Sphere. In Holmes, D. (ed.) *Virtual Politics: Identity and Community in Cyberspace*. London: SAGE.

Putnam, Robert. 2001. *Bowling Alone: The Collapse and Revival of American Community*. New York: Simon & Schuster.

Qin, Jialun, Yilu Zhou, Edna Reid, Guanpi Lai and Hsinchun Chen. 2007. Analyzing terror campaigns on the internet: Technical sophistication, content richness, and Web interactivity. *International Journal of Human-Computer Studies* 65(1): 71–84.

Ramsay, Gordon. 2011. *The Evolution of Televised Election Coverage in Britain and its Impact on the Democratic Political Process*. PhD Dissertation. University of Glasgow.

Rash, Wayne. 1997. *Politics on the Net: Wiring the Political Process*. New York: W. H. Freeman.

Remington, Thomas F. 2001. *The Russian Parliament: Institutional Evolution in a Transitional Regime, 1989-1999*. New Haven, CT: Yale University Press.

Reporters Without Borders [Reporters Sans Frontières]. November 17, 2005. *The 15 Enemies of the Internet and Countries to Watch*, available online at http://en.rsf.org/the-15-enemies-of-the-internet-and-17-11-2005,15613.html (last accessed September 1, 2012).

Reuter, John and Thomas F. Remington. 2009. Dominant party regimes and the commitment problem: The case of United Russia. *Comparative Political Studies* 42(4): 501–26.

Rheingold, Howard. 1995. *The Virtual Community: Finding Connection in a Computerised World.*
London: Minerva.

Richter, Andrei. 2011. *A Landmark for Mass Media in Russia.* Strausbourg, France: European
Audiovisual Observatory.

Rogers, Richard. 2009. *The End of the Virtual: Digital Methods.* Amsterdam: University of
Amsterdam Press. Pre-print version available for free download at http://www.govcom.org/
publications/full_list/oratie_Rogers_2009_preprint.pdf, last accessed April 6, 2012.

Rohozinski, Rafal. 2000. How the Internet Did Not Transform Russia, Current History 99:
334–51.

Rose, Richard and Neil Munro. 2002. *Elections Without Order: Russia's Challenge to Vladimir Putin.*
Cambridge: Cambridge University Press.

Russian Federal Agency on the Press and Mass Communication. 2011. *Internet v Rossii: Sostoyanie,
tendentsii i perspektivy razvitiya (The Internet in Russia: Conditions, Trends and Perspectives on
Development).* Moscow: Regional Public Centre for Internet Technology. Available at:
http://www.fapmc.ru/magnoliaPublic/rospechat/activities/reports/2011/item6.html
(July 16, 2011).

Sakwa, Richard. 2011. *The Crisis of Russian Democracy: Dual State, Factionalism and the Medvedev
Succession.* Cambridge: Cambridge University Press.

Salmi, Anna-Maria. 2003. Health in Exchange: Teachers, Doctors and the Strength of Informal
Practices in Russia. *Culture, Medicine & Psychiatry* 27(2): 109–30.

Saunders, Robert A. 2009. Wiring the Second World: The Geopolitics of Information and Com-
munications Technology in Post-Totalitarian Eurasia. *Russian Cyberspace* 1(1): 1–24.
Online at http://www.digitalicons.org/issue01/issue1/robert-saunders.php?lng=English.
Last accessed August 9, 2010.

Schudson, Michael. 1995. *The Power of News.* Cambridge, MA: Harvard University Press.

Scott, James C. 1977. *The Moral Economy of the Peasant: Rebellion and Subsistence in Southeast Asia.*
New Haven, CT: Yale University Press.

Semetko, Holli and Natalya Krasnoboka. 2003. The Political Role of the Internet in Societies in
Transition: Russia and Ukraine Compared. *Party Politics* 9(1): 77–104.

Shenk, David. 1997. *Data Smog.* San Francisco, CA: Abacus.

Siebert, Fred S., Theodore Peterson and Wilbur Schramm. 1963, reprinted 1994. *Four Theories of
the Press.* Chicago: University of Illinois Press.

Slider, Darrell. 2010. How united is United Russia? Regional sources of intra-party conflict. *Journal
of Communist Studies and Transition Politics* 26(2): 257–75.

Smyth, Regina. 2006. *Candidate Strategies and Electoral Competition in the Russian Federation:
Democracy Without Foundation.* New York: Cambridge University Press.

Smyth, Regina, Anna Lowry and Brandon Wilkening. 2007. Engineering victory: Institutional
reform, informal institutions, and the formation of a hegemonic party regime in the Russian
Federation. *Post-Soviet Affairs* 23(2): 118–37.

Sparks, Colin. 2000. Media Theory after the Fall of European Communism: Why the Old Models
from East and West Won't Do Anymore. In James Curran. And Myung-Jin Parks (eds)
De-Westernizing Media Systems. London: Routledge: 35–49.

Steger, Wayne P., Christine B. Williams and Molly Andolina. 2010. Political Use of Social
Networks. Paper presented at the Annual Meeting of the American Political Science Association, Washington, D.C. Download via open paper archive at http://papers.ssrn.com/
sol3/JELJOUR_Results.cfm?form_name = journalbrowse&journal_id = 1621378T.

Street, John. 2001. *Mass Media, Politics and Democracy.* New York: Palgrave Macmillan.

Strandberg, Kim. 2009. Online campaigning: an opening for the outsiders? An analysis of Finnish
parliamentary candidates' websites in the 2003 election campaign. *New Media and Society,*
11(5): 835–54.

Sunstein, Cass R. 2009. *Republic.com 2.0.* Princeton, NJ: Princeton University Press.

Suvorov, Gleb. January 2012. *Kto zhe vse-taki byl na Bolotnoi i na sakharova? Analiz profelei 20,000 uchastnikov mitinga [Who was really at Bolotnaya and Sakharov?: An Analysis of the Profiles of 20,000 Meeting Participants]*. Moscow: Basilisklab. Available online at http://basilisklab. com/boloto-analis-posetitelei.html, last assessed April 6, 2012.

Taubman, Geoffrey. 1998. A Not-So World Wide Web: The Internet, China, and the Challenges to Nondemocratic Rule. *Political Communication* 15(2): 255–72.

Teubner, Gunther. 2004. Societal Constitutionalism: Alternatives to State-Centred Constitutional Theory? In Christian Joerges, Inger-Johanne Sand and Gunther Teubner, *Transnational Governance and Constitutionalism*. Oxford: Hart Publishing: 3–28.

Toffler, Arthur and Heidi Toffler. 1995. *Creating a New Civilization: The Politics of the Third Wave.* Atlanta, GA: Turner Publications.

Trombetta, Lorenzo. 2012. Altering Courses in Unknown Waters: Interaction between Traditional and New Media during the First Months of the Syrian Uprising. *Global Media Journal* (German edition but printed in English). Volume 2(1): 1–6.

Turbine, Vikki. 2007a. Russian women's perceptions of human rights and rights-based approaches in everyday life. In Rebecca Kay (ed.) *Gender, equality and difference during and after state socialism*. Basingstoke, Palgrave: 167–87.

Turbine, Vikki. 2007b. Women's Perceptions of Human Rights and rights-based approaches in everyday life: a case study from provincial Russia. PhD Thesis, University of Glasgow.

Turnšek, Maja and Nicholas W. Jankowski. 2008. Social Media and Politics: Theoretical and Methodological Considerations in Designing a Study of Political Engagement. Paper presented at Politics: Web 2.0: An International Conference, Royal Holloway, University of London. Archived at http://newpolcom.rhul.ac.uk/politics-web-20-paper-download/.

Voltmer, Katrin. 2000. Constructing Political Reality in Russia: *Izvestiya*—Between Old and New Journalistic Practices. *European Journal of Communication* 15(4): 469–500.

White, Stephen. 2011. *Understanding Russian Politics*. Cambridge: Cambridge University Press.

White, Stephen and Sarah Oates. 2003. Politics and the Media in Postcommunist Russia. *Politics* 23(1): 31–37.

White, Stephen, Sarah Oates, and Bill Miller. 2003. The 'Clash of Civilizations' and Postcommunist Europe. *Comparative European Politics* 1(2): 111–27.

White, Stephen, Richard Rose, and Ian McAllister. 1996. *How Russia Votes*. Washington, D.C.: CQ Press.

White, Stephen, Matthew Wyman, and Sarah Oates. 1997. Parties and Voters in the 1995 Russian Parliamentary Elections. *Europe-Asia Studies* 49(5): 767–98.

Wilhelm, A. G. 2000. *Democracy in the Digital Age: Challenges to Political Life in Cyberspace*. New York: Routledge.

Wright, Scott. 2006. Design Matters: The Political Efficacy of Government-Run Discussion Boards. In Sarah Oates, Diana Owen and Rachel K. Gibson (eds) *The Internet and Politics: Citizens, voters and activists*. London, Routledge: 80–99.

Wu, Wei and David Weaver. 1996. On-line Democracy or On-Line Demagoguery? Public Opinion "Polls" on the Internet. *Harvard International Journal of Press/Politics* 2(4): 71–86.

Zygar, Mikhail. December 18, 2009. Kremlin hand hovers over Russia's internet. London: openDemocracy. Available at http://www.opendemocracy.net/od-russia/mikhail-zygar/ kremlin-hand-hovers-over-russias-internet (last accessed July 16, 2011).

Index